Integrated Marketing Communications
2001–2002

The Chartered Institute of Marketing/Butterworth-Heinemann Marketing Series is the most comprehensive, widely used and important collection of books in marketing and sales currently available worldwide.

As the CIM's official publisher, Butterworth-Heinemann develops, produces and publishes the complete series in association with the CIM. We aim to provide definitive marketing books for students and practitioners that promote excellence in marketing education and practice.

The series titles are written by CIM senior examiners and leading marketing educators for professionals, students and those studying the CIM's Certificate, Advanced Certificate and Postgraduate Diploma courses. Now firmly established, these titles provide practical study support to CIM and other marketing students and to practitioners at all levels.

**The Chartered
Institute of Marketing**

Formed in 1911, the Chartered Institute of Marketing is now the largest professional marketing management body in the world with over 60,000 members located worldwide. Its primary objectives are focused on the development of awareness and understanding of marketing throughout UK industry and commerce and in the raising of standards of professionalism in the education, training and practice of this key business discipline.

Integrated Marketing Communications 2001–2002

Chris Fill and Tony Yeshin

Published on behalf of
The Chartered Institute of Marketing

OXFORD AUCKLAND BOSTON JOHANNESBURG MELBOURNE NEW DELHI

Butterworth-Heinemann
Linacre House, Jordan Hill, Oxford OX2 8DP
225 Wildwood Avenue, Woburn, MA 01801-2041
A division of Reed Educational and Professional Publishing Ltd

$\mathcal{R}$ A member of the Reed Elsevier plc group

First published 2001

British Library Cataloguing in Publication Data
A catalogue record for this book is available from the British Library

ISBN 0 7506 5311 6

For information on all Butterworth-Heinemann
publications visit our website at www.bh.com

Typeset by Avocet Typeset, Brill, Aylesbury, Bucks
Printed and bound in Italy

Contents

Welcome to the latest edition of the Coursebook for the CIM Diploma paper on Integrated Marketing Communications.

The syllabus is designed to build on the knowledge of the promotional tools developed in the study of Marketing Operations and is designed to specifically focus attention on the management process associated with organizing and implementing integrated marketing communication activities.

Structure

This Coursebook has been subject to considerable structural revision. What this means is that as you work through the units you are building the knowledge in the right order so that you have a strong command of the subject and of course, are better placed to pass the examination.

This Coursebook is divided into units which are presented in the order best suited to help you learn about IMC. Please work through them in numerical order and complete as many of the activities as possible.

The syllabus for the Integrated Marketing Communications module is provided at the end of the book for your reference. However, we can assure you that all the topics are covered, but in a different order. This is so that your learning process is easier and builds incrementally.

Support

This edition of the Coursebook has been written so that you can develop an understanding of the subject quickly, have easy reference to all the topics that you need to know about and be able to work through a series of activities to assist your understanding of the subject. It has been deliberately kept slim and manageable, designed to provide you a programme of learning about Integrated Marketing Communications (IMC).

However, this is not a text book, it is a Coursebook designed to help you learn and understand. We strongly recommend that you do not rely on the Coursebook alone for your studies. Reference should be made to one of the essential texts recommended by the CIM and for this particular module the text is:

Chris Fill (2002) *Marketing Communications, Contexts, Strategies and Applications, 3rd edit*, London: Prentice Hall Europe.

If you cannot get a copy then please use the second edition.

This book provides the depth of analysis that is required on a postgraduate course and will enable you to appreciate why certain actions are recommended as well as the 'how-to' aspect. Therefore, please use the two learning resources in tandem.

In addition to these books you are encouraged to read the weekly trade papers, in particular *Marketing, Marketing Week, Campaign, PR Week* and *Revolution*. You should also have a look at MarketingOnline, the exciting new online learning resource provided by Butterworth-Heinemann. Each month I post current details about the subject, news items and study and hints which build towards the examination. If you are able to use all of these resources then we are confident that you will not only be successful in the examination, but you will enjoy learning about this fast-changing subject.

Good luck with your studies and with the examination itself.

Chris Fill and Tony Yeshin

July 2001

Authors' acknowledgements

We would like to thank all those who have given their time, skills, knowledge and patience to the development of this Coursebook.

In particular we would like to acknowledge our families for their understanding and forbearance during the writing period.

An introduction from the academic development advisor

Over the past few years there have been a series of syllabus changes initiated by the Chartered Institute of Marketing to ensure that their qualifications continue to be relevant and of significant consequence in the world of marketing, both within industry and academia. As a result I and Butterworth-Heinemann have rigorously revised and updated the Coursebook series to make sure that every title is the best possible study aid and accurately reflects the latest CIM syllabus.

The revisions to the series this year include both restructuring and the inclusion of many new mini cases and examples. There are a number of new and accomplished authors in the series commissioned both for their CIM course teaching and examining experience, and their wide general knowledge of the latest marketing thinking.

We are certain that you will find the new look-books a highly beneficial study tool as you prepare for the CIM examinations. They will guide you in a structured and logical way through the detail of the syllabus, providing you with the required underpinning knowledge, understanding and application of theory.

The editorial team and authors wish you every success as you embark upon your studies.

Karen Beamish
Academic Development Advisor

How to use these Coursebooks

Everyone who has contributed to this series has been careful to structure the books with the exams in mind. Each unit, therefore, covers an essential part of the syllabus. You need to work through the complete Coursebook systematically to ensure that you have covered everything you need to know.

This Coursebook is divided into units each containing a selection of the following standard elements:

- **Objectives** tell you what part of the syllabus you will be covering and what you will be expected to know, having read the unit.
- **Study guides** tell you how long the unit is and how long its activities take to do.
- **Questions** are designed to give you practice – they will be similar to those you get in the exam.
- **Answers** (at the end of the book) give you a suggest format for answering exam questions. *Remember* there is no such thing as a model answer – you should use these examples only as guidelines.
- **Activities** give you a chance to put what you have learned into practice.
- **Debriefings** (at the end of the book) shed light on the methodologies involved in the activities.
- **Exam hints** are tips from the senior examiner or examiner which are designed to help you avoid common mistakes made by previous candidates.
- **Study tips** give you guidance on improving your knowledge base.
- **Insights** encourage you to contextualize your academic knowledge by reference to real-life experience.
- **Definitions** may be used for words you must know to pass the exam.
- **Summaries** cover what you should have picked up from reading the unit.

While you will find that each section of the syllabus has been covered within this text, you might find that the order of some of the topics has been changed. This is because it sometimes makes more sense to put certain topics together when you are studying, even though they might appear in different sections of the syllabus itself. If you are following the reading and other activities, your coverage of the syllabus will be just fine, but don't forget to follow up with trade press reading!

Objectives

In this introductory unit you will:

- Consider and define what Marketing Communications are
- Evaluate the relationship between marketing and marketing communications.
- Explore the elements of marketing communications
- Appraise the role of personal influences on the communication process.

By the end of this unit you will:

- Appreciate the different elements of marketing communications
- Discuss the variety of uses for which marketing communications can be used
- Understand the principles of communication
- Evaluate the impact of personal influences on the effectiveness of marketing communications.

This unit covers syllabus sections: 1.1.1, 1.1.4, 1.2.3

Study guide

The first unit of this Integrated Marketing Communication Coursebook is designed to establish a broad base for the study of marketing communications. You may have completed the CIM Advanced Certificate in Marketing or the new paper in Marketing Operations or will have an understanding of the practical issues of marketing communications through your other studies.

This unit will reacquaint you with the broad area of marketing communications and examine their role within the context of the marketing mix. The material has been designed to be straightforward and easy to use, and provides the foundation for your study of the subsequent material.

Exploring and defining marketing communications

Study tip

Organize your material carefully and systematically from the beginning of your course Ideally, keep all of your material together in a single file.

Use file dividers to keep broad topic areas indexed and the relevant materials with the pertinent notes.

Look out for appropriate articles and current examples which will be useful to illustrate your examination answers.

Organizations use an increasing variety of marketing communication tools and media in order to convey particular messages and encourage us to favour their brand or products. As consumers, we are exposed to a vast amount of information on a daily basis – everything from news reports on television, radio and in the press, to weather forecasts, traffic information, store signs, product packaging, instore point-of-sale material, and so on. Advertising is just one of the elements with which the consumer must deal every day.

The tools of the marketing communications mix are:

- Advertising
- sales promotion
- public relations
- personal selling
- and direct marketing.

Now, these five basic tools are supplemented by other forms of marketing communications. For example, you may have been thinking about sponsorship and telemarketing, or exhibitions and the Internet.

Well, these are either subsets of the five basic tools or they are media. So, sponsorship is a part of public relations, telemarketing is a part of direct marketing, exhibitions are part of personal selling and the Internet is technically not a tool of marketing communications, it is a communications medium.

A communications medium is a part of the range of media available to carry promotional (often advertising) messages. Tools and media are separate.

Advertising is any form of paid-for media (television, press, radio, cinema, outdoor) used by the marketer to communicate with his or her desired target audience(s).

Public relations consists of all forms of planned communication between any organization and its publics with the objective of establishing and maintaining mutual understanding. This understanding may relate to the organization or to its products. It is important to note, however, that public relations is not publicity, nor is it free advertising.

Sales promotion is the use of short-term, often tactical, techniques (money-off, coupon offers, gifts, contests) to bring forward future sales. In other words, it is a bribe so that by adding value a sale might be achieved now, rather than possibly at some point in the future.

Direct marketing is an interactive system of marketing which uses one or more advertising media to effect a measurable response and/or transaction at any location (British Direct Marketing Association).

Personal selling is the process by which a (sales) person using face-to-face communications with one or more prospective purchasers, attempts to make sales.

Activity 1.1

Identify an example of each of the marketing communications mix components.

Define the task that each has been designed to fulfil and decide whether it is likely to achieve its primary goals.

The promotions mix is the use of any or all of the above-described elements in a unified and cohesive manner designed to achieve specifically defined and measurable promotions objectives. It is important to understand at this stage that these are the tools used in all forms of marketing communication, whether they be for packaged consumer goods, consumer durables, industrial products or services. In terms of marketing communications planning, the nature of the product or service which is to be promoted makes little difference – the same communications tools will be employed. Each component of the marketing communications mix will, however, have a specific task to achieve and it is the deployment of the tools to achieve the objectives which will be an important part of the overall understanding of the subject.

The tools of the marketing communications mix all have different properties and different potential to achieve different tasks. Therefore, managers must mix the tools in such a way that they achieve the actual tasks at hand, within the resources available.

Activity 1.2

Identify a product (this may be something from a supermarket or chemist) and a service (such as banking or dry cleaning).

Do some research and make a list of the elements of marketing communications which are used by the company to support the brand.

Obviously, each component of the marketing communications mix can be used on its own. In fact, though, this is rarely the case. Most companies use some combination of the marketing communications tools in order to achieve their objectives. Most advertising campaigns will be supported with sales promotions activities, or public relations or both. A direct mail campaign may follow media activity designed to stimulate interest in the product. Most companies use point-of-sale material to remind the consumer of their advertising message at the point of purchase, and so on. A recent yet long running Vauxhall campaign included, among other things, a major television, print and poster advertising, public relations activity resulting in major articles in the national press both about the car and the advertising, dealer support activity, exhibitions, sponsorship and direct mail.

What is important, and vitally so, is that each element of the communications mix should integrate with the other tools in the mix in order to achieve the communication of a single and unified message. Clearly, the impact of the message will be enhanced if it is reinforced by other parts of the mix, and the campaign objectives will be achieved in a more cost-effective manner.

Activity 1.3

Find examples of each of the tools of the marketing communications mix. Write these down in your file. Now find another set of examples and work out how they are used differently by the two organizations.

Recent years have seen an explosion in all forms of media. Apart from the five land-based television channels (BBC1, BBC2, ITV, Channel 4 and Channel 5) we have an increasing number of satellite and cable stations, and the number will continue to grow as the technology improves. The arrival of digital television in the form of Sky Digital and OnDigital has already delivered a considerable number of new television channels, with more being introduced on a regular basis. However, as yet, comparatively few people have the appropriate receivers, but that will change over time. We have radio on FM, medium wave and long wave and, apart from the national and local BBC stations, the UK also has three national commercial stations (Classic FM; Virgin 1215 on AM; and Atlantic on long wave) and more than 150 regional and local commercial radio stations. There are national and regional, morning and evening, daily, weekly and Sunday Newspapers. There are over 3500 magazines, covering every form of interest area imaginable. There are a wide range of outdoor media, not just fixed poster sites, but also posters on the sides of buses and taxi cabs, on the Underground and at railway stations. And many of us have become walking advertisements for the brands we wear, with our clothes bearing logos for all to see.

Activity 1.4

Find examples of the different media available to organizations.

Marketing Communications are an essential part of the Marketing Mix – sometimes described as the 'Four Ps'. It is important to understand that each of the elements interacts with each of the others. Thus, the nature of the product – and its appeal to the customer – will be influenced by the price which is charged. Similarly, the availability of the product at specific retail outlets and through different dealerships may influence a customer's perception of the quality of the product. And marketing communications – the fourth P – affect all the other components of the marketing mix.

Marketing Communications are just a part of the marketing mix and its role is to communicate the marketing plan to target audiences. However, it is not as simple as this might imply, its role may vary according to circumstances and the particular task at hand.

So, marketing communications may be required to provide information, to persuade a potential customer to buy a product or it may be used to remind a lapsed customer of the need to purchase brand *X* at the next opportunity. Indeed, there is a fourth role, a strategic role associated with the positioning of a brand so that a customer might understand quickly what the brand offering is and what the value might be to them. This is all part of the differentiation role that marketing communications have to play.

The role of Marketing Communications are to either:

- Differentiate a product/brand (to make it different to a competitor's brand)
- Remind and reassure a target audience (to encourage (re)purchase)
- Inform a target audience (e.g.of a new brand or flavour)
- Persuade an audience to take a particualr set of actions (e.g. buy a brand)
- These four roles might be more easily remembered as the DRIP roles of marketing communications.

Activity 1.5

Find examples for each of the DRIP roles.

Relationship marketing

Before progressing any further with a definition of marketing communications it is useful to consider them in conjunction with a development of marketing known as relationship marketing. With the ability to reach customers on a highly segmented or even one-to-one basis has come the recognition that the process itself can become two way. Hitherto, marketing communications are primarily concerned with the process of communicating to the end customer. By encouraging the process of feedback, we can now communicate *with* the customer. In other create a dialogue rather than a monologue.

Increasingly, companies such as Nestlé and Heinz have announced moves into club formats which enable the establishment of a direct relationship between the manufacturer and the consumer. Many loyalty programmes, such as the Frequent Flyer and Frequent Stayer programmes now run by most international airlines and hotel groups, have a similar objective of establishing a relationship with the consumer, to their mutual benefit.

The encouragement of a 'feedback' loop is a facet of marketing communications which is destined to grow apace over the next few years and, as companies perceive the benefits of encouraging a positive relationship with their customers, their consumers, their suppliers and others, so we will witness the growth of developed two-way marketing communications programmes. Much attention has been focused on this type of activity with the introduction of loyalty cards by almost all the major supermarket chains. Here, consumers are rewarded with points proportionate to their spend within the store, and one chain – Sainsbury – is advertising bonus points on particular product lines.

The real significance of these cards is not so much in terms of the rewards that they provide to consumers, rather in the amount of knowledge that can be built up about those individuals. Each time the consumer makes a purchase, information can be placed on the database regarding the items bought by the customer, the amount spent and, over time, the retailer can obtain a complete picture of the brand preferences, frequency of purchase and so on for every individual who shops in their store.

Activity 1.6

Why is there a growing trend towards relationship marketing? What are the benefits to the company? What are the benefits to the consumer?

It has to be recognized that contemporary marketing is more complex than at any time in the past. No longer is it sufficient to rely on the traditional marketing mix variables to achieve differentiation between manufacturers. Areas such as product design and development, pricing policies, and distribution are, in themselves, no longer capable of delivering the long-term differentiation required.

With an increasing level of convergent technologies, product innovation may be going on in parallel between rival manufacturers, even without their knowing what the other is doing. Even where this is not the case, any new feature can rapidly be copied by the competition. Where once a new feature, ingredient, or other product attribute would enable a manufacturer to achieve a unique stance for an extended period, this is no longer the case. One has only to look at the area of the rapid innovation within the soap powder and detergent markets to see just how speedily rival manufacturers catch up with each other.

With the concentration of distribution into relatively few hands, the opportunities for achieving sole distribution of brands is minimized. Indeed, the retailers themselves represent an increasing threat to the manufacturers' brands as their packaging moves ever closer to that of the manufacturers' own.

Pricing, once a major area of differentiation, similarly provides less scope. The pressure on margins brought about by the increasingly competitive nature of retailers' own products has restricted the scope to use price to differentiate effectively. Clearly, this is particularly true of fast-moving consumer goods where price dissimilarity can only operate over a very narrow range. Other products, such as perfumes and toiletries, and luxury goods ranging from hi-fi to cars still have more flexibility in the area of price.

We are left, therefore, with only one of the four marketing mix variables which can be utilized to achieve effective brand discrimination – marketing communications. Many now argue that marketing communications are the only opportunity of achieving sustainable competitive advantage. If all other things are equal – or at least more or less so – then it is what people think, feel and believe about a product and its competitors which is important. Since products in many areas will achieve parity or comparability in purely functional terms, it will be the perceptual differences which consumers will use to discriminate between rival brands. It may be perceptions at product, or increasingly at corporate brand level, but only through the use of sustained and integrated marketing communications campaigns will manufacturers be able to achieve the differentiation they require. This then refers to one of marketing communications roles, identified earlier, namely to differentiate a brand.

To appreciate the impact of this statement, it is worth looking at a market which replicates many of the features described above. In the bottled-water market, several brands co-exist, each with unique positionings in the mind of the consumer. Yet, in repeated blind tastings, few consumers can identify any functional characteristics which could be used as the basis for brand discrimination.

A definition of marketing communications

The attitudes of the customer towards a particular product/brand will, to a substantial extent, be a reflection of the nature of the marketing communications elements that are used to support a brand. The task of Marketing Communications are to present the product or service in the most appropriate manner. In that respect, it must be considered a logical extension of the fundamental principles of marketing itself.

> **Definition**
>
> Marketing communications
>
> 'Marketing communications are a management process through which an organization enters into a dialogue with its various audiences. Based upon an understanding of the audiences communications environment, an organization develops and presents messages for its identified stakeholder groups, and evaluates and acts upon the responses received. The objective of the process is to (re)position by influencing the perception and understanding of the organization and/or its products and services, with a view to generating attitudinal and behavioural responses' (Fill, 2002)

As mentioned earlier, it is important to establish two-way communications, hence the need for *dialogue*. It was also established that there is a need to differentiate a product, hence the *positioning* theme. Customers are active problem solvers, people think at different levels about the value to them of a communication or an intended purchase, hence the *cognitive response* aspect of the definition.

Marketing communications are used by organizations to communicate with a wide array of stakeholder audiences, not just customers (not just consumers). In order to achieve the desired marketing and marketing communications objectives, a company may well have to communicate with governmental agencies (to influence existing or potential legislation); the city, financial institutions and shareholders (in order to raise the necessary funds to pursue its marketing programmes); distributors and retailers (to encourage them to stock the product); the media and other opinion formers (to ensure that they think and write positively about the product); the community at large; and its own employees. All of these stakeholders will need to be communicated with and, importantly, the nature of the message may need to be varied to reflect the differing needs of these groups.

The communications process

It is not surprising that with all this 'noise' surrounding us, the task of marketing communications has become increasingly difficult. For any message to get through, it must break through the surrounding noise and grab hold of the potential consumers' attention. To understand the complex process of marketing communications, we have to recognize that each and every one of us has to use some form of filtering system, in order to extract the information we need from everything that surrounds it.

Activity 1.7

How do we decide what information to absorb, and which to ignore?

We can look at a simple model which describes the various stages. At its simplest level, we can describe the model as having three elements. The first is the sender of the message. The second is the message itself, and the third is the recipient of the message. This could be depicted as shown in Figure 1.1. Unfortunately, this model oversimplifies the nature of the process. It makes no allowance for the fact that the message may not be understood by the recipient; nor does it take into consideration the means by which the message is transmitted to the receiver.

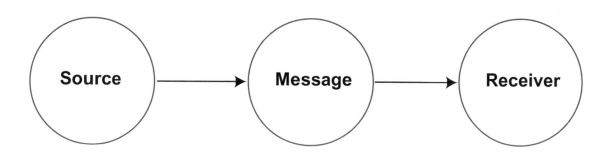

Figure 1.1
A simple model of the communication process

A better understanding of the process is provided by the more detailed model shown in Figure 1.2. A number of new elements have been introduced which illustrate the more complex nature of communications. In order to convey any message, we need to encode it into some form of symbolic representation. This may take the form of words, colours, shapes or pictures. Advertising is usually a combination of both words and pictures which combine to convey a desired impression of the product or service to the consumer. The message to be transmitted will need to be placed into some form of medium or carrier which the sender believes will be seen or heard by the intended receiver.

This may be the conventional media, such as television, the press, radio, or posters, but may also include point-of-sale material and the packaging of the product. Later on in the text, we will explain how the medium itself may play an important part in assisting or changing the intended message.

Importantly, we must recognize that the message is only one of many which the intended receiver will be required to deal with. To understand that, think of yourself reading a colour magazine. The advertiser who wants to tell you something about his product must compete for your attention not only with the variety of other advertisements included in that issue, but also the diversity of articles for which you bought the publication in the first place. The resultant noise may well interfere with the effective communication of the message. The reader may not spend enough time reading the advertisement, and may only glean enough information to form an impression of the intended message. This is an important aspect of the process of communications which we will return to in later units.

In addition, there is all the 'surrounding noise' with which we have to deal. Few of us have the opportunity to consider an advertisement in splendid isolation. Invariably there will be a whole variety of things going on around us which may detract from our ability to concentrate and to extract the full message being sent by the advertiser. The decoding process may, therefore, be incomplete or confused. In any case it will be influenced by the recipient's preconceptions of the sender. If he or she regards the company as being reliable and trustworthy, then it is likely that the message will be interpreted in that light. However, if the individual has previously had some form of negative experience with another product or service from the same company then it is less likely that the message will be interpreted in a positive manner.

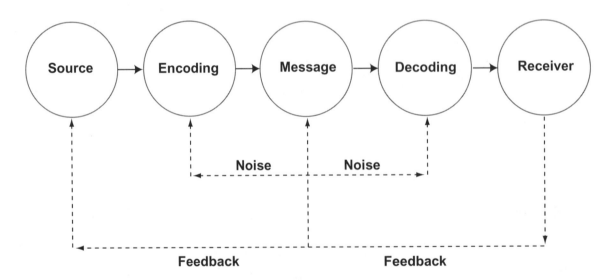

Figure 1.2
A linear model of the communication process

A recent police recruitment press campaign deliberately used elements of the decoding process to elicit a specific response. The advertisements showed a police officer chasing an individual dressed in casual clothes. The casual reader might conclude, consistent with normal decoding of information, that the person being chased was a criminal. In fact the advertising revealed him to be a plain clothes officer going to help someone else.

The response which the receiver makes will vary according to the nature of the message and these extraneous factors. Some advertisements simply convey information, others contain some form of invitation to purchase. The response of the receiver to the specific message will be of great importance to the sender, who will need to build in some form of feedback mechanism in order to understand better the nature of the response and, if appropriate, be in a position to change the message if that response is negative. This is of course the dialogue that we identified earlier as an important aspect of marketing communications.

One final comment on the communication process, – the effectiveness of communication is determined partly by the elements we have highlighted here. However, there are a number of other elements that need to be considered when developing marketing communications and these concern the environment in which the communications are expected to work and the behaviour (e.g. mood) of the people involved in either sending or receiving communications. These are referred to as contextual elements in that they define the overall conditions in which communications work. These contextual aspects are considered in more detail in unit 'Context 2 – Other contexts'.

Personal influences

The communication process is influenced by a wide range of other factors. One of the skills of the communication manager is to manage these other elements in such a way that they enhance the effectiveness of the communications and improve the efficiency of the communications spend.

One of these factors is the influence other people can have. Messages received from individuals rather than the media have the potential to deliver a stronger message than those delivered through media alone. One of the ways in which this can be effected is through the use of opinion formers. These are people who are either experts or are actively involved in the subject area. Messages received from these people are more likely to be believable as they contain higher levels of credibility. For example, journalists relay information and are percieved to be objective in their analysis and the comment they pass on.

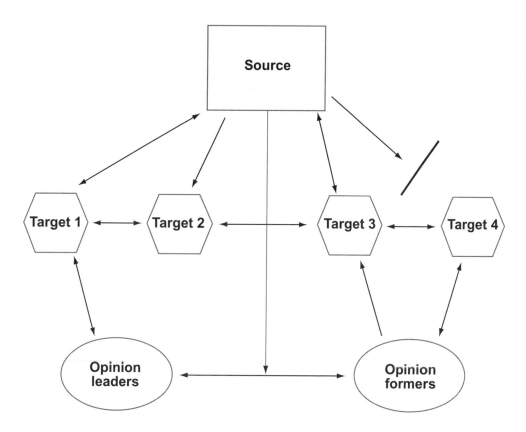

Figure 1.3
Opinion formers and opinion leaders in the communication process

Opinion leaders on the other hand are usually members of our own peer group. Their expertise is based upon their own interest as a hobby or pastime in the subject areas. It is certainly not their career or part of their job. Therefore word-of-mouth communications from these individuals carries even higher levels of credibility than those borne by by opinion formers. See Figure 1.3.

It is not surprising therefore that some campaigns seek to generate word-of-mouth recommendation as this form of personal influence has a far greater impact than advertising, sales promotion or direct marketing is ever likely to achieve.

In the world of new media this idea of personal influence is used through viral marketing. This involves the transmission of e-mail messages from friend to friend and is referred to as word-of-mouse communications.

How does marketing communications work?

The shortest answer to this question is that we don't really know! Although a great many theories have been put forward to explain the mechanical operation of marketing communications, many of them have either been too simplistic or have simply not stood up to empirical examination.

Originally proposed (1925) to explain the process of personal selling, the AIDA model was rapidly adopted to explain the process of communications in advertising. The basic tenant was that, in order to have effect, the first task of any campaign was to gain the *attention* of the viewer or reader. The second stage is the stimulation of an *interest* in the proposition. In most cases, it would be reasonable to assume that if the first requirement – attention – had been met, the second would follow on almost automatically.

The third stage is to create a *desire* for the product or service being promoted. Often, this will take the form of a 'problem-solution' execution in which the advertiser seeks to position the product as the answer to a problem which has previously been identified.

Activity 1.8

Identify at least three examples of current advertising (not including the markets mentioned above) where the problem-solution approach is currently employed.

The fourth and final stage of the AIDA model is the stimulation of some form of response on the part of the audience – the action stage. Most advertisements have a specific call to action, and many are linked with promotional offers designed to induce a purchase of the product or some other desired end result.

From the outset, it was recognized that a fundamental aim of communication was to cut through the surrounding clutter and arrest the attention of the potential purchaser. Moreover, it suggested that the process of communications required the audience to pass through a series of sequential steps, and that each step was a logical consequence of what had gone before. The principle of sequential activity or learning is used commonly in many marketing models, and is often referred to as a *hierarchy of effects*. It is clear that the attention phase is key to the process, since whatever follows will be of little value if the attention of the audience has not been achieved.

However, this model and other 'hierarchy of effects' models are now discredited as valid interpretations of how advertising (marketing communications?) work. Many other models have been developed to explain the consumer interaction with advertising and the processing of advertising messages, the **'heightened appreciation model'** is a valuable tool for explaining some of the mechanics of the advertising message and, importantly, assists in determining advertising strategy. What the model suggests is that, by identifying a desirable attribute of a product (through the use of consumer research) and linking it directly with the brand, the consumer is both made more aware of that, attribute and associates it with the brand. The direct result of this activity is to create a more positive awareness of the product or service, which results in more frequent usage and the building of a better image.

A good example of how the manufacturers' focus on a specific attribute can arouse heightened appreciation of that attribute can be seen in the soap powder market. For many years, the primary benefit of all products within the category has been their ability to get clothes whiter. As a result of changes in the formulation of the product, the focus has shifted towards colour fastness. The majority of advertising in the category stresses this benefit, with the result that the consumer now compares competing products against this dimension rather than the degree of whiteness which is delivered by the product.

Contemporary thoughts about how marketing communications (very often just advertising) work tend to be less specific and less inclined to suggest that buyers move sequentially. The learn-feel-do sequence suggested by the hierarchy of effects models is now generally considered to be out-of-date and inaccurate.

Today, ideas such as Hall's four frameworks, Jones's Strong and Weak theories of advertising (and Ehrenberg's ATR model) and general descriptions such as Prue's Alphabetical model are more widely accepted as suitable interpretations.

What emerges from this is that integrated marketing communications work through an interaction between the brand and the communications that surround it. As we will see later in this Coursebook, brand-related communications can be orientated to the rational factual aspects of a product or may be orientated to image and emotional brand associations. Brands can remind people about needs (need more *x*) and they can also remind about the advertising and the associations that surround a brand.

Advertising can work by persuading people to buy a brand (Strong theory) or they might work by reminding people of a need they may have (Weak theory). Advertising and marketing communications work in different ways in different situations (contexts) and it is not right to say that it works by any one single method.

Exam tip

The Senior Examiner expects students at this level to understand that AIDA is no longer a suitable model. Students need to be familiar with the general ideas associated with the Strong and the Weak theories and to appreciate the relationship that may exist between a brand and the advertising that surrounds it. A more detailed exploration of these topics can be found in chapter 20 of the essential text that accompanies this module (Fill, 2002).

Summary

In this unit we have:

- Begun the process of understanding the nature and role of marketing communications andtheir position within the marketing mix.
- Considered a definition of marketing communications and discovered the depth and significance of this complex subject.
- Explored some of the difficulties which marketing communications messages must confront in an increasingly crowded media environment and the various stages through which the message must pass on its way to the recipient.
- Revisited communication theory and developed our understanding of the role which personal influences can play on the communication process.
- Discussed some of the problems associated with the AIDA model and introduced more contemporary ideas about strong and weak theories, triggers and brand associations.

Further study and examination preparation

See Question 2 of the examination paper for June 2000 in the appendices.

Objectives

In this unit you will:

- Study the nature of marketing communications strategy.
- Examine the need for and characteristics associated with integrating marketing communications.
- Discover a framework for the development of marketing communications plans.
- Move through the important stages which must be followed in the planning process.

By the end of this unit you will:

- Understand the nature and importance of strategy in the context of marketing communications.
- Appreciate the strategic importance of integrated marketing communications.
- Be aware of the forces that affect marketing communications strategy.
- Have developed an understanding of the role of planning.
- Know of the Marketing Communications Planning Framework and know what the sequence of activities is.

This unit covers syllabus sections 1.1.1, 1.1.2, 1.1.3, 1.2.2.

Study guide

This unit is concerned primarily with providing a comprehensive understanding of the strategic implications of marketing communications and, especially, the dynamics of integrated activities.

This is a particularly important unit, since it establishes key principles which will affect your understanding of the further processes involved in the discipline.

The development of a carefully structured marketing communications plan is a critical facet of the communications process. If there is any lack of clarity in the planning phase, this will have significant consequences for the activity which follows. It is therefore important to ensure that your understanding of the topic is comprehensive.

You are advised to attempt the various exercises contained in this unit which have been specifically designed to reinforce your learning, and answer the short questions which have been included for the same reason.

Introduction to marketing communications strategy

Study tip

Remember that it is the Marketing Plan (document) that holds a great deal of this information. We are not interested in repeating all the analysis and preparation of the preferred marketing strategy – it has already been completed.

Marketing communications have an important strategic role to play within organizations. In 2001 the Boots Co announced that it was redefining its overall business and marketing strategy, was going to reformat its high street shops into 'convenience' and 'Wellbeing' stores and that its alliance with Granada will see the launch of a digital interactive shopping channel. These are fundamental changes to strategy and it will be incumbent upon marketing communications to deliver messages that reflect the new strategy, that inform and advise customers, potential customers and other stakeholders of the benefits Boots will offer in the future. In order to implement and sustain this new approach Boots needed to restructure their internal organization, put in place new systems and procedures and perhaps retrain and/or refocus the way staff work.

Another way of looking at this is that Boots have redefined their business activity and as a result they needed to reposition themselves so that customers understood what the Boots brand promises to deliver. The issues here concern marketing strategy, staff and customer perceptions, positioning and branding. All these are important aspects of marketing comunications strategy and each is considered in more detail later in this book.

Strategy is not necessarily the same as planning. Strategy might be considered as the purpose and direction of the organization whereas planning might be considered to be the articulation of the strategic intent. In other words strategy is about where an organization is headed and planning is about the detail concerning how that strategy is to be accomplished.

Marketing communications strategy is about how an organization can successfully communicate and deliver its marketing strategy and this inevitably involves a rich complexity of organizational, market, human, product and corporate branding issues.

Integrated marketing communications

For Boots to be successful it is likely that it will need to integrate its activities. A major contemporary issue in the field of Marketing Communications is the drive towards integrated activity. There are a number of reasons for this fundamental change in thinking which needs to be examined.

Key to the issue is the fact that the customer does not see advertising, public relations, sales promotion and other marketing communications techniques as separate and divisible components. As the receivers of a variety of messages from an equally wide range of sources customers build up an image – either favourable or unfavourable – of a company, its brands and its services. As far as they are concerned, the source of the message is unimportant. What they will be concerned with is the content of the message and to what degree the brand promise is actually delivered.

A parallel consideration is the fact that the communicator desires to achieve a sense of cohesion in the messages which he or she communicates. If, for example, advertising is saying one thing about a brand and sales promotion something different, a sense of dissonance may be created with the customer left in some doubt as to what the brand is really trying to say.

Definition

IMC

IMC are 'The management process associated with the strategic development, delivery and dialogue of consistent, coordinated messages, that stakeholders perceive as reinforcing core brand propositions. (Fill, 2002)'.

There is little doubt that marketing communications funds spent on a single communications message will achieve a far greater impact than when a series of different or contradictory messages are being sent out about a brand. With increasing pressure on funds, marketers desire to ensure that they present a clear and precise picture of their products and services to their customers. This is particularly true in those instances where a company with a comparatively small budget seeks to take on competitors with significantly larger levels of expenditure.

The NSPCC is a good example of how a small player can use its marketing communications efforts to achieve significant impact. By adopting a coordinated campaign towards its policy of reducing child abuse, and communicating it effectively through a simple message delivered through a set of integrated marketing communications activities, the charity has achieved a significant impact in making this issue more visible.

Few companies are specifically concerned with issues of whether to spend their money on advertising, sales promotion, public relations, or elsewhere. They are concerned with ensuring that they develop a cohesive marketing communications programme which most effectively communicates their proposition to their customers. The specific communication route is of far less important than the impact of the message. In budgetary terms, companies need to consider where their expenditure will best achieve their defined objectives. The previous notions of separate and distinct advertising, sales promotion, public relations, and other budgets fail to appreciate that the considerations of the marketing communications budget need to be addressed as a matter of priority.

At the heart of the debate is the recognition that the customer must be the focus of all marketing communications activity. If we return to the CIM definition of marketing we can see that the primary need is the anticipation and satisfaction of customer wants and needs. It is the development of an understanding of the customer and his or her wants and needs that will ensure that marketing communications works effectively to achieve the objectives defined for it. This represents a fundamental change of focus. A shift from the functional activity of creating marketing communications campaigns to an attitudinal focus in which the customers' needs are at the heart of all marketing communications planning.

There are many reasons why organizations seek to establish IMC and some of the advantages and disadvantages are listed in Table 2.1.

Table 2.1: Advantages and Disadvantages of IMC (Fill, 2002. Used with kind permission)

Advantages of IMC

1	Provide opportunities to cut communication costs and/or reassign budgets
2	Have the potential to produce synergistic and more effective communications
3	Can deliver competitive advantage through clearer positioning
4	Encourage coordinated brand development with internal and external participants
5	Provide for increased employee participation and motivation
6	Have the potential to cause management to review their communication strategy
7	Require a change in culture and fosters a customer focus
8	Provide a benchmark for the development of communication activities
9	Can lead to a cut in the number of agencies supporting a brand.

Disadvantages of IMC

1	Encourage centralization and formal/ bureaucratic procedures
2	Can require increased management time seeking agreement from all involved parties
3	Suggest uniformity and single message
4	Tendency to standardization might negate or dilute creative opportunities
5	Global brands restricted in terms of local adaptation
6	Normally require cultural change upon employees and encourages resistance

7 Have the potential to severely damage a brand's reputation if incorrectly managed

8 Can lead to mediocrity as no single agency network has access to all sources of communication expertise

The task of developing and implementing marketing communications campaigns is becoming increasingly divergent. No longer is the task in one pair of hands. As the specialist functions develop further, the marketer must seek and co-ordinate the input from a number of different sources. Many organizations will retain an advertising agency, a public relations consultancy, a sales promotion company and, perhaps, even a media specialist. Ensuring that all of these contributors work to the same set of objectives and deliver a cohesive message to the customer is a task which is an increasingly challenging one. All of these contributors need to be involved in the process of IMC.

Activity 2.1

Find two examples of an integrated marketing communications programme. Describe the variety of communications techniques used, and how they are integrated with each other.

In addition to these factors there are major difficulties implementing IMC. General reluctance to change, financial systems and brand management structures all serve to impede progress. However, on a more positive note it is becoming evident that the development of interactive technologies is encouraging organizations to reconsider their communications and as a result some are more prepared to develop integrated activities.

So far the idea behind Integrated Marketing Communications are that customers perceive a single consistent message. This is true and many people refer to IMC as the coordination of the tools of the promotional mix. However, this is not the full story as the other elements of the marketing mix communicate as well and for integration to be achieved these elements need to be harnessed within the chosen strategy and delivered consistently.

Product

All products are multi-dimensional in their nature. At the most basic level there are a series of functional features designed to meet the essential requirements of the target consumers. Sometimes referred to as the 'core product', this consists of the assembly of ingredients which provide the basic character of the product. Thus a car consists of an engine, a passenger compartment and four wheels; a washing powder is a collection of ingredients designed to ensure that clothes are washed clean; and so on. Clearly, however, these describe only the basic characteristics. At this level, many consumers are unable to distinguish between competing products within the same category.

An example of this differential perception is given in *Creating Powerful Brands,* by L. de Chernatony and M. McDonald (Butterworth-Heinemann, 2nd ed, 1998). In a blind taste test of the two leading carbonated diet beverages, when the brand identity was concealed, 51 per cent of those sampled preferred Diet Pepsi, 44 per cent preferred Diet Coke, and 5 per cent said that they were the same or that they couldn't tell the difference. When the products were sampled in an open test, with the brand identities revealed, only 23 per cent indicated that they preferred Diet Pepsi, with 65 per cent preferring Diet Coke, and 12 per cent saying that they were equal or didn't know. The key differentiating factor was the brand identity, which provided additional values to the consumer, overriding the physical characteristics of the products.

Manufacturers invest vast sums of money into the development of other facets of the product which are designed to assist the consumer in their identification of a brand in a crowded marketplace. The brand name and the packaging all serve to add other dimensions to the core product. Again, at a basic level, these facets may only be there to provide a clear identification of the product on the supermarket or chemist shelf. However, in most cases, they go much further and invest the core product with a series of intangible values which, to a much greater degree, serve to assist in the discrimination of one manufacturer's product from that of a competitor. Names, logos and pack designs and colours all provide the consumer with the ability to recognize a particular manufacturer's product and determine whether or not it is likely to meet their specific needs and wants.

Much more important in the overall purchasing decision are the intangible aspects of a product – the image dimensions and perceptual factors which are the real discriminators in brand purchase. It is here that marketing communications play a key role. The key brand dimensions relating to awareness, image, brand values, etc., are, for the most part, the direct result of the work done within marketing communications.

Price

As with product, price is an important dimension of the overall proposition to the consumer, and will have important implications from the perspective of marketing communications. In a purely marketing context, pricing decisions will be considered as a distinct element of the marketing strategy. However, it is important to remember that all pricing decisions will have an impact on consumers' perceptions of the product or service. In this context, therefore, pricing can be seen to have a promotional dimension which we will consider below.

It may be a cliché, but many consumers relate price to quality expectations. Thus, a more expensive product is innately assumed to be of higher quality, while a cheaper one may be perceived as being of lesser quality. It is important, here, however, to distinguish between perceptions of value for money. All consumers make a fundamental equation between price, performance and value for money. Economic circumstances may dictate that a cheaper product is purchased, but many consumers continue to separate this decision from overall product performance.

In many instances, price is an important discriminator between private label products and those produced by major manufacturers. Advertising is often used to reinforce the values associated with manufacturers' brands to ensure that, despite the higher price charged, the product still represents superior value for money. Advertising for Fairy Liquid has stressed the product quality and longevity of use against cheaper rival brands, for example.

The price of a product will often be used as a reference point by consumers. If, in a given market, brands are segmented by price, then the price of a product will serve to identify the relative position of an unknown brand. In, say, the market for compact disc players, some manufacturers will charge £75, others around £150, and yet others at prices in excess of £500. A new product entering the market at a price of £175 will immediately be perceived as a contender in the middle range.

Of course, as consumers learn more about the various competitors and their respective product offerings, the absolute price may recede in importance. However, it is important to remember that in many instances, particularly where the consumer lacks sufficient information to compare all the available brands on the basis of the features which they offer, price will be an important guide.

In some instances, a high price can reinforce the prestige image of a brand. If the price of a product is well known, then ownership of the particular product can reinforce the social prestige. This is particularly true of premium-priced jewellery and watches, but may also relate to the use of perfumes and items of clothing.

Place

Where the product is sold may, similarly, have a considerable impact on consumer perceptions of a brand. The nature of the outlet which stocks a particular brand may transfer certain dimensions of image to the brand itself and make it more or less desirable as a purchase. Products which are uniquely stocked by high-quality outlets tend to be perceived as high quality, while those stocked by discount stores may have the image of those outlets transferred to the brand and encourage consumers to perceive those brands as being of lower quality. The presentations of the major perfume houses stressed this aspect of their marketing activity to the Monopolies and Mergers Commission to prevent their prices from being discounted in 'cheap price' outlets.

The retail environment may play a significant part in establishing credibility for a product within its category. In the case of many ethical pharmaceutical products, manufacturers can choose the nature of their distribution. On the one hand, they can achieve a wider reach of the marketplace by encouraging the major supermarket chains to stock their products. On the other, they can restrict their distribution to specialist chemist outlets. With the latter, however, there is the clear transference of the professional authority of chemists to these products. In some respects, this may be regarded by the consumer as a professional endorsement of the efficacy of the product, which is clearly not derived from other outlets. Thus, a clear choice must be made between the reference value of the stockist and the wider distribution gained through a broader range of outlets.

Many manufacturers deliberately restrict distribution to ensure the projection of a desired image for a brand – watches, jewellery, hifi. Recently Levi lost a court decision to prevent Tesco and other major grocery retailers from selling their jeans at discounted prices. Their objections are based on the detrimental impact this might have on the images of the Levi brand and Tesco taking advantage of the huge financial investment Levi have put into building the brand to make them desirable. It can be seen, therefore, that marketing and marketing communications are inextricably linked so the strategic approach of one area must equally be applied to the others.

Activity 2.3

Find other examples of the contribution to marketing communications made by each of the other Ps of the marketing mix.

Marketing communications are not only about the promotional mix or the marketing mix, they are also about how representatives of a company (employees and managers) actually behave. They are about attitudes and the degree of care that customers perceive when they are engaged with an organization. Therefore a lot of work 'behind the scenes' needs to take place if consistency is to be achieved. Really effective IMC occur through an incremental process, by changing the procedures and actions of a company, by refocusing the culture and then by bringing together the internal and external communications so that the messages say and deliver the same brand promise. See Figure 2.1

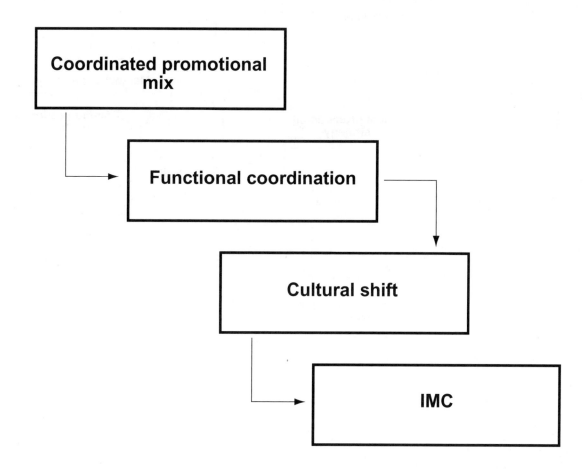

Figure 2.1
Incremental development of IMC

Look at B&Q. Here is a retail organization that deliberately uses its staff in all of advertising. Not only do customers recognize and appreciate the B&Q brand promise being spoken for by the type of people they will encounter when visiting a store, but staff also feel valued and that they are able to control the message that is transmitted and uphold what they promise.

Planning and frameworks

The development of a cohesive and integrated marketing communications plan demands the adoption of a systematic process to ensure that all dimensions of the plan are carefully and thoroughly considered. There is no such thing as the 'ideal' planning format. Each plan must be adapted to meet the specific circumstances which need to be addressed. However, a planning framework can help ensure that all necessary aspects are considered when developing a marketing communications campaigns.

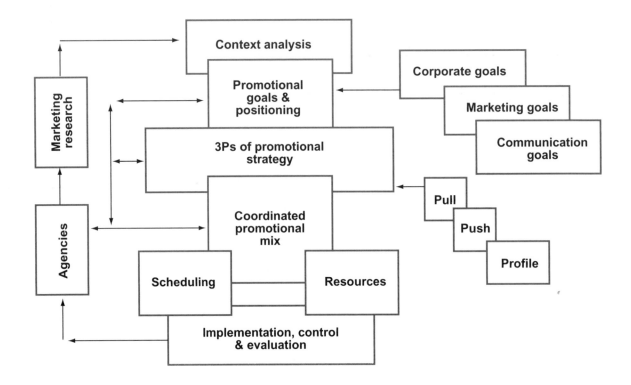

Figure 2.2
The marketing communications planning framework (Fill, 2002).

Figure 2.2 sets out the marketing communication planning framework (the MCPF). This serves a number of purposes. One is to identify specific aspects of such a plan, the general order in which they occur and to suggest that all the parts are integrated as part of an overall plan. There are linkages between the many parts and these linkages are the 'oil' that makes the plan mobile, that makes it work.

Exam hint

Knowing this plan and how the parts are interrelated is important. The examiner often asks questions that either require students to demonstrate their knowledge of the different parts or they are required to use the framework in order to answer a specific question (e.g. to develop a marketing communications plan in response to a mini-case question)

Using the MCPF

In order to utilize the MCPF, information is required. In real life, this information can be gathered from a variety of sources over a predetermined period of time. With experience the data collected can be used to feed subsequent campaign plans. In an examination however, you will be working in a very restricted time period and you will not have access to all the information you require. In these circumstances you need to concentrate on the salient points and make judgements about the information you have (as in real life) and to make reasonable assumptions about the information you do not have or would like to have.

In some instances, information will be readily accessible. In others, the task of collecting relevant data will be more difficult. In all cases, the need to conduct specific programmes of marketing research will be important to identify key customer issues.

The remaining parts of this unit briefly consider each of the elements of the MCPF. These are explored in more detail in subsequent units; the goal at this stage is to give you a taster for the issues to be managed.

Context analysis

The starting point for any determination of strategic direction, must be a comprehensive and thorough analysis of the background situation along a number of key dimensions. As we saw when looking at ideas about communication processes it is useful to consider the context within which marketing communications occur. Therefore, it is necessary to consider four main contextual areas: the market (or business context), the customer/audience characteristics (the customer context), the company (or internal context) and the general environment (or external context).

These four areas are examined in greater depth in the next unit, however, a brief overview is presented here.

The business context

The first context to examine is that of the marketplace and the company's preferred overall approach to achieving its objectives in the light of market conditions and competitor behaviour. In simple terms, the issues can be summarized as follows in Table 2.2

Table 2.2: Questions to be asked in an analysis of the business context
What business are we in and how do we compete?
What are its key products and services?
How are these differentiated from those of its competitors?
How they satisfy potential customers?
What are the significant trends?
Who are our customers?
Where are they?
How do we segment them?

These and other questions should already have been answered and documented as part of the Marketing Plan. What is required now is a deeper insight into the market conditions, competitor activities, audience characteristics and to derive a more meaningful insight into how communications can be made more effective.

The segment information feeds different aspects of the MCPF. The attitudinal aspects feed the media requirements and the behavioural information feeds the message and creative aspects of the message.

Activity 2.4

For any market with which you are familiar, identify possible market segments. What might be the implications for marketing communication messages for each segment?

In those situations where the company operates with several brands, it will be important to understand the role that each of them has within the overall portfolio. Clearly, a fundamental need will be to ensure differentiation between them in the eyes of potential customers. This will minimize the likelihood of share steal from one of the company's brands by another. Similarly, the brand position will need to be carefully considered to determine whether it is one that needs to be sustained or, if weak, requires modification. Lucozade, for example, used marketing communications to change the position which the brand occupied in the minds of customers – from a drink that restored health to one that replaces energy lost through sporting exertion.

In the same way, the historic brand values may well dictate the tone and direction of the marketing communications campaign, since there may be elements associated with, for example, the advertising campaign, which need to be underpinned in any future activity.

The customer context

You will recall from your previous marketing studies that understanding buyer behaviour can be very important. What we need to understand are the perceptions, motivation and attitudes that our target audiences experience when considering our product category and our brand. We also need to understand the risks they perceive and the levels of involvement they have when making these purchase decisions.

The reason for having this information is that we can then design marketing communications campaigns that are more likely to be effective. We may have identified negative attitudes – in which case marketing communications need to change attitudes. We may have found that the target audience completely misunderstands what our product does – in which case our marketing communications must inform them more clearly. It may be that the price is perceived to be too high, in which case marketing communications must convey the value added more effectively and in doing so reduce levels of perceived risk.

Activity 2.5

Find an advertisement for a direct marketing organization (often to be found in the weekend colour supplements). What sort of risks might they be trying to reduce?

Turn to Unit 3, page 42, for a list of the perceived risks most commonly experienced by buyers.

So far in this book there has been a tendency to see customers as consumer. This is not always the case as customers may be businesses and the buyers may be professional managers buying on behalf of large corporations. Because the characteristics of the buying process can be so very different in these circumstances we need to be aware of the implications for business-to-business communications.

There are a wide array of other factors that can influence the shape and nature of customer behaviour and when dealing with international marketing communications this can be very important.

The internal context

Since marketing communications are inextricably linked with marketing strategy, we need to develop an understanding of the organization, its employees, culture and ooverall approach. Remember, we are trying to develop 'integrated marketing communications' and this means developing a set of internal core values that are appreciated and valued by staff (motivation and involvement) and customers (consistency, credibility and the delivery of promises).

We also need to understand the functional capabilities of the organization and importantly, the level of financial resources likely to be available to support the intended and required marketing communications. If, for example, the company has only limited financial resources, then it will not be able to undertake a costly communications exercise. If there are gaps, say, in the sales force, then a communications plan which depends to a high degree on personal selling is unlikely to achieve its targets – unless the company's own personnel are augmented from an external force, or new recruits are employed and trained before the plan is implemented.

Setting the communications budget is an important aspect of the marketing-communications plan and is considered in more detail towards the end of this unit and again in unit Financial resources. At the very least, the examiner will expect you to be able to justify your identification of an appropriate budget for the task set within a particular question and you must have a full understanding of the important aspects of this topic. A common student error is to misjudge the balance between the level of available financial resources and the campaign that they propose. So, 30 secs of television advertising on Coronation Street costs £140,000 (station average price). With production costs running at £500,000 you can see that a substantial promotional budget is necessary.

At this stage of the planning process, a check needs to be made to determine the overall amount of available funding, as this can act as a guide to future decisions. A more precise budget is worked out later once it is known which promotional tools (and media) are to be used.

Activity 2.6

Why is budget determination a critical phase of the marketing communications planning process?

Having completed the internal company analysis, we can begin to examine the other dimensions. It is not necessary to carry out these activities in any particular sequence, as long as by the end of the exercise all of the key dimensions have been covered fully.

The external context

It is equally important to establish an understanding of the broader environment in which the company operates. This may be either a domestic or international context. Here, there are a number of important factors which are, substantially, outside the control of the organization, although to varying degrees it may be possible to exert some form of influence.

The external context is normally considered through use of the PEST framework. These political, economic, social and technlogical factors are, by definition, outside the control of any one organization. The essence of the analysis is see how any of these forces might impact on the marketing *communications* specifically (not just the company or its marketing).

For example, a change in social values such as families no longer eating their evening meal together can be reflected not only in different product offerings but also in the way families are depicted in advertisements. For over 30 years Oxo used typical family scenes to show their brand but this was stopped in 1999 when a fresh approach was taken to repesent contemporary family life.

Marketing objectives and positioning

The next step is to work out the objectives for the campaign. These are derived from the Context analysis and not from any arbitrary notion of what might be required. It is important to be clear as to the distinction between marketing and marketing communications objectives.

Marketing objectives are the specific goals that need to be achieved during the timescale of the plan. They will often refer to such targets as: increasing brand share by x per cent or to y per cent; increasing the return on capital investment; maintaining or increasing distribution; and penetrating an identified sector of the market.

Marketing communications objectives, as we will see later, are concerned with specific goals relating to communications. As such, they will relate to areas such as: increasing awareness; informing the market of specific features or attributes of a product; suggesting new uses for a product; explaining how a product functions; and altering perceptions of a product or service.

These goals help define what is to be achieved and how the campaign is to be evaluated at a later date.

Positioning is one of the key strategic issues associated with marketing communications. Marketing communications need to be designed so that the objectives are met and the desired position 'in the minds of members of the target audience' is the achieved. You may remember that one of the roles is to differentiate a brand, in other words position it so that stakeholders perceive the brand clearly and separately from all other competing brands. The task at this stage is to identify how the brand should be positioned and whether to use marketing communications to reposition it in order that it be perceived and valued more clearly.

Marketing communications strategy

Marketing communications strategy is about two main elements. The nature of the target audience and the message that the audience needs to receive and understand.

The target audience

The target audience can be considered as one of three parts:

1. End users customers (b2b and b2c) – Pull
2. Members of the marketing channel – Push
3. All other stakeholders – Profile

These three audiences comprise the 3Ps of marketing communications strategy, pull, push and profile. Each is considered in more detail later in the book.

Identification of the core message

Analysis of the customer context should contribute to the identification of the most appropriate message. It is vitally important to understand the way customers think, feel and behave towards your company, products, services or brands. For example, it is necessary for camera manufacturers to understand their customers purchase patterns, needs, usage, preferences and buying motivations as this information can be used to identify the most effective message that needs to be conveyed.

Another way of looking at this is to analyse the criteria customers use for brand selection. These criteria may relate to the individual – in terms of their desires and aspirations – while others relate to the product – both its physical properties and levels of emotional appeal. It is the combination of these characteristics into a single and cohesive message that is clearly understood by the target customer which will ensure the development of effective marketing communications. The core message therefore refers to whether customers need to understand how the brand is to be (re)positioned, if they are to be reminded, informed or if an attempt is to be made to persuade them to take a particular action (se.g. calling for a brochure, buying the product, visiting a web site etc).

Activity 2.9

Find several examples of advertising campaigns for products in the same product category.

How does the core message differ for each of them?

The development of the promotional mix

Although it is important to develop the individual components of a campaign with great care and attention to detail, it is arguably more important that we should ensure that all communications devices offer a single and consistent message to the target audience. It follows then that we can only begin the process of identifying the campaign elements once we have determined the precise nature of the message we wish to communicate.

We will need to consider all dimensions of marketing communications – as indeed we will in the following units of this Coursebook – in order to examine the precise contribution that each of them can make to the delivery of the communications strategy. But we should not take a fixated view as to which components we include in the campaign. Equally importantly, we must determine at the outset which of the various areas should take the lead in our activity. In most cases this will follow logically from the work that we have done in the development of our communications plan.

If the primary task is to increase levels of awareness of our brand, then we will be driven into a consideration of the relative merits of advertising, public relations and direct marketing. If we wish to offer a specific inducement to sample the product, then it is likely that we will use the variety of sales promotions techniques available to us, although the communication of the message may remain with advertising. If our audience is highly defined, then a direct marketing approach may be preferable to a broad-based advertising campaign, and so on.

It is highly likely that there will be several options open to us, and it is important to consider the relative merits of each approach. In some instances, budgetary considerations and time frames may dictate that a series of subjective decisions be taken. However, in an ideal situation, we should be prepared to test the various elements of the communications mix.

Activity 2.10

Although you will not need to have detailed knowledge of media costs, some limited understanding will be important to your being able to allocate a budget to the various elements of the communications mix. To help you in this process, identify the following:

- The cost of a 30-second television commercial.
- The cost of a full-page black and white press advertisement in a national newspaper.
- The cost of a one-minute radio advertisement.

Implementation: Resources and Co-ordination

It is vitally important that, in order to maximize campaign effectiveness, the implementation programme be carefully co-ordinated. In simple terms, this means the allocation of the right resources (primarily financial) and the adoption of a critical timing plan (Gantt chart) to ensure that each aspect of the campaign breaks at the right time. There are a number of elements which need to be considered in this respect.

Resources

For the purposes of this unit, it will suffice to list the various methods of budget determination. It is important, however, that you carefully consider the topics covered in unit Financial resources later in your study programme.

There are a variety of different methods of determining a marketing communications budget, and the approach taken will largely depend on the particular nature of the circumstances. These will include:

- Marginal analysis
- Percentage of last year's turnover or sales
- Percentage of gross profit margin
- Residue of last year's surplus
- Percentage of anticipated profit
- Unit or case sales ratio
- Competitive expenditure levels
- Desired share of voice
- Media inflation
- Objective-and-task
- Experimentation
- What we can afford
- New product considerations

Co-ordination

The first priority will be to ensure that the sales force is fully briefed both as to the nature and the objectives of the campaign. Their enthusiasm will need to be stimulated to ensure that all other elements can, reasonably, be put in place at the right time. At the same time, it is important to ensure that they are equipped with the appropriate sales aids to communicate the message to their immediate audience of wholesalers and retailers.

Equally important is the fact that sufficient time must be built in not only to allow them to communicate the proposition but also, in turn, to enable the distribution channels to take up appropriate volumes before the campaign breaks. If, for example, the campaign depends on a sales promotion incentive, then adequate stock of the specially prepared packaging needs to be in store to meet anticipated customer demand. Even if the campaign is designed to build awareness of the brand, or to stimulate trial of existing product, it is important to ensure that, as far as possible, the trade is made aware of the campaign *before* it breaks to the public. Not only will this enable the selling in of stocks against demand but, more important, it will serve to develop the relationship between the retailer and the company.

The functional aspects of campaign implementation are important. Sufficient time needs to be planned for promotional labels to be printed, television commercials and press advertising to be delivered to the media, direct marketing lists to be profiled and duplicated, public relations activities to be prepared and placed in the media channels, and so on. Care also needs to be taken to ensure that all aspects of the campaign integrate well with each other. To repeat what has been said previously, the more closely integrated the various elements of the campaign are, the more effectively will the message be communicated to the target audience. Not only will we avoid confusion between different elements of the campaign, but we will also ensure that the single message is continuously reinforced.

Contingencies

A wise general once said: 'There is no such thing as success, only limiting the damage of failure'. In marketing communications this statement is particularly relevant. However great the efforts taken to eliminate the possibility of errors creeping into the campaign, and in testing the effectiveness of the variables, one key dimension cannot be assessed in advance – the nature of competitive response. Only once the campaign is fully implemented will it be possible to identify the specific nature of competitive activities. Although these may take some time to implement, the planner can be reasonably certain that the competition will not sit idly by and watch as the campaign erodes their strengths. What form this might take can certainly be considered in advance, although its true nature will not be known until it, too, is implemented. Sufficient funds must be kept aside to make necessary adjustments to the planned campaign to ensure that the objectives can be met.

Evaluating and monitoring performance

It is important that all aspects of the campaign are carefully monitored during their implementation. Even the best laid plans go wrong, and if a proper monitoring process is followed minor errors can be identified and corrected.

Even with careful pre-testing, there is no substitute for the real thing. The performance of the campaign in a live situation is what matters and it is vitally important that some continuous assessment of campaign achievement is implemented – possibly in the form of a tracking study, or some other form of periodic research – to identify the impact of the campaign on the target audience.

Most important, the information gathered will ensure that subsequent campaign planning is enhanced by the additional knowledge. Some form of feedback mechanism must be built in to enable the proper evaluation of the campaign activities against the established objectives to determine the extent to which those objectives have been met.

Summary

In this unit we have seen that:

- There is a need to understand not only what strategy is but how it differs from planning.
- IMC are a deeper and complex subject than is often considered. They are more than the coordination of the promotional mix, it involves culture, functional coordination and a blend of internal and external messages.
- The MCPF provides a structure upon which it is possible to develop marketing communication activities.
- Each stage of the framework fulfils an important role, each stage feed other elements of the structure and the framework needs to be seen as a system of interacting parts.
- It is important that the objectives are clearly defined and specific tasks for the communications programme, are designed to communicate to a defined audience to a defined degree, within a specific time frame and against a predefined budget.

Further study and examination preparation

See Question 4 of December 2000 exam paper in the appendices

Objectives

This and the unit 'Contexts 2 – Other contexts' are designed to build your understanding of how to prepare marketing communications by developing a sound knowledge of buyer behaviour. By analysing the different contexts in which marketing communications occur a far deeper insight can be achieved.

This unit will help you:

- Appreciate the role context analysis plays in the development of marketing communications
- Understand the significance of the ways in which buyers process information and its impact on marketing communications
- Consider the impact of customer decision making on marketing communications

By the end of this unit you will be able to:

- Relate your understanding of marketing communications to the key aspects of buyer behaviour.
- Discuss elements of information processing
- Demonstrate an understanding of the decision making processes buyers use when making purchase decisions.

This unit covers syllabus sections: 1.1.2, 1.2.1, 1.3.1.

Study guide

There are a number of important issues covered in the units and, in many respects, they will underpin your ability to deal with the topics contained in the units 'Contexts 2 – other contexts' and 'Promotional objectives and positioning'. Try to go over each of the topics carefully and, if necessary, reread them to make sure that you have grasped all the points that are raised.

Under the Diploma syllabus, it is quite likely that you will be called upon either to discuss the various concepts presented in this unit, or to apply the principles of these models in order to demonstrate an understanding of the relevance of theory to practical applications. For this reason, it is important that you should develop a clear understanding of the individual aspects of each of the concepts described. Think about why they have been developed and their relationship to the 'real' world.

Introduction to contexts

Study tip

This unit will require you to spend some time developing an understanding of some quite complex frameworks and ideas. You should practise drawing the important examples from memory, so that you can illustrate them in your answers in the examination.

Marketing communications, by their very nature, exist in a dynamic environment. All around us things are changing constantly. The underlying reasons for the purchasing of a product or service are affected by a variety of important factors. The economic environment will play a substantial part in forming people's attitudes to their patterns of expenditure. What is considered 'essential' at some times, will be regarded as something of a luxury when family income is under pressure, either because of the broad economic circumstances, or individual factors such as continuity of employment or the 'feel-good factor'.

The variety of elements that impact on organizations AND the way they communicate must be understood if truly effective marketing communications are to be developed. Marketing communications occur at a point in time, for a particular reason, to accomplish a particular task. Therefore, it is incumbent upon those responsible for the design and management of marketing communications to fully understand the current and immediate conditions in which communications are to be delivered.

Thinking back to the linear model of communications you will recall that there is a realm of experience that envelopes both sender and receiver. If the sender identifies that the target audience is male, aged 34 to 55 and likes football then messages containing information about ballet and classical music are unlikely to be very effective.

This aspect of preparing the marketing communications plan is referred to as a 'context analysis'. It seeks to define the relevant situation, isolate key variables that might affect the marketing communications and it determines the objectives that need to be accomplished.

To help make sense of the vast array of variables that can affect marketing communications, the context analysis is split into four main components. These are:

- The customer context
- The business context
- The internal context
- The external context.

The customer context is considered during the rest of this unit while the remaining contexts are looked at in unit Context 2 – Other contexts.

Students are advised that a much fuller explanation of the Information Processing and Decision Making aspects can be found in the recommended Essential Text for this CIM Diploma unit: Chris Fill. *Marketing Communications: Contexts, Strategies and Applications*. 3rd edn, 2002 .

Exam hint

The Senior Examiner has stated frequently that it is vital to have a good understanding of this topic area. He has backed this up by examining these topics often. He believes strongly that it is important to have a firm understanding of Information Processing and Buyer Decision Making in order to develop effective marketing communications.

The customer context

Customers, lapsed customers and potential customers lie at the heart of marketing and marketing communications. Our purchasing behaviour and the way we understand the world around us is influenced by many different factors. You will be aware of many of these from your previous studies so no attempt is made here to go over all the aspects of buyer behaviour. We have tried to distil these into the key factors, the ones that the Senior Examiner has indicated are critical, the ones that are likely to have an immediate influence on the design and effectiveness of marketing communications.

There are three main elements associated with buyer behaviour:

1. General factors,
2. Information processing
3. Buyer decision making.

These are considered in turn.

Element A – General factors

General factors are largely demographic and relate to externally generated issues.

Social class

The social class to which we belong will have an important bearing on the way in which we interpret messages, whether they come from the area of marketing communications or elsewhere. All societies operate some form of class system which establishes clear sets of values in the minds of the members of the class. In very real terms, classes differ in their occupations, lifestyles, their way of speaking, their educational expectations, their possessions, and so on. Most individuals perceive that different classes within society have differing amounts of status, privilege and power.

Most important, class will impinge on people's behavioural patterns. It will affect such things as the clothes they wear, the food they eat and the newspapers they read. From the perspective of marketing and marketing communications, we need to be concerned with such issues as how the buying patterns of the social classes differ from each other since they inherently represent a major opportunity for market segmentation.

Age and sex

These are two further variables which will affect our attitudes towards products and services. Again, such areas as clothing and foods will have different appeals to people of different age and sex. Both the nature of the clothes worn and, importantly, the brands which are perceived to have desirable attributes, will be affected by the age of the individual.

Clothing products bearing the names of manufacturers such as Chipie, Benetton and the various designer labels have a particular appeal to young or more affluent consumers. Others, like Jaeger and Burberry, will tend to have greater appeal to a somewhat older audience. Older consumers tend to be more 'traditional' in their food consumption patterns. Snack foods and convenience meals have a far greater acceptance among the young than the old, for example.

Again, these factors will be important considerations in the process of market segmentation, which we will examine in more detail later.

Family

The influences of the family on patterns of consumption are important to understand. Products which were consumed as part of childhood and growing up tend to continue to be purchased even after the individual has become independent and left home.

Race and religion

All races and religions have fundamental beliefs which impact upon purchasing decisions. This may occur either because they are included within accepted doctrines, or simply because of familiarity.

Income

This is an obvious consideration in the process of segmentation. The ability to purchase products and services is an important factor. While it is obviously desirable that all products should be aspirations of their target audiences, aspiration will not of itself sell products. The consumer must have sufficient disposable income to be able to at least consider purchasing a product offered to them.

Roles

All of us occupy different roles at different times. The same person may be an employer, a son, a father, a husband, a member of a club, and so on. Importantly, these roles will affect our purchasing decisions since, even within the same category, different products may be considered more or less appropriate to the role being fulfilled.

If a man was, for example, contemplating buying flowers, the purchase decision would be substantially influenced by the role and environment in which those flowers would be seen. Thus, the flowers selected for his office would very likely be different from those bought as a gift for his wife or partner.

Reference groups

All of us, similarly, relate to reference groups within society. As with roles, it will be important to the individual to adopt the style and traits of the reference group to which they belong or wish to belong. An immediate example would be the style of clothing. While in the office, a person would be likely to wear formal clothing in keeping with other employees. That same person might wear more casual clothing at home or for leisure, but equally might buy specific clothes similar to those worn by other members of, say, a sports club or other membership group. Many students, for example, wear Levi jeans to ensure consistency with the attitudes of their peer group.

Family life cycle

The nature of the products purchased will be influenced to a substantial degree by the stage which the individual occupies within the overall family life cycle. Typically, family life cycles may be divided into several distinct stages, as shown in Figure 3.1.

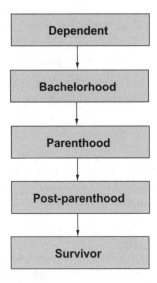

Figure 3.1
The family life cycle

The *dependent* individual is typically under 18 years old and living at home with his or her parents. At a very early age, all purchasing decisions are made on his or her behalf, although as the individual becomes older there may be an increased level of consultation. Even very young people may exert a considerable influence on purchasing decisions, especially in terms of the selection of brands.

As age increases, so too does the level of independence, even within the family environment. The break up of the nuclear family has resulted in, on occasion, separate meal times and a consequent personal selection of the foods to be consumed.

The *bachelorhood* stage is that of a young single adult living away from parents. The individual may be employed or unemployed and this will have a substantial bearing on the nature of products and services consumed. There will, however, be strong evidence of family influence on purchasing decisions, typically in the areas of which familiar brands of fast-moving consumer goods will continue to be purchased. At the same time, the individual will be seeking to stress his or her independence, and some purchase decisions will be specifically made to enhance this feeling. This stage will most commonly be followed by the *honeymoon* period. Whether the couple are married or living together, the key features are the enhanced wealth – derived from two income earners – and the relative lack of commitments. This affords a more indulgent lifestyle and the consumption of luxury products. This may evolve into the nest-building stage in which consumption patterns will be dictated by the expenses involved in setting up a permanent home.

The period of *parenthood* will be typified by the diversion of income to the problems of bringing up children. Financial resources will often be stretched considerably and former purchases will sometimes be deferred. The purchase of a new car, for example, may be given lower priority in the context of feeding and clothing one or more children. Here again, the period will embrace a number of significant changes. Income will tend to increase over the period. However, as the children become older their needs will change, resulting in a diversion of income to other expenditure areas, such as education.

The penultimate stage is that of *post-parenthood*. Here the children have left home, leaving the parents with a relatively high disposable income. Most of the household needs will have been purchased previously and, except for replacement, monies can be spent on a new form of indulgence – travel and holidays, leisure pursuits, and so on.

The final stage is that of the *survivor*. This stage occurs with the death of one spouse. Here, again, purchase patterns will change. There will be an increased tendency to purchase packaged convenience food products, and in many cases the pursuit of a more economical lifestyle.

A proper understanding of the family life cycle is an important facet in the determination of marketing communications strategies. The appropriate positioning of products and services to individual life-cycle groups will be an important ingredient in the successful communication of the supporting message.

Activity 3.1

Identify six products which might have special appeal for each of the lifecycle stages described above.

Changes in family composition

The notion of the family comprising two adults and 2.4 children is long gone. In all countries, the notion of family itself has different meanings. Some communities perceive the family as a small integrated unit, others adopt a model of the extended family with the elder children having responsibility for ageing members of the family – either parents or grandparents. The increasing levels of divorce and the growing acceptance, by some, that marriage is not a norm to which they wish to comply, has resulted in growing numbers of single-parent families. In all these situations, the needs and expectations of different families will be substantially different from each other, and effective marketing communications needs to recognize and respond to these underlying changes in society.

The ageing population

In many countries, improved standards of living and better health care have resulted in two parallel changes. On the one hand, in order to sustain living standards, people are deferring having children or are having fewer of them. On the other hand, life expectancy is improving as medical care is enhanced. These forces have resulted in a progressively ageing population in most developed markets, and with it a change in the values, needs and wants which consumers exhibit with regard to products and services.

Element B – Information Processing

There are a number of topics associated with information processing. However, you are required to know about perception and attitudes and how they influence and are influenced by marketing communications.

Perception

As noted in unit Introduction to marketing communications, consumers are continuously bombarded with vast quantities of information. Whether the information is orchestrated by the marketer or the media in general is less relevant than the fact that there is simply too much information for the average consumer to process effectively. The inevitable consequence is that much of the material is simply screened out and discarded. The result is that the consumer may make purchasing decisions based on limited knowledge, or even a misunderstanding of the real facts. The individual is far less concerned with the average advertising message, which makes the task of ensuring appropriate communications with the target audience an even more daunting prospect.

As consumers, our awareness of specific advertising messages is treated in a similar way. Some form of trigger mechanism is usually required to encourage us to pay attention to the variety of marketing communications messages. Usually, this is an internal recognition of an unfulfilled need which heightens the levels of awareness of pertinent advertising and other information. The principle can be commonly observed. If, for example, you have recently purchased a new car, your awareness of the marque will be enhanced and you will immediately become aware of similar vehicles all around you.

However, in the process of attempting to find better and more effective ways of communicating, we have also gained a greater appreciation of the nature of marketing communications. Much work has been done in the area of model construction and theoretical examination which has helped us to enhance areas of implementation. However you do not need be concerned with some of the complex models of buyer behaviour.

The process of decoding a message, whether it be from an advertiser or simply in the form of an article which interests us, will be substantially influenced by a number of perceptual factors. All of us, whether we think about it consciously or not, are influenced by a number of factors in our perception of a situation. And, as we will see later, perception itself is a key factor in the field of marketing communications.

Often, the consumer will possess only limited information on which to base a purchase decision. Some of that information, gleaned from other sources, will be incomplete.

Value judgements will be based on that limited understanding since, for the individual involved, their perceptions are reality. It is irrelevant that what they understand about the nature of a product or service is lacking or even wrong. In the field of marketing communications we must deal with those perceptual values and either play to them or seek to change them if that be the appropriate course of action.

Essentially, perception is about how we manage the various stimuli that we encounter. From a marketing communications perspective we are dealing with advertisements, promotions, members of the salesforce, direct mailers, etc. all of which represent stimuli. The perception of stimuli involves three components – attention getting, organising and interpretation.

Getting the attention of the target audience is an essential prerequisite of the other levels of the process. If the attention of the potential consumer is not secured by the marketing communications message, then it is impossible to communicate salient aspects of that message. In some respects, attention is determined by the consumer's attitudes towards the product category and the brand within it. If there is little interest in the product category, then gaining attention will be a difficult task. By the same token, however, if the consumer has become interested in the particular category (heightened awareness) for some reason, then significantly more attention will be devoted to the advertisement and its contents. This may come about, for example, because the consumer has decided to purchase a new car. Following that emotional decision, advertisements for cars, particularly those in the area of interest and relevance, will be more readily perceived. Typography, colour, shape, presentation, sex, music, tone of voice, brand name, voice overs are all variables used to get attention.

Activity 3.2
Find five advertisements and determine the devices used to get your attention.

The organization of the stimuli, once perceived, is necessary in order for us to understand what it is that has attracted our attention. Various devices are available but of these contour and grouping are often used techniques. So, our attention is drawn to a bottle with a dark liquid, it means Coca-Cola because we understand the shape of the bottle. This is an extreme example but it illustrates the principle well.

New or misunderstood products can be shown with products and brands that are well known and understood so that we learn that the weaker product is similar to the recognised brand. So healthy foods are pictured next to a gymnasium, top sporting stars or people working out.

Finally the organised stimuli need to be understood or *interpreted*. The Coca-Cola stimuli means something about American life and quenching thirst. This aspect of perception is influenced by our background, family values, the society in which we live and the culture to which we belong. All exert a significant impact on our own decision- making process. A product which is wholly acceptable in one society might be taboo in another because of social, religious or moral values. Even the colour of the packaging may mean something different in different markets. The advertiser must be conscious of these factors when developing a communications campaign.

Perception is at the heart of positioning. This part of the context analysis provides information that feeds the objectives, positioning, message content and media vehicle scheduling.

Attitudes

As we have seen elsewhere, the consumer holds a series of *attitudes*, some of which may relate to the brand and the purchasing decision. Although most of these attitudes will be formed by external factors – age, sex, class, the influence of relatives, friends and peer groups, cultural factors and so on – some are the direct result of the impact of an advertising message. In some instances, the *advertising* will serve to reinforce existing beliefs; in others, it will modify existing attitudes. If the consumer already believes that a well-balanced diet is essential to good health, then a product which promotes itself with this proposition is likely to be well received. The advertising will reinforce held beliefs and attitudes and strengthen the perception of the brand. In some instances, the advertising message may modify attitudes, perhaps by presenting a potential solution to a problem which the consumer previously felt could not be resolved.

Attitudes are an expression of an individual's feelings towards a person or object, and reflect whether they are favourably or otherwise disposed towards that person or object. Attitudes are not directly observable, but can be inferred either from behavioural patterns or by some form of interrogation, typically using market-research methods. Attitudes consist of three main components, cognitive, affective and conative. These are more easily remembered and understood as learn, feel and do. See Figure 3.2

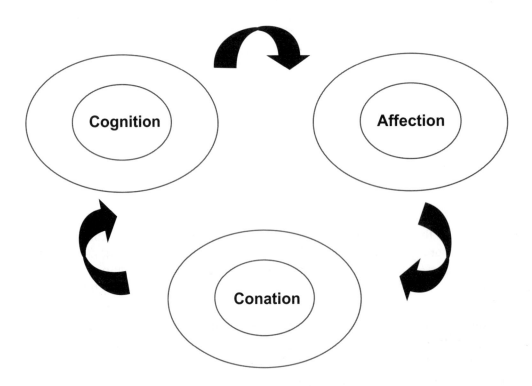

Figure 3.2
The three-component attitude model

What this means is that we when we buy something we learn something first, then feel something (about the product) and then do something (reject it, buy it ask for more information).

These feelings (the affective component) are often attached to significant attributes (tangible or intangible). So, when looking at attitudes towards, say, tinned soup, the feelings (like/dislike) may be a reflection of the taste (tangible attribute) or the brand name and the associations that they bring to the individual (intangible). Marketing communications can play a very important role in modifying the attitudes people have. By changing negative attitudes into positive attitudes, a person's predisposition to buy that brand at the next opportunity increases.

Marketing communications can change attitudes by the following methods:

- **Change the physical product or service element:** at a fundamental level, attitudes might be so engrained that it is necessary to change the product or service.

- **Change misunderstanding:** by product demonstration it is possible to change misunderstanding about the function of a product.
- **Build credibility:** through use of an informative strategy based on product demonstration and hands-on experience (e.g. through sampling) it is possible to build credibility, a brand to be relied on.
- **Change performance beliefs:** by changing perceptions held about the attributes, it is possible to change the attitudes about the object. So, if product performance is in doubt, provide evidence to correct the misperception.
- **Change attribute priorities:** a strategy to emphasize a different attribute can change attitudes. By stressing the importance of service attributes, airlines might have an advantage over their rivals who stress punctuality.
- **Introduce a new attribute:** this action might create a temporary advantage if it is valued by the target audience.
- **Change perception of competitor products:** by changing the way competitor products are perceived it is possible to differentiate your own brand.
- **Change or introduce new brand associations:** by using celebrities or spokespersons with whom the target audience can identify, it might be possible to change the way a product is perceived on an emotional basis rather than relying on attributes and a more rational argument.
- **Use corporate branding:** by using the stature of the parent company it is possible to develop a level of credibility and brand values that other brands cannot copy.
- **Change the number of attributes used:** today, two or even three attributes are often combined with strong emotional associations in order to provide a point of differentiation and a set of benefit-orientated brand values.

A fuller account of this important aspect of marketing communications can be found in the essential text for this unit (Chris Fill, 2002).

Activity 3.3

Select a market sector (airlines, bottled water, financial services, etc.), determine the leading brands and find examples of their communications. How have they used attributes to communicate. Are any of them trying to change the attitudes held of the target audience?

Attitudes towards products and services are an important dimension, since they will affect the individual's propensity to purchase. Products for which favourable attitudes are held are far more likely to be purchased than are those which create negative attitudes.

It is important to recognize that attitudes are not easy to change. Most consumers adopt fairly consistent behavioural patterns which can only be changed over time. If the consumer is of the view, for example, that all drink is evil, then no amount of advertising for alcoholic beverages is likely to alter that attitude.

Activity 3.4

Identify examples of advertising which:

- Seeks to change existing beliefs
- Seeks to reinforce beliefs.

However, we have to recognize that the consumer will not necessarily take in all of the advertising message, or may modify the content of the message to suit their existing views. Advertising promoting healthcare insurance will be irrelevant if the consumer believes that they are too young, for example, to be likely to fall seriously ill.

In turn, these attitudes will influence the *purchasing* decision. In some instances, held beliefs will arouse interest in a product category or a brand. Exposure to a specific advertising message may induce the consumer to go and buy the product. It is important to recognize that this is a two-way process. If the consumer is dissatisfied with the purchase, or feels that it does not live up to the promises of the advertising, then a process of dissonance will take place. Their attitudes towards the brand will be modified to reflect this lack of satisfaction and the advertising message will be viewed in a different light.

Activity 3.5

If a consumer's initial experience with a product is poor, how can the manufacturer use marketing communications to overcome the resistance to repeat purchasing with the introduction of a new formulation of the product?

Attitudes in general reflect changing patterns over time. The activities of pressure groups, peer groups and others will make some purchases more desirable, while others are less so. One only has to look at the growth in the awareness of environmental issues to see how brands have had to respond. Product ingredients which were once widely accepted can now no longer be included if the brand is to enjoy wide acceptance. Fashion exerts a similar influence. Once popular brands are now scorned by consumers as being unfashionable, while others have grown from limited acceptance to broad popularity as fashion dictates their purchase.

Element C – the decision-making process

Depending on the nature of the product or service that we are intending to buy, we tend to follow a series of distinct 'steps' which form the decision-making process. Commonly, we recognize five stages in the decision-making process, although it must be noted that not every purchase decision involves each of the stages, nor can we say that the consumer always begins the process at the beginning and ends at the end! A model of the purchase decision-making process is shown at Figure 3.3.

Figure 3.3
Stages in the purchase decision process

Problem recognition

The starting point in the purchasing process is the identification of a problem or unfulfilled need on the part of the consumer. In some instances, these will be basic human needs relating to, say, hunger or thirst. In other instances, the stimulus to problem recognition may be derived from some external source – the comment of a friend or relative, seeing a television commercial or press advertisement, and so on. In all cases, the consumer recognizes that there is a difference between the actual state and the desired state, and that in order to resolve the imbalance, a purchase may need to be made.

The search for information

In many purchase decisions, there is little time between the identification of the problem and the purchase of the product to fulfil the need. Impulse purchase decisions typically illustrate this type of decision making. The consumer may, for example, pass a confectionery outlet and feel slight pangs of hunger. He or she will enter the outlet and select a product, say a bar of chocolate, to satisfy that hunger. We will see, shortly, that this is indicative of what is known as *routine problem solving*. Indeed, many purchase decisions, particularly of fast-moving consumer goods, are of this nature. In essence, the consumer has previously stored sufficient information about the product category in order to make an appropriate brand selection without any need for additional information. Think about the last occasion on which you purchased a bar of chocolate. Did you go into the outlet to buy a specific brand or did something in the store trigger a purchase response? Perhaps it was the recognition of the Cadbury's wrapper, or an item of point of sale for, say, Twix or Galaxy, which suggested the solution to the problem.

In more complex purchasing decisions, such as the decision to buy an expensive item such as a hi-fi, television or car, such spontaneity is impossible to contemplate. Even if the consumer recognizes that their existing hi-fi no longer performs in the desired manner, it is extremely unlikely that he or she would simply go down to the nearest electrical retailer and purchase the appropriate equipment. Prior to embarking on the purchase, the consumer will seek as much information as possible to aid the purchasing decision.

Some of this 'information' may come from friends and relatives, who may describe their personal experiences with a particular make or model. Further information might be obtained from independent sources, such as consumer evaluation magazines – *Which?* or *What Hi-fi,* etc. In many instances, the consumer will consult specialist retailers for advice. Needless to say, the latter is less than likely to be totally unbiased, but will nonetheless contribute to the sum of knowledge that the consumer is building up about products that might be appropriate. Marketing communications, in the form of advertising, public relations and sales promotion will also play a significant part in this information-building process.

Evaluation of alternatives

The third stage of the process will be a consideration of the alternatives available to satisfy the need. Some of the criteria will be self-referenced. For example, the purchase may be restricted by the availability of funds. Accordingly, products which are too expensive to be affordable will be discarded. Other criteria might be the performance of the product. What output does it have? Will the look and appearance fit in with my existing decor? The scope of the equipment – does it, for example, play records, tapes CDs and DVDs?

Here again, marketing communications make an important contribution to the evaluation process. As we will see later, some advertising is specifically designed to identify appropriate criteria on behalf of the consumer. Indeed, much advertising for expensive consumer durables is of this nature in which comparisons are made between the advertiser's product and those of his competitors in order to assist the consumer in the purchase selection.

Only when the consumer has gathered sufficient information and evaluated the various alternatives against the established criteria, will the consumer pass to the next stage – the decision to purchase.

Activity 3.6

What are the factors which, in your opinion, influence the evaluation of alternatives?

Relate this question to a recent purchase of an infrequently purchased item, which you have made.

Purchase decision

Even having passed through the previous stages, it would be naive to assume that the process invariably ends with a decision to purchase. Personal or other considerations may dictate that the consumer either defers the decision or abandons it completely.

If, as was suggested earlier, the consumer has insufficient money to purchase the 'best' equipment at that time, they may feel that cheaper items lack some of the desired features. Accordingly, the decision might be made to delay the purchase until such time as the desired product is affordable.

Alternatively, the consumer might feel that none of the available alternatives really satisfies the need. Perhaps the improvement sought represents too great an investment and it would be better to remain with the existing equipment, at least for the time being. However, it is equally reasonable to assume that many consumers reaching this stage of the decision-making process end it by making a purchase selection.

Post-purchase evaluation

Once the consumer has returned home with the selected item, a stage known as 'post-purchase evaluation' begins. We have already seen that the consumer has built up an idealized image of the desired purchase during the earlier stages of the process, resulting from a variety of internal and external influences. Inevitably, they will make comparisons of the performance of the product with those criteria.

Where the consumer is satisfied that the product meets the level of expectations, then we have consumer satisfaction. Obviously, this may well impinge on the purchase decisions of other consumers, since the purchaser will, in this instance, comment favourably on the performance and other attributes of his or her purchase to others seeking advice and input.

However, where the consumer feels that the product does not live up to expectations, he or she is said to experience 'dissonance' or 'post-purchase dissatisfaction'. The latter may be brought about, for example, by an advertising message which overclaims for the product. Or there may be an imbalance between the true needs and the product delivery. In either case this post-purchase dissatisfaction is an important element to understand. Consumers who have this response will comment unfavourably on the product, perhaps undermining the impact of marketing communications campaigns. They may write letters of complaint to the manufacturer or, in extreme cases, begin their own programme of publicity by writing to newspapers, specialist publications, and so on. Certainly it is extremely unlikely that they would purchase the same brand again on another purchase occasion.

Television programmes such as *Watchdog* may serve to accelerate this dissonance. By exposing deficiencies in product performance, some viewers may be motivated to re-evaluate their own recent purchasing decisions. Yet others may conclude that their intended purchase is inappropriate, given the new information. Major brands such as Hoover and Hotpoint have been the subject of investigation by the programme, with a resultant negative impact on their sales.

Activity 3.7

Why is a consideration of post-purchase satisfaction so important in the context of marketing communications?

What does this suggest for the creation of marketing communications messages?

The nature of purchasing

We have already seen that purchase decisions will be made more or less spontaneously, depending on the nature of the purchase. We can distinguish between three types of decision according to the nature of the 'problem solving' in which the consumer is involved:

- Routine problem solving
- Limited problem solving
- Extensive problem solving.

Routine problem solving

As we have already seen, many purchases, especially those involved with low-priced, fast moving consumer goods, are of this type. In many cases, because the consumer has prior experience of the product category and the variety of brands that are available, little information seeking is involved in the process. Moreover, where the price of the item is comparatively low, little risk is involved in the purchase decision. Hence the decision will tend to be taken quite quickly and in a routine and automatic way.

Activity 3.8

Some consumers purchase products spontaneously. What role do marketing communications play in this context?

Limited problem solving

Sometimes, when a consumer is considering the purchase of a new or unfamiliar brand, even when it is within a familiar product category, there may be a limited amount of information seeking, and the consumer will tend to spend slightly more time before making a purchase decision. This is also associated with slightly more expensive purchases, where the cost involves a slightly more detailed consideration or where there is a degree of risk in the purchase. The selection, for example, of over-the-counter medicines is likely to involve some careful consideration of the ingredients, the identity of the manufacturer and so on, before the decision to purchase is made.

Extensive problem solving

The consumer will become involved in a more detailed search for information and the evaluation of alternatives in those instances where the product category is unfamiliar or where a purchase is made on a very infrequent basis.

Obviously, purchases which involve a high capital outlay on the part of the consumer (durable items, cars, houses) or a high degree of personal commitment (life insurance, membership of clubs and societies) will be of the extended problem solving variety.

Activity 3.9

Identify four examples of:

- A routine purchase
- A purchase involving limited problem solving
- An extended problem solving purchase.

Perceived Risk

Our propensity to involve ourselves in the purchase decision process is partly a reflection of the level and type of perceived risk that we each see in these decisions. These risks may be a function of the following six elements:

- Performance risk – will the product wash my clothes clean?
- Financial risk – is this good value? Will I get the goods (e.g. Internet shopping fears)
- Social Risk – what will my friends think?
- Ego risk – how will I feel about myself ?
- Physical risk – will the product harm me or others?
- Time risk – how long have I to make this decision, buy this product?

These risks will be present in all decisions, but to varying degrees according to product/category experience, confidence, wealth, education, etc. The risks will vary across product sectors for each individual.

Activity 3.10

Find some examples of direct mail advertising. Which risks are being addressed in the advertisement?

Exam tip

The areas of perception, attitudes and risk are tested in examinations on a regular basis. You need to know the components and understand how they are affected by and can affect marketing communications. Find some examples and apply these concepts.

Summary

In this unit we have seen that:

- The key to the development of an effective and fully integrated marketing communications plan is the adoption of a systematic process of analysis.
- In order to identify the appropriate brand positioning and creative proposition, it is vitally important to have a comprehensive understanding of the meaningful consumer dynamics.
- Issues of importance are perception, attitudes and perceived risk and marketing communications can be used to change, moderate or influence these elements.
- At the same time, it is equally essential to develop an understanding of the broader environment in which the product or service is sold, and of the factors which are likely to affect its development.

Further study and examination preparation

See Question 5 of the examination paper for December 2000 in the appendices.

Objectives

In this unit you will:

- Examine the need for and characteristics associated with the business, internal and external contexts.
- Read about how ethical issues are an important consideration when developing marketing communications.
- Explore issues concerning how these elements can impact on the nature and role of marketing communications.

By the end of this unit you will:

- Understand how an appreciation of segmentation can affect the content of a message and the media used in marketing communications.
- Explain how internal marketing communications can improve the effectiveness of an organization's marketing communications.
- Be able to discuss the impact of internal communications on integrated marketing communications.
- Be aware of the external forces that affect marketing communications strategy and know that it is the impact on communications (not marketing) that is important.

This unit covers syllabus sections: 1.1.5, 1.3.2, 1.3.7.

Business, Internal and External perspectives

This unit is designed to to help you understand more about the business, internal and external contexts which influence marketing communications. These three areas are explored in turn and at the end of it you should have a sound platform to develop your marketing communication skills and understanding.

The business context

The business or market context is important as it is necessary to appreciate the trading/operating conditions, to know whether the market is growing or shrinking, to understand the communications and positions being taken by competitors and to understand the different segments in which all players are operating.

At the root of the business context analysis is the Marketing Plan. This document highlights the strategy, the marketing mix detail and the timescales and resources that are available. It is important to realise that the preparation of a marketing communications plan does not require all this work to be repeated. What happens is that the marketing plan needs to be developed. Certain parts need to be refined, inspected more closely and issues teased out in order that those working on parts of the marketing communications plan (e.g. creative teams, media plans, searchers) have a much more detailed understanding of various parts of the market and the brands operating in them.

This part of the analysis requires an understanding of the market, general trends, competitor strategies and communications (positioning is important) and the segment characteristics.

For example, since the UK government introduced fees for eye sight tests the number of people having eye tests has fallen (predictably). Research into the market and to the way competitors positioned themselves led Specsavers Opticians, the UK's leading retail opticians to position themselves based upon added values. As a result they introduced marketing communication campaigns featuring David Shepherd (an artist) and Stephen Hawking (phyicist) who use their sight in different ways, one who interpretes the world and the other who has an inner sight. The goal was to stimulate interest in the market, to remind people of the value of their sight and to generate an increase in the number of people visiting Specsaver Opticians. All of this was generated by understanding the business context: the market conditions, competitor behaviour and segment characteristics.

Segmentation

You will be familiar with the various principles associated with segmentation, so there is no need to repeat them here. However, if you are in doubt it may be a good idea to try the next activity before progressing any further.

Activity 4.1

Write down the five main bases by which markets can be segmented. As a clue, one of them is demographics (and this includes age, sex, income, religion, education). So, what are the other four?

Research among consumers has shown that specific lifestyle factors in terms of shared beliefs, attitudes, activities and behavioural patterns often transcend other forms of differentiation.

Activity 4.2

Why do marketers use techniques other than basic demographics to develop a better understanding of market segment opportunities?

Lifestyle segmentation (a part of pychographics) tends to group people on the basis of their interests, activities and opinions and, as such, provides a much fuller picture of consumers than conventional demographic segmentation is able to provide. Indeed, it is the use of a multilayer approach to segmentation that provides the richest insight.

Lifestyle segmentation measures three key facets of the individual:

- *Activities* – how they spend their time
- *Interests* – the dimensions of personal interest in their surroundings
- *Opinions* – the factors which are important to them.

Several attempts have been made to group people according to lifestyle characteristics. Typical of these is the work done by the Stanford Research Institute in the USA, known as VALS. This divides the population into groupings according to their self-orientation – these are listed below at Table 4.3.

Table 4.3	
Actualizers.	Successful and sophisticated individuals with high self-esteem and high resources who seek to develop and express themselves in a variety of ways.
Fulfilleds	Mature, satisfied and comfortable individuals who tend to seek knowledge concerning their surroundings. They tend to be less concerned with images than functionality and value for money.
Believers	A group with comparatively conservative beliefs, with a strong attachment to tradition and the community. As such, they are relatively slow to change their purchasing patterns and rely on familiar brands.
Achievers	Tendency to be successful in their careers and are in control of both themselves and their lives. Their purchases tend to reflect this in terms of those items which display their success to others.
Strivers	These are very image conscious and tend to emulate those whom they perceive as having done well. Although their income will tend to be limited, they spend their money in ways which, they hope, will secure the approval of those they wish to be like.
Experiencers	Mainly young and impulsive. They are very much the followers of fashion and, while rejecting conformity, tend to be avid trialists of new products and experiences.
Makers	These are practical individuals who have a belief in their own skills. They tend to be absorbed in the home and family and enjoy participation in practical hobbies such as DIY, wine making, gardening, and so on.
Strugglers	This group tend to be of poor health and of low income and who represent relatively limited markets for most consumer goods and services.

This approach has been developed in the UK market as the Social Values approach. Turn to the essential text by Chris Fill (Fill, 2002) for an insight into the UK research. The above discussion shows that there are a wide variety of opportunities to engage in *market segmentation*. In essence, manufacturers are continuously examining ways in which consumers can be grouped together in different ways in order to present their product or service in a unique light.

There can be no single prescription for the process of market segmentation. What is important is that companies have a deep understanding of their potential consumers and their needs and respond to them with an appropriate array of products and services specifically designed to meet those needs. From our perspective, the purpose of this work is to develop an insight into how best to communicate with the target audience, to know which promotional tools, what sort of message and which media might be most effective.

Activity 4.3

How do the major manufacturers in the soaps and detergent markets differentiate their products from those of their competitors?

In those situations where the company operates with several brands, it will be important to understand the role that each of them has within the overall portfolio. Clearly, a fundamental need will be to ensure differentiation between them in the eyes of potential customers. This will minimize the likelihood of share steal from one of the company's brands by another. Similarly, the brand position will need to be carefully considered to determine whether it is one that needs to be sustained or, if weak, requires modification. Lucozade, for example, used marketing communications to change the position which the brand occupied in the minds of customers – from a drink that restored health to one that replaces energy lost through sporting exertion.

In the same way, the historic brand values may well dictate the tone and direction of the marketing communications campaign, since there may be elements associated with, for example, the advertising campaign, which need to be underpinned in any future activity.

Ethical considerations in marketing communications

With regard to the business context, one major issue remains to be dealt with. This relates to the ethical and legal considerations which apply to the field of marketing communications. It has to be recognized that marketing communications are often described as an immoral business activity, responsible for exerting a pernicious influence on society in general. By the promotion of products and services which are beyond the reach of many consumers, marketing communications are held responsible for many of the underlying ills of society.

Undeniably, marketing communications stimulates the desire of individuals to aspire to a superior lifestyle and, with it, to have access to a wider range of goods and services. However, whether this is a reflection of the values of marketing communications, or of society as a whole, is a more difficult question to resolve.

Activity 4.4
Defend the position of advertising against the argument that it creates unnecessary needs and wants.

It is a fundamental dimension of human nature to 'seek to improve one's lot'. What was an acceptable lifestyle 20 or 30 years ago would be significantly below the level of today's desires. Products which were then considered aspirational are now considered to be the very staples of existence. Inevitably, it is a facet of an open society that individuals have the right to choose the products and services which they wish to have access to. The alternative is a more rigid society in which choice is restricted – based on the value judgements of others.

On a more fundamental level, criticisms of advertising often relate to the issues of selective emphasis and exaggeration. Since advertisers choose to highlight only those areas in which their product performs well, or better than their competitors, rather than providing a comprehensive analysis – warts and all! – such advertising may be criticized as failing to communicate the true nature of the products or services it promotes. By the same token, some advertisers use exaggerated claims to promote the appeal of their products.

Ultimately, there are a series of responses common to all societies which will limit these excesses. It may be a cliché, but if the product or service fails to deliver against the expectations of consumers – largely created by marketing communications – the product will fail. We have already seen that the area of post-purchase satisfaction (or dissatisfaction) is an important dimension of marketing communications. Manufacturers who seek to use marketing communications to promote inferior products, or whose claims for performance exceed their ability to deliver will rapidly appreciate the impact of the dissonance which such activity creates.

However, it must remain true that there are a number of areas in which the consumer must be protected against the excesses which might otherwise be against their interests. To this end, the governments of most countries have created a variety of legal and other regulatory frameworks which ensure that marketing communications perform in a manner which is acceptable to the public at large. These, in turn, are augmented by self-regulatory procedures which have resulted in the creation of codes of conduct to which practitioners are required to subscribe.

There has been a progressive realization that those practising marketing have an ethical responsibility towards society. This area has proved to be contentious since it is difficult to define the nature of ethical behaviour. The fundamental role of marketing is to satisfy the needs of consumers. However, there may be times when although seeming to satisfy those needs, they are in fact being misdirected. A recent *Watchdog* programme demonstrated that many products labelled as 'light', implying a low-fat content, in fact were higher in fat than regular versions of the same brands.

In the same vein, an increasing number of products claim to be 'environmentally friendly'. However, when their packaging fails to meet standards of biodegradability, can they really substantiate this claim? Often products serve to satisfy the needs of one group of consumers, but at the expense of others. Environmental pressure groups have demonstrated that products containing CFC gases may work efficiently, but in so doing they deplete the ozone layer. Here again, there is an ethical conflict.

These examples serve to illustrate that, while it may be accepted that a company must first serve the needs of its customers, there are increasing concerns that companies should also recognize their responsibilities to society as a whole.

In recent years, a wide variety of issues have been raised to further the debate:

Advertising to children:

In many countries it is permissible to advertise products directly to children. Elsewhere, as in Sweden such activity is banned. However, opponents of the ban point to the restricted availability of children's products – toys and confectionery – and the relatively higher costs of those products.

The depiction of women in advertising:

Concern has been expressed over the way that women are shown in advertising campaigns. Many believe that these serve to reinforce stereotypical roles. Database marketing Some observers regard the collection of information about consumers to be an invasion of privacy.

Product labelling:

There is increasing pressure on companies to declare the full contents of their products on labelling, particularly of those ingredients which might result in harm to some consumers or where their consumption might conflict with their beliefs.

Confusion pricing:

It is argued that many companies deliberately use different bases of pricing to preclude the consumer from making direct price comparisons.

The issue of the ethical responsibility of companies is a complex one. As noted earlier, companies which pursue policies which are in conflict with contemporary beliefs will often find that consumers respond by rejecting their products or services. However, the issue remains as to whose ethics should be followed.

In some countries, providing a financial incentive to an intermediary to secure a contract is regarded as an accepted part of the selling process. In the West, such activity would be regarded as bribery!

Similarly, some commentators regard the provision of inferior products to developing countries as being immoral. However, supporters of these policies would argue that even inferior products represent a significant improvement on what is currently available!

It is important that you appreciate the ethical and moral concerns which relate to both marketing and marketing communications practices. The Senior Examiner has expressed a desire to ensure that candidates are able to argue these issues as they relate to examination questions.

Activity 4.5

What are the roles of legal and self-regulatory controls within marketing communications?

In the UK, for example, the codes of practice of the Institute of Practitioners in Advertising, the Institute of Public Relations and the Institute of Sales Promotion, among others, provide detailed guidelines for the best practice within their respective fields of activity.

Activity 4.6

Identify examples of codes of practice which apply to advertising and public relations.

What do they seek to achieve?

How are they enforced?

The ultimate sanction rests with the consumer. The historical development of marketing and, with it, marketing communications, has entered a new phase. As described by Kotler, P. (2000) we are entering a new phase in which marketers must balance their own needs with those of society in general.

> 'The social marketing concept holds that the organisation's task is to determine the needs, wants and interests of the target markets and to then deliver the desired satisfactions more effectively and efficiently than competitors in a way that maintains or improves the consumer's and the society's well being.'

Kotler, P. (2000) *Marketing Management,: the Millennium Edition*, Englewood Cliffs, NY : Prentice Hall

The underlying changes in consumer attitudes will result in the exertion of a number of pressures on marketing organizations. The ultimate power of the consumer remains the freedom of choice. If manufacturers fail to recognize and respond to these changes, then they must accept that they will be forced to accept the consequences of their actions, or lack of them. If manufacturers act in ways that consumers find detrimental or harmful to their well-being, they will reject their products. By the same token, if they are seen to be taking positive steps to improve the general environment in which the consumer exists, those same consumers will reward them by buying their products.

Activity 4.7

How should marketers adapt their marketing communications programmes to reflect the requirements of societal marketing?

These concerns should not be overstated. An annual survey conducted by the Advertising Association repeatedly reports that the level of those expressing concern or disapproval with advertising is falling progressively. Only 7 per cent of the population express such mistrust. For most, the field of marketing communications makes a positive contribution to society in general. It communicates information about products and services efficiently and cheaply and provides consumers with confidence in the goods and services that they purchase. It stimulates competition to produce new products and to improve old ones, and helps to ensure choice on the part of consumers. It helps to fuel economic prosperity, with the subsequent contribution to employment, by the opening up of new growth areas. And it expands media choice, by funding diverse and independent media which, substantially, rely on the income derived from advertising.

Marketing Communications are a function within all developed economies which, despite comments to the contrary, make a valid and realistic contribution to economic well-being.

The internal context

The internal audience, comprising management, other executives and the workforce are, similarly, the recipients of messages from the organization. Importantly, how they interpret messages will have a bearing on the way in which they deal with and respond to outside audiences.

You will recall that when we looked at ideas about integrated marketing communications we saw that organizations communicate through the behaviour of their managers and employees as well as through the tools of the promotional mix. When we consider the internal context we need to account for the degree to which employees believe in the organization, its values and how they communicate with others outside of the organizations. In addition to this we need to account for the financial resources and understand the the broad amount of funds that are likely to be made available. We look at the internal communications here and the detail concerning the financial resources are considered in Unit Financial resources.

Employees constitute an internal market, and in that sense need to be communicated with just as much as external (or non-members) stakeholders, through effective marketing communications. Marketing communications should be used to differentiate, remind/reassure, inform and persuade (DRIP) employees, just as much as any other target segment.

Activity 4.8

Apply each of the elements of the DRIP roles of marketing communications to employees.

Organizational identity is concerned with what individuals think and feel about the organization to which they belong. When their perception of the organisation's characteristics is in balance with their own self-concept, organizational identity is said to be strong. These shared perceptions and feelings (with other employees) form a collective sense of organizational identity.

There may well be variances between the perceptions of employees and external stakeholders, and this may be a cause of confusion, misunderstanding or even conflict. In general, the closer the member/non-member identification, the better placed the organization will be to achieve its objectives.

There are a number of occasions when identity is critical. These may be during periods of rapid growth or decline, during merger and acquisition or when a major part of the organisation's identity 'kit;' is lost, (for example when a founder member retires or leaves the organization).

The strength of organizational identity is a reflection of the culture that binds (or not) the organization together. Although it is possible to see various levels of organizational culture it is really the basic beliefs, values and assumptions that are shared by members of an organization, that define an organisation's view of its self.

Culture and communication

Organizational culture is not static; the stronger the culture the more likely it is to be transmitted from one generation of organizational members to another, and it is also probable that the culture will be more difficult to change if it is firmly embedded in the organization. Most writers acknowledge that effective cultural change is difficult and a long-term task.

The focus of internal marketing communications has evolved through notice boards and training and development programmes to one that is more frequent, informal and often based around new technology. Video conferencing, internal televison, e-mail, Intranets, bulletin boards and newsletters and magazines constitute an array of appropriate communication devices. External communications need to take account of staff reaction, get their cooperation and support and depict them in a positive and motivating manner.

The development of integrated marketing communications has to be based on internally generated communications blending and reinforcing externally orientated communications. An understanding of organizational identity and culture is the foundation of corporate reputation strategies.

It is essential to understand and manage organizational identity to minimise any discrepancy between members' and non-members' perceptions of what is central to and distinctive about the organization. If you think about your own experiences buying clothes, music or books food, part of your perception of the organization you are buying from is influenced by how staff treat you and how attentive or caring they appear to be. The quality of the interface (or point of interaction) between staff (members) and customers (non-members) is a reflection of the degree to which their marketing communications are integrated.

Remember, organizations communicate with customers and other external stakeholders through their employees. IMC is more likely to work when the behaviour and signals delivered by employees reinforce the messages delivered through the promotional mix to external audiences.

The internal context provides the overall frame within which the marketing communications activities can occur.

The external context

The external environment is largely uncontrollable yet can have a major impact on an organisation's marketing communications. As you will know from previous studies, a useful acronym as an aid to remembering the dimensions of the external environment is PEST. Each of these initials represents an important dimension of the external environment which will need to be considered in order to determine how changes in the external environment might impact on marketing *communications*. See Figure 4.1.

Figure 4.1
Elements of the external environment

Political factors

Political influences are likely to be significant in the future development of a company's business. Inevitably, a change of government brings with it a new political agenda which may favour some aspects of business, while diminishing the prospects of others.

The government of the day may introduce specific pieces of legislation which curb or control particular business functions. High on most political lists is the desire to control certain perceived anti-social activities. These include smoking and the consumption of alcoholic beverages. Government action, for example, may limit access to the media either in part (as in the UK) or entirely (as in other parts of the EEC). A change of government may manifest itself in the form of higher levels of taxation, which are specifically applied, and which make particular goods and services more expensive to the customer. Equally, it may take the form of specific controls on the importation of certain products in order to protect domestic markets for domestic producers.

The converse may equally be true. Governments may provide direct incentives to encourage certain forms of customer behaviour which, in turn, encourage them to buy particular goods and services. In the UK and elsewhere, government action has specifically benefited the growth of private health-care provision and personal pensions, for example.

Some of the actions of government may be anticipated to occur in the short term – the annual budget statement, for example, will have a sizeable impact on the performance of the economy by the tightening or relaxation of personal taxation levels and interest rates. Both these factors affect the potential for growth of a company's sales.

Although the longer term is less easy to predict, a company must nevertheless attempt to anticipate likely changes which may impact on the way that its business is likely to perform.

Economic factors

By the same token, the economic elements will inevitably affect sales potential. Recent years have seen a worldwide recession which has significantly dampened down economic performance. While governments have made various attempts to stimulate their economies, with varying degrees of effectiveness, the underlying factors have resulted in a reduction in levels of employment and the preparedness of individuals to embark on specific patterns of expenditure. Both of these influences have considerably reduced the sales volumes of specific goods and services.

Activity 4.9

Write out the segments of the beverage market. Consider all the various options available (e.g. hot, cold, alcoholic, nonalcoholic).

Taking any one segment, consider the additional segmentation possibilities.

Although currently experiencing a slight recovery, car sales have sustained a considerable downturn over recent years. Similarly, house sales have been depressed compared to previous years. However, although these factors have impacted on direct sales, there have been positive benefits in other areas. Because some people have deferred the purchase of a new car, many of them have spent more on car maintenance and the purchase of accessories – to the direct benefit of the companies operating in these areas. Similarly, there has been a growth in some areas of house and garden improvements, either because home owners have sought to improve their own personal environments, or because they have tried to make their houses more attractive to potential purchasers. Again, the suppliers of goods and services in these areas have been the direct beneficiaries. These examples serve to illustrate the fact that it is important to examine not only the broad-scale impact of economic changes, but also the effects on related areas which may experience growth.

Social forces

We have already seen that there is a series of fundamental changes in both customer attitudes and behaviour patterns within the social environment. Here again, it is important to be aware of these factors in order to anticipate their likely impact on business performance. Since most of these will be the direct result of observable changes, it is somewhat easier to foresee their effect. A few examples will illustrate this point.

Life expectancies have increased dramatically throughout this century in most developed countries. In the UK, for example, in 1901 the average life expectancy for men at birth was only 45 years, but today it is close to 73 years. For women, the comparable figures are 48 and 78 years, respectively. Indeed life expectancy will continue to increase as a direct consequence of the underlying improvements in eating habits, living conditions and medical knowledge. This has been accompanied, for many, by a considerably enhanced standard of living. Many of these individuals have long since paid off their mortgages and, now that their children have left home, can 'trade down' their properties in order to gain access to their capital. The result has been a dramatic growth in the sales of specific products and services which are targeted to appeal to these more affluent older individuals.

A similar trend can be seen as a result of the progressive reduction in the number of births – resulting in a smaller youth market and a dampening down of demand for many products aimed at this segment.

The increased number of working women has brought about changes in the retail environment. Since they can no longer access their preferred stores during the 'normal' hours of 09.00 to 17.00, retailers have been forced to adopt longer trading hours, even opening during weekends to ensure that their customer needs are satisfied.

Smaller family units, single-parent families and similar factors have resulted in a growth in the demand for small product sizes, and so on.

An increased concern with the impact of particular goods and services on the environment has, similarly, resulted in both manufacturers and retailers being forced to become more aware of their responsibilities in these areas. Sometimes the direct result of governmental action and in other instances the result of customer pressures, manufacturers have been forced to respond by changing the nature of their products (to eliminate chloro-fluorocarbons (CFCs) and chlorates) or their packaging in order to minimize the wastage of scarcer resources.

Inevitably, this brief overview can only consider a few of the important dimensions of social change. A comprehensive plan must consider them all and isolate the communication impact.

Activity 4.10

The key social changes which might affect the marketing communications planning process for:

- Family shampoo
- A low-cost airline
- A charity seeking donations.

Impact of the external analysis

It is important to recognize that a company's ability to deliver products that perform in the manner which customers expect will often be related to the technological dimensions of production. Most organizations maintain a research and development function, part of whose purpose is to ensure that products are continuously up-dated to take advantage of new technologies. Sometimes, these reflect 'in-house' development of new ingredients and formulations; in others, they are a response to competitive improvements as the company seeks to identify the basis on which competitors' products achieve their results.

Equally, other aspects of technological change need to be considered for their likely impact on the planning of marketing communications activities. Some of the important changes which are taking place include:

- *Speed of communication*

  Information is transmitted rapidly from one market to another.

- *Campaign coordination*

  Facilities such as ISDN and video conferencing enable discussions to take place between people in different markets without the need for travel.

- *Targeting*

  New technology enables the rapid analysis of data enabling more effective targeting of audiences.

- *New media channels*

  Digital technology has opened up opportunities to communicate with target audiences in new and different ways. Web sites, for example, enable companies to augment their conventional marketing communications activities. Similarly, they can provide a new level of interactivity between the company and its customers.

- *Retail opportunities*

  New technology has opened up new channels of distribution. Manufacturers can use the Internet to sell direct to customers, bypassing conventional retailers.

Activity 4.11

Carry out a PEST analysis for a product or service of which you are aware and determine whether there are likely to be any significant factors that might impact on its marketing communications.

The external factors will be equally relevant to the determination of the objectives, strategy and the process of implementation. The results of the PEST analysis may indicate some new dimension which will affect the nature of the communications message. For example, new legislation may restrict the ability to make particular claims for the brand. Similarly, changes in the economic environment may affect the ability of the customer to afford the brand or to purchase at the same level of frequency as previously.

The outcomes of all of these elements of the analysis will guide the establishment of objectives and the strategy determination. This will affect all aspects of the marketing communications plan, which will need to match the available financial resources and personnel skills previously identified, but must equally be appropriate to the achievement of the specific objectives identified.

Similarly, the identification of the communications message will be determined by the need to support the brand appropriately given the understanding of the brand promise. The delivery of the message will affect the selection of the marketing communications tools and the identification of the appropriate media channels used (assuming that a media-based campaign is appropriate).

Media will need to be selected based on the ability to deliver and reinforce the desired message within the budgetary limitations.

Most organizations will have direct access to some of the required information but may also require specific market research programmes to supplement their knowledge and understanding of the important issues. Overall, it can be seen that the analysis of the current situation affects all aspects of the marketing communications plan, since any errors made at this stage will have a detrimental impact on the ability to achieve the desired goals.

Summary

In this unit you will have:

- Discovered how understanding the business context, and in particular market segmentation, can help shape the marketing communications used by an organization.
- Seen how market conditions and competitor communications can help shape the nature of the marketing communications mix.

- Been introduced to the critical nature and impact that ethical and moral issues can have on marketing communications.
- Considered the integrative nature of well managed internal marketing communications and explored the various dimensions of organizational culture and its potential impact on marketing communications. These issues are reexamined as part of corporate identity and corporate branding later in this Coursebook.
- Been introduced to the impact of the external contextual conditions and understood that while using the PEST factors as the main framework, we are only interested in the impact on communications not marketing or business strategy.

Further study and examination preparation

See Question 5 of the examination paper for June 2000 in the appendices.

Objectives

In this unit you will:

- Consider the nature and derivation of promotional objectives.
- Explore the complexity of the different types of goals
- Familiarize yourself with positioning and related concepts
- Learn about different positioning strategies

By the end of this unit you will be able to:

- Determine appropriate objectives from an understanding of the prevailing context
- Discuss the advantages and disadvantages of sales and communication related goals
- Set objectives in terms of the SMART framework
- Appraise the positioning strategies followed by other organizations
- Recommend positioning strategies in the light of information derived from perceptual maps.

The unit covers syllabus section 1.3.3

The role of marketing communications objectives

The important role that objectives play in management is clearly understood and accepted by most practising managers. Whether they set appropriate objectives is another question and is the main topic of this unit.

It is important that, in establishing marketing communications objectives, certain 'rules' are followed. These are not hard and fast rules, but are intended to provide guidelines for the establishment of realistic objectives which can be agreed upon, adhered to and monitored.

Be succinct

A marketing communications objective should be a succinct statement of the specific communications tasks within the overall marketing plan.

As we have already seen, it is vitally important that the tasks of marketing communications are distinguished from those of marketing. As such, they must state the specific tasks that marketing communications techniques are uniquely qualified to perform and should not encompass aims that require the use of other marketing techniques. Moreover, since Marketing Communications are a relatively abstract area, it is even more important to have clearly defined objectives in order to provide real substance to any debate.

Written and measurable

Marketing communications objectives should be written down in finite and measurable terms.

It is not sufficient to define marketing communications objectives simply as, for example: 'To increase awareness, to build loyalty, to encourage trial'. Such statements fail to establish the necessary targets which are required to be met and, perhaps more importantly, do not allow for the proper evaluation of the campaign upon completion. If the level of awareness has increased by, say, 10 per cent or we have 15 per cent more loyal users, can we agree that the campaign has worked? It is important to include these levels at the outset in order both that the appropriate strategy can be determined and that the outcome of the campaign can be properly tested and evaluated.

Agreed by everyone

It is important that marketing communications objectives are agreed upon by everyone involved in the process.

From the management to the creative team, all the people involved in the process of marketing communications must agree, at the outset, what the specific objectives are. By ensuring this level of agreement, everyone involved knows precisely what is required and, equally important, has a benchmark against which to assess recommendations.

Are the techniques recommended capable of achieving the objectives? Does the proposition communicate the desired position to the target audience, and so on. The absence of agreed objectives can result in considerable wastage of both time and effort, since the parties involved do not hold a unified view of what is to be achieved. Moreover, the objectives themselves will provide a focus for debate and the means of resolving differences of opinion.

There is little doubt that people can achieve more when they are given a precise statement as to what they must aim at. This is increasingly important as the costs of marketing communications multiply, and the need to avoid waste becomes more pressing.

The statement of objectives should not conflict with the creative process. while it remains true that we are always looking for the 'big idea', it is more likely that we will find it if the work is properly focused. Clearly defined objectives assist the process of creative thought. By establishing a precise definition of what it is that we wish to communicate, the creative team can concentrate their efforts on deciding how best to say it. In the absence of clear and definite objectives, there is a tendency towards 'compromise'. By being precise, the tasks can be more readily achieved.

Planning process

The process of planning must be separated from that of implementation.

As much time must be spent on determining what needs to be said and to whom, as how to say it. The fundamental requirement is to ensure that the delivered message is consistent with consumer needs and wants. It follows that determining which segment of the overall audience represents the target for a marketing communications campaign, and precisely what it is that they require of the product category, are essential prerequisites to the creation of a campaign designed to communicate that proposition. Similarly, the planning process must be based on an intimate knowledge of the markets and consumer buying behaviour. Hence the customer context analysis.

Markets, and consumers within them, have become increasingly volatile. Few people can claim to have a precise understanding of the particular requirements at any moment of time without accessing additional information.

The introduction of new products, with new properties and attributes will serve to change expectations of how an existing product should perform. And, as we will see, we need to be concerned as much with perceptions as with the reality of product performance and delivery. What the consumer *believes* about a product is far more important than the reality.

Where are we now?

The Marketing Communications Planning Framework, introduced in Unit 2, provides a checklist of the activities that need to be completed. As with most planning tools the start position is some realistic assessment of the current situation, in this case the Context Analysis. Part of this process involves working with and developing aspects of the Marketing Plan.

If there is no Marketing Plan then for the objectives of the communications plan to be useful and realistic, an assessment of the current position of the product or service must be made. If a brand already has a high level of awareness, for example, then it is unlikely that expenditures in this area will achieve much. If the brand is failing to make progress, then it can be assumed that it is in some other area that there are shortcomings. These need to be determined before campaign objectives can be set.

At the same time, the task of taking awareness levels from, say, 20 to 50 per cent will be markedly different from that of improving to, say, beyond 80 per cent. There will be significant implications for target definition, media selection and so on, which we will consider in later units.

The important point to be made here is that the Context Analysis unearths the objectives that the communications plan needs to achieve. It is by analysing the customer, business, internal and external contexts that the real goals are revealed.

These goals not only provide the focus for the development of the campaign but they also establish a series of benchmarks against which objectives can be set. In other words, they provide the main form of campaign evaluation.

Monitoring and control

It is important that agreement is achieved in advance as to the methods to be employed for evaluation and control. Again, as we shall see, there are a wide variety of measurement techniques pertinent to the area of marketing communications. However, the different techniques are themselves designed to monitor different aspects of marketing communications. It is important that the relevant approaches are employed to monitor performance, since the use of the wrong technique may fail to assess performance within the desired areas.

It is important to establish that monitoring is not an end in itself. The purpose of using techniques such as market research is to aid the process of learning and understanding, and to enable the accurate assessment of the cost-effectiveness of the techniques employed.

Activity 5.1

Identify three examples of markets where the physical product differences are minimal.

What are the differences that marketing communications seeks to communicate in those markets?

Activity 5.2

Without referring to the previous section, outline the important requirements when defining marketing communications objectives.

Determining marketing communications objectives

A starting point for the process is the *determination of objectives*. To begin with, it is vital that we discriminate and distinguish the aims of marketing communications from those of marketing in general.

Marketing communications objectives are specific communications tasks to be achieved among a defined audience to a defined extent and within a specific time frame. To this might be added the words 'within a predefined budget'.

In many instances, the objectives outlined for marketing communications remain imprecise and vague, or are confused with the overall marketing objectives.

Objectives written as:

- To increase our share of market
- To encourage more young users to purchase the brand
- To ensure a wider level of distribution

are all areas in which the process of marketing communications can make a contribution.

However, they are properly the province of marketing rather than marketing communications. Moreover, they lack the necessary precision which will enable us to monitor whether, after the completion of marketing activities, these objectives have been met adequately and cost-effectively.

By the same token, statements written as:

- To improve the company image
- To develop favourable attitudes towards the brand
- To establish the product as a leader in its field

while more properly the province of marketing communications, are similarly vague and imprecise. It is imperative that all marketing communications objectives are clearly defined and understood.

Activity 5.3

For a recent campaign with which you have been involved, or of which you have awareness, attempt to define:

- The marketing objectives
- The marketing communications objectives
- Examine how they differ and how they relate to each other.

Which objectives?

Most people when asked the question 'what is the purpose of using marketing communications?' will answer 'to increase sales' or 'to improve market share'. While these answers are not incorrect they might not cover the full range of objectives nor do they reflect the full responsibility that all the other elements of the marketing mix have for contributing to sales and profitability.

For example, if sales fall is that the responsibility of marketing communications? The answer is usually 'no' as poor sales may result from poor quality products, inappropriate pricing, ineffective distribution strategies, changes in fashion, competitor actions or even a downturn in the overall economy.

By focusing on sales alone there is a tendency to lose sight of other needs. For example, when launching a new product or service, the objective has to be to increase awareness in order that sales might be achieved in the longer term. Other goals might be to provide information, generate leads, direct customers to events or web sites or even to maintain a competitive presence in the marketplace.

Activity 5.4

Select a company that is experiencing trading difficulties (e.g. Marks and Spencer) and consider some of the reasons that might explain the situation they are in.

Is it all because of poor marketing communications?

What should start to be clear is that a single objective is not normally sufficient. What we must determine are *three* different types of objectives:

- Corporate
- Sales
- Communications.

The first relates to corporate image and reputation, embodied in the perceptions and preferences of other stakeholders. The second relates to sales volume, market share, profitability and revenue. The third relates to buyers of the product or service offered by the organization.

Corporate objectives stem from a clear organizational purpose, which may be documented in a mission statement. This is the root of the strategic approach to marketing communications. If this has changed, if the overall strategy has altered then this will need to be reflected in the messages communicated about the organization, as part of its overall profile (see unit Marketing communications strategy – the '3 Ps') and it may need to be reflected in product level communications.

Objectives, then, translate the mission into a form that can be understood by relevant stakeholders. They are the *performance requirements* for the organization and will be broken down into targets for each functional area, such as Finance, Human Resources, Production, Sales and Marketing. Some will be short-term and some long-term. They may change over time.

The various organizational objectives are of little use if they are not communicated to those who need to know what they are. Traditionally, such communication has focused upon employees, but there is increasing recognition that the other members of the stakeholder network need to understand an organisation's purpose and objectives.

The content of promotional objectives has also been the subject of considerable debate. Two distinct schools of thought emerge: those that advocate sales-related measures as the main factors and those that advocate communication-related measures as the main orientation.

Sales objectives

As we saw recently, many managers see sales as the only meaningful objective for promotional plans. Their view is that the only reason an organization spends money on promotion is to sell its product or service. Therefore, the only meaningful measure of the effectiveness of the promotional spend is in the sales results. These results can be measured in a number of different ways. Sales turnover is the first and most obvious factor particularly in business-to-business markets.

Sales objectives may do little to assist the media planner, copywriters and creative team associated with the development of the communications programme, despite their inclusion in campaign documents such as media briefs.

Sales-orientated objectives are, however, applicable in particular situations. For example, where direct action is required by the receiver in response to exposure to a message, measurement of sales is justifiable. Such an action, (termed a behavioural response), can be solicited in direct-response advertising. This occurs where the sole communication is through a particular medium, such as television or print.

The retail sector can also use sales measures, and it has been suggested that packaged goods organizations, operating in markets which are mature with established pricing and distribution structures, can build a databank from which it is possible to isolate the advertising effect through sales.

For example, if a supermarket based its advertising on celebrities talking about their favourite recipes, it would be possible to monitor the consequent stock movements of the particular ingredients supported by the celebrity. This should also enable the supermarket to evaluate the success of particular campaigns and particular celebrities. However, it is arguable that this may ignore the impact of changes in competitor actions and changes in the overall environment.

Furthermore, the effects of an organisation's own corporate advertising, ad stock effects (impact or carryover effects of previous advertising) and other family brand promotions need to be accounted for if a meaningful sales effect is to be generated.

The sales school also advocates the measure on the grounds of simplicity. Any manager can utilize the tool, and senior management does not wish to be concerned with information which is complex or unfamiliar, especially when working to short lead times and accounting periods. However, it ignores the complexity of consumer behaviour and the purchase process and so may result in wasting some of the investment made through marketing communications.

Communications objectives

The context analysis may reveal situations where the aim of a communications campaign should be to enhance the image or reputation of a product or where promotional efforts are to be seen as communication tasks, such as the creation of awareness or positive attitudes towards the organization or product. In other words sales are not regarded as the only goal.

Colley (1961) proposed that the communications task be based on a hierarchical model of the communications process:

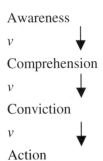

Awareness

v

Comprehension

v

Conviction

v

Action

Awareness of the existence of a product or an organization is necessary before purchase behaviour can be expected. Awareness, therefore, needs to be created, developed, refined or sustained, according to the characteristics of the market and the particular situation facing an organization at any one point in time.

                                    Involvement
                    High   **Low**

```
          ┌─────────────────────────┬─────────────────────────┐
          │                         │                         │
          │                         │        Refine           │
   High   │    Sustain awareness    │      awareness          │
          │                         │                         │
          │                         │                         │
          ├─────────────────────────┼─────────────────────────┤
Awareness │                         │                         │
          │                         │                         │
          │    Build awareness      │    Create brand with    │
   Low    │        rapidly          │    product class need   │
          │                         │                         │
          │                         │                         │
          └─────────────────────────┴─────────────────────────┘
```

Figure 5.1
Different forms of awareness

Figure 5.1 sets out different forms of awareness depending upon the buyer's previous experience and involvement. In situations where the buyer experiences high involvement and is fully aware of a product's existence, attention and awareness levels need only be sustained and efforts need to be applied to other communication tasks, which may be best left to the other elements of the communications mix. For example, sales promotion and personal selling are more effective at informing, persuading and provoking purchase of a new car once advertising and direct marketing have created the necessary levels of awareness.

Where low levels of awareness are found, getting attention needs to be a prime objective in order that awareness can be developed in the target audience.

Where low involvement exists the decision-making process is relatively straightforward. With levels of risk minimized, buyers with sufficient levels of awareness may be prompted into purchase with little assistance of the other elements of the mix.

Recognition and recall of brand names and corporate images may be sufficient triggers to stimulate a behavioural response. The requirement in this situation would be to refine and strengthen the level of awareness in order that it provokes interest and stimulates a higher level of involvement during recall or recognition.

Where low levels of awareness are matched by low involvement, the prime objective has to be to create awareness of the focus product in association with the product class.

Organizations use awareness campaigns and invest a large amount of their resources in establishing their brand name.

Comprehension cannot always be automatically assumed simply because there was awareness. For comprehension there needs to be knowledge about the product or service and this is often stimulated by providing specific information about key brand attributes. These attributes and their associated benefits may be key to the buyers in the target audience or may be key because the product has been adapted or modified in some way. This means that the audience needs to be educated about the change and shown how their use of the product may be affected. For example, in attempting to persuade people to try a different brand of washing powder, it may be necessary to compare the product with other powders and provide an additional usage benefit, such as an environmental claim.

Conviction follows when buyers become determined to try a particular product at the next opportunity. The audience's beliefs about the product need to be moulded, and this can be accomplished by using messages that demonstrate a product's superiority over its main rival or by emphasizing the rewards conferred as a result of using the product; for example, the reward of social acceptance associated with many fragrance, fashion clothing and accessory advertisements, and the reward of self-gratification associated with many confectionery messages.

High-involvement decisions are best supported with personal selling and sampling, in an attempt to gain conviction. Low-involvement decisions rely on the strength of advertising messages, packaging and sales promotion to secure conviction.

Action should result from an effective marketing communications programme. Advertising can be directive and guide buyers into certain behavioural outcomes; for example, to the use of free telephone numbers (0800 and 0500 in the UK), direct mail activities and reply cards and coupons.

For high-involvement decisions the most effective tool in the communications mix at this stage is personal selling.

In the light of this, the overriding task of the campaign is to position the brand so that buyers can distinguish it from its competitors and understand the brand values. This represents the strong strategic dimension of marketing communications and is discussed in more detail later in this section.

SMART objectives

To assist managers, there is a set of guidelines referred to as SMART objectives. This acronym stands for Specific, Measurable, Achievable, Relevant, Targeted and Timed.

The process of setting SMART objectives requires managers to consider exactly what is to be achieved, when, where, and with which audience. This clarifies thinking, sorts out the logic of the proposed activities and provides a clear measure for evaluation at the end of a campaign.

Specific: Is it awareness, perception, attitudes or some other element that needs to be completed? Whatever it is, it must be clearly defined and must enable precise outcomes to be determined.

Measurable: Make sure that a measure of activity is set, against which performance can be assessed. For example, this may be a percentage level of desired prompted awareness in the target audience.

Achievable: Ensure that the objectives are attainable, otherwise those responsible for their achievement will lack motivation and a desire to succeed.

Realistic: The tasks must be relevant to the brand and the context in which they are set.

Targeted and Timed: The target audience must be clearly defined and the campaign should have start and end dates clarifying the period over which results are to be considered.

To bring this part of this unit to a close, the objectives for a marketing communication campaign are derived from an understanding of what needs to be done relative to the particular situation an organization or product brand is in. This means that the objectives are determined through the context analysis.

Promotional objectives need to be defined in SMART terms and need to relate to corporate, sales and communication tasks.

The positioning concept

One of the roles of Marketing Communications are to differentiate a product (or organization). Part of this differentiation is concerning with positioning. This is the process whereby information about the organization or product is communicated in such a way that the object is perceived by the consumer/stakeholder to be different from the competition, and thus to occupy a particular space in the market.

Positioning, therefore, is the natural conclusion to the sequence of activities that constitute a core part of the marketing strategy. Market segmentation and target marketing are prerequisites to successful positioning. From the research data and the marketing strategy, it is necessary to formulate a positioning statement that is in tune with the promotional objectives. The positioning concept is a very important strategic term of marketing communications. This importance of establishing a distinct image of a brand in people's minds has developed mainly because of increasingly competitive market conditions. Increasingly there is little material difference between many products. Organizations, as well as products, are positioned relative to one another, mainly as a consequence of their corporate identities, whether they are deliberately managed or not. Sometimes, the perception of an organization may even be the only means of differentiating one product from another. Therefore, it is important to position organizations as brands in the minds of actual and potential customers, as well as the other stakeholders.

Positioning is about what the buyer thinks about the product or organization. It is not the nature of the product that is important here, but how the product is perceived. You may recall the importance that was attached to perception studied in unit Context 1 – the customer context.

It is important to understand that brand images are not fixed. They can be amended or changed completely by the appropriate use of marketing communications tools. For example, Hellman's, have transformed salad dressing from an old fashioned to a modern and desirable accompaniment to food.

Activity 5.6

Taking recent examples of marketing communications (use current television commercials and press advertisements), contrast the relative positionings adopted by four main-stream car manufacturers.

The competitive pressures within the retail market have resulted in a number of campaigns focusing attention on price. ASDA position themselves on low price relative to Sainsbury's, Safeway and Tesco while Curry's in the retail electrical market, B&Q in the DIY market, among others, have all run campaigns which stress their price competitiveness, reinforced by the proposition that they will match any other retail price on the same goods and variously improve on it. The consequence is that price comparison becomes an increasing facet of consumer attention.

Altering brand images

Most consumers are responsive to a 'bargain' proposition. Certain assumptions are made, particularly in relation to well-known and familiar brands. If a potential consumer sees a product on sale in a market environment, there is some expectation that the price will be lower than, say, in the normal retail environment. If the brand name is well established, then it is likely that they will be able to draw from it the confidence and reassurance which will be necessary to the making of a purchase decision. Indeed, there is considerable evidence that these perceptual factors, influenced by the environment, will for some consumers, induce them to make a purchase, even though they might have been able to purchase the same product at a lower price elsewhere.

Many retailers have recognized this situation and have adopted a position relative to their competitors of low price. By marking down the prices of a narrow range of products, they encourage the consumer to believe that all products are similarly discounted. This 'everyday low prices' (EDLP) strategy has been followed by a number of major manufacturers as well, including Procter and Gamble.

The result is that the consumer will decide to make all of his or her purchases at that outlet, based on the perceptions derived from a limited comparison of those brands upon which the retailer has focused marketing communications activity. Since few consumers are in a position to make objective comparisons across a wide range of comparable outlets, these perceptions are accepted and become the reality.

The situation is compounded by the fact that price is only one consideration in a purchase decision. Most people have an ideal view of a price and quality combination. Needless to say, such a view is highly personal and subjective, but becomes the basis of making subsequent purchase decisions for that individual. Thus reputation, both for retailers and brands, will be an important consideration in the purchase selection

Whatever the position, either deliberately chosen or accidentally occupied, it is the means by which customers understand the brand's market position.

Types and strategies

All products and all organizations have a position. The position determined by each stakeholder can be managed or it can be allowed to drift. However, brands may be positioned in one two main ways: one uses a rational approach the other uses an emotional or expressive approach. See Figure 5.2

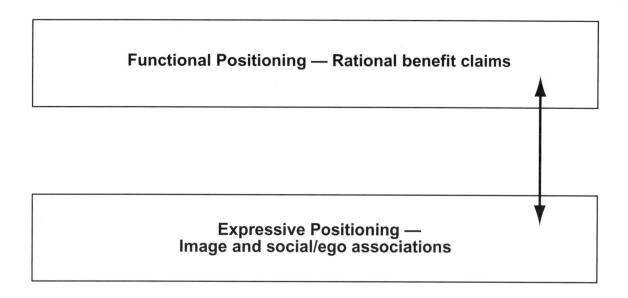

Figure 5.2
Two main ways of positioning brands

Rational positioning

Some purchasing behaviour is conditioned by the need to take rational decisions as to the nature of purchase. In those instances, it is important to provide the consumer with hard factual evidence which will occasion their purchase. This may take the form of a promotional device, such as a lower price or extra product free. In other instances, it may be some statement of the functional performance of the brand, such as lasting longer than its competitors. In the case of more expensive purchases this may take the form of long copy advertising, factual comparisons, etc.

Expressive positioning

Many products and services are purchased more because of the image that is associated with them, than the purely functional benefits. In such instances it is important to consider the style and the image which is conveyed by the advertising, or the possibility of developing an association with famous names or personalities. This form of positioning stresses the emotional or expressive associations and marketing communications role is to convey in a consistent and uniform manner the desired position.

Positioning guidelines

Increasingly, organizations are trying to manage their brand positions and are using positioning strategies to generate an advantage over their competitors. This is particularly important in markets that are very competitive and where mobility barriers are relatively low. In intensely competitive markets where buyers have great choice, an offering with a clear identity and orientation to a particular target segment's needs will not only be stocked and purchased but can warrant a larger margin through increased added value.

To manage the position the following schedule is recommended:

1. Which positions are held by which competitors?
   This will almost certainly require consumer research to determine attitudes and perceptions and possibly the key attributes that consumers perceive as important.
2. From the above, is it be possible to determine which position, if any, is already held by the focus brand.
3. From the information gathered so far, is it possible to determine a positioning strategy; that is, what is the desired position for the brand?
4. Is the strategy feasible in view of the competitors and any budgetary constraints? A long-term perspective is required, as the selected position has to be sustained.
5. Implement a programme to establish the desired position.
6. Monitor the perception held by consumers of the brand, and their changing tastes and requirements, on a regular basis.

Perceptual mapping

In order to determine how an offering is perceived, the key attributes that stakeholders use to classify products in the market need to be established. A great deal of this work will have been completed as part of the research and review process prior to developing a communications plan. The next task is to determine perceptions and preferences in respect of the key attributes as perceived by buyers.

The objective of the exercise is to produce a perceptual map where the dimensions used on the two axes are the key attributes, as seen by buyers. Each product is positioned on the map according to the perception that buyers have of the strength of each attribute of each product. By plotting the perceived positions of each brand on the map, an overall perspective of the market can be developed. Figure 5.3 shows that the key dimensions for the washing machine market are price and economy of use.

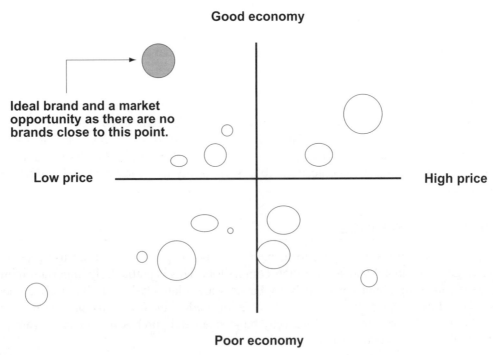

Figure 5.3
A perceptual map for the washing machine market.

68

The closer products are clustered together, the greater the competition. The further apart the positions, the greater the opportunity to enter the market, as competition is less intense.

It is also possible to ask buyers and other stakeholders what an ideal brand would consist of. This perfect brand can then be positioned on the map, and the closer an offering is to the ideal point the greater its market share should be, as it is preferred more than its rivals. These maps are known as preference maps. By superimposing the position of an ideal brand on the map, it is possible to extend the usefulness of the tool.

Perceptions of what constitutes the right amount of each key attribute can assist management in the positioning exercise. Marketing communications can, therefore, be designed to convey the required information about each attribute and so adjust buyers' perceptions so that they are closer to the ideal position, or to the position on the map that management wants the brand to occupy.

Perceptual mapping is an important tool in the development and tracking of promotional strategy. It enables brand managers to identify gaps and opportunities in the market and allows organizations to monitor the effects of past marketing communications.

Positioning strategies

The development of positions which buyers can relate to and understand is an important and vital part of the marketing communications plan. In essence, the position adopted is a statement about what the brand is, what it stands for, and the values and beliefs that customers should associate with the particular brand.

There are a number of overall approaches to developing a position. These can be based on factors such as the market, the customer or redefining the appeal of the brand itself; see Table 5.1.

Table 5.1: Positioning approaches (Fill, 2002. Used with kind permission)		
Approach	Type of application	Examples
Market-related	First into a market	Heineken (refreshment position)
	Redefine the market:	AA (repositioned as the Fourth Emergency Service)
Customer-related	A unique buying reason	Fairy Liquid (lasts longer, greater value)
	Particular type of buyer	Tia Maria (a girl's magic not just a drink to be consumed on special occasions)
Appeal-related	Distinct personality	Pepperami (crazy/mad, 'bit of an animal')
	Decision criteria	Virgin Upper Class (a sensible business decision, not a whim or a risk)
	Imaginative or interesting	Castrol (made oil into liquid engineering)

Within these three broad approaches, a number of strategies are available.

Product features

This is one of the simpler, and more commonly used, positioning concepts. The brand is set apart from the competition on the basis of its relative attributes, features or benefits.

For example, Pantene makes hair shine and beautiful and Ronseal 'Does what it says on the tin'.

Price/quality

Price itself can be a strong communicator of quality, with a high price denoting high quality – for example, luxury brands such as Cartier and Alfred Dunhill whose high prices signal quality and exclusivity. Similarly, the alcoholic lager Stella Artois, which is positioned as 'refreshingly expensive'.

At the other end of the spectrum EasyJet offer 'cheaper fares'.

It may be more difficult to establish a position of reasonable price *and* good quality, but it is often attempted – for example, Sainsbury's, 'where good food costs less'.

Use

By informing markets when or how a product can be used, a position can be created in the minds of the buyers – for example, Lastminute.com for late holiday and theatre bookings, Nurofen 'Meltlets' to relieve pain when no liquid is handy to wash down a tablet.

Product class dissociation

Some markets are essentially uninteresting, and most other positions have been adopted by competitors.

The Alliance and Leicester Building Society used to proclaim that 'not all building societies are the same'. The suggestion was that they were different from the rest and hence offered better services and customer care.

User

An extension of the target marketing process is to position openly so that the target user can be clearly identified – for example, 'Flora for all the family' or Saga 'for the over 50s'.

Competitor

For a long time, positioning oneself against a main competitor was regarded as dangerous and was avoided. Burger King and McDonalds contest the high street fast food market even though McDonalds have over 70 per cent market share. Lawnmower manufacturers such as Flymo and Qualcast still compete against each other as do credit card issuers such as MBNA and Capital One.

Benefit

Positions can also be established by proclaiming the benefits that usage confers on those that consume. Sensodyne toothpaste appeals to all those who suffer from sensitive teeth, and a vast number of pain relief formulations claim to smooth away headaches or relieve aching limbs or sore throats.

Cultural symbol

An appeal to cultural heritage and tradition, symbolized by age, particular heraldic devices or visual cues, has been used by many organizations to convey quality, experience and knowledge. Churchill Insurance represented by a British Bulldog, Kronenbourg 1664, 'Established since 1803' and Aspreys 'By appointment' to members of the British Royal family, are just some of the themes used to position organizations.

Activity 5.7

Find alternative examples to represent each of the positioning strategies described above.

Positioning plans, may be based on one or a combination of the above strategies. Whatever the position adopted by a brand or organization, both the marketing and promotional mixes must endorse and support the position so that there is consistency throughout all communications.

For example, if a high-quality position is taken, such as that of Rayban, then the product quality must be high compared with competitors, the price must be correspondingly elevated and distribution synonymous with quality and exclusivity. Sales promotion activity will be minimal and advertising messages visually affluent and rich in tone and copy, with public relations and personal selling approaches transmitting high-quality, complementary cues.

The dimensions used to position brands must be relevant and important to the target audience and the image cues must be believable and consistently credible. Positioning strategies should be developed over the long term if they are to prove effective, although minor adaptations to the position can be carried out in order to reflect changing environmental conditions.

Repositioning

If a position is strong and it is continually reinforced with clear simple messages, then there may be little need to alter it. However, technology is developing quickly, consumer tastes evolve and new offerings and substitute products enter the market. This means that the relative positions occupied by different brands in the minds of buyers are likely to be challenged on a frequent basis. This may mean that repositioning is necessary, especially if there has been substantial drift away from the original position and the brand is underperforming.

There are a number of reasons why repositioning may be necessary:

- Changing market opportunities and developments
- New (revised) business strategies
- Mergers and acquisitions
- Changing buyer preferences (which may be manifested in declining sales)
- The current position is either inappropriate or superseded by a competitor,
- Attitudes have changed or preferences surpassed.

When Brut was launched (an aftershave manufactured by Fabergé) it was positioned at the premium end of the market and at the time represented a significant shift in male attitudes towards this category. However, some years later with a host of competitors and new attitudes towards male grooming, repositioning was necessary. This was achieved through a significant price reduction, accompanied by a change in the pattern of distribution, and supported by a major communications campaign. This strategy served to reposition the brand in the minds of consumers – with a considerable impact on the value of sales generated. However, repositioning can be difficult to accomplish, often because of the entrenched perceptions and attitudes held by buyers towards brands.

Summary

In this unit we have seen that:

- Promotional objectives are necessary if effective marketing communications are to be generated. They provide direction, coordination, integration and a means of evaluating the success of the campaign.
- Appropriate objectives are derived from a context analysis, not from what people think is necessary. Objectives need to be drawn from an understanding of market and customer needs. They need to have a corporate, sales and communications related element.
- Once determined promotional goals need to be framed in SMART terms.

- Positioning is about how people perceive brands, how they see them relative to competing brands. Successful positioning requires an understanding about what is important to particular (target) customers.
- There is a range of different positioning strategies available for new brands and for repositioning established brands.

Further study and examination preparation

Try Question 4 of the examination paper for December 1999 following the guidelines provided below.

Question 5.1

You have decided to speak to your Marketing Team in order that they better understand the role of objectives in the integrated communication planning process.

Prepare notes for your presentation explaining the role of objectives, and identify which of the different elements of the communication process might be influenced by the objectives set.

See the question guidelines in Appendix 5.

Objectives

In this unit you will:

- Be introduced to three main types of communication strategy
- Consider the characteristics associated with each of the strategies
- Explore the nature of the core message that is an integral part of the strategy
- Examine the role of crisis management and its key dimensions, and consider the process of handling a crisis.

By the end of this unit you will be able to:

- Describe marketing communication strategy
- Explain pull, push and profile strategies
- Discuss the differences between them
- Determine the nature of core messages
- Know how to assess which strategies are appropriate for specific tasks.
- Have an understanding of the areas of corporate identity and crisis management

This unit covers syllabus sections 1.1.3, 1.1.4, 1.3.4, 1.3.5, 1.3.6.

Introduction

In order to accomplish the promotional objectives or goals that have been established it is necessary to formulate ways of achieving them. Strategies are used to meet the goals that we seek to achieve.

Some people regard marketing communication strategy as simply the combination of activities in the communications mix. The key issues really concern the overall direction of the programme, how it fits in with marketing and corporate strategy, and the targeting of primary messages in order to establish effective positions.

From a 'customer' perspective it is possible to observe three different types of customer need and from that deduce that there could be three different types of communication objective and strategy to meet those needs. There are those customers who are endusers, there are those who do not consume the product or service but add value to it as part of the marketing channel and finally there are all stakeholders whose focus is not the product or service but the organization itself.

The first group of 'customers' require product/service based messages that aim to increase levels of awareness, build and/or reinforce attitudes, and so motivate them to buy the offering. They expect it to be available when they decide to enquire, experiment or make a repeat purchase. This approach is known as a *pull* strategy as it encourages consumers to pull the products through the channel network.

Members of the marketing channel require messages that encourage them (retailers, wholesalers and dealers) to take stock, be motivated and committed to their partner organizations or participate in the movement of the product/service so as to make it available to end user customers. Communication strategies in these circumstances are referred to as *push* strategies.

There are occasions when stakeholders need to understand how or what an organisation's position is regarding particular issues. This approach seeks to influence attitudes towards the company and is referred to as a *profile* strategy. These three strategies are considered in turn.

Therefore, the three main types of audience can be identified broadly as customers, members of the marketing channels and all other stakeholders who are connected to the organization or the brand in question. Communication strategy may be referred to as the 3Ps:

- **Pull** – strategies to reach customers (consumers and businesses)
- **Push** – strategies to reach members of the marketing channel
- **Profile** – strategies to reach all relevant stakeholders.

Each of these strategies will now be explored in turn.

Pull Strategies for customers

Where the objective is to stimulate demand by encouraging consumers (and end user businesses) to 'pull' products through the marketing channel network, a pull strategy is necessary, see Figure 6.1. However, a pull strategy requires a core message to support it, to reflect the different opportunities that are available to position a brand.

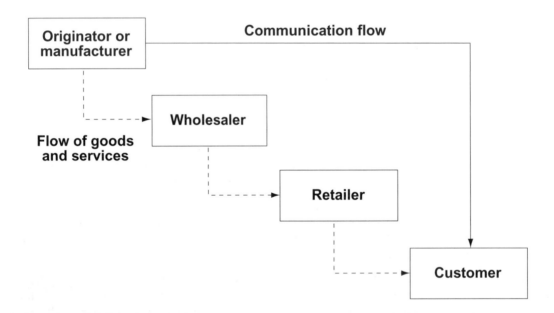

Figure 6.1
Direction of communications in a pull strategy

Activity 6.1

Write down what DRIP stands for without referring back to section 1.

You will have remembered that this means to differentiate, remind/reassure, inform and persuade and audience.

A pull strategy might be used to reposition a brand, to *differentiate* a brand from its competitors and to add value so that a customer clearly understands what the brand means and what it can do for them. For example, Thorntons, the chocolate manufacturers and retailers, have recently repositioned themselves so that they now wish to be seen as a part of giving gifts. The message therefore is about differentiation and gifts.

A campaign objective might be to *remind* lapsed customers of the brand values and so encourage them to begin buying the band once again. For example, Specsavers Opticians use marketing communications generically to build associations between the need for good eye sight and their brand. In some instances the strategy serves to ensure that the brand is brought towards the front of the consumer's mind. In others, it will seek to communicate specific benefits or uses of the brand which may have been forgotten. Or, perhaps it will suggest new uses which will make the brand more relevant to the consumer's needs. Alternatively the strategy might be to *reassure* customers that their recent purchase was a wise one. At the time of writing, a massive reassurance campaign is being used to reassure potential overseas tourists that Great Britain is a safe place to spend a holiday.

Many campaigns aim to keep audiences informed in order to keep a brand alive in their minds. New variants (e.g. tastes, colours, packaging and performance ability) may need to be communicated. Very often the goal is to build awareness levels so that when a customer thinks of a product category they immediately think of a particular brand. So, dog owners need tinned dog food (product category) and then think of their (dog's) preferred individual brand.

Activity 6.2

Find examples of campaigns where the goal was to build awareness.

At various times in the life of a brand, it is important to raise the level of awareness among target consumers. Inevitably, this is most often associated with the introduction of a new product. However, either because of competition or other pressures (perhaps a reduction in the levels of marketing communications support), the levels of awareness of a particular brand may fall, and it is necessary to improve these levels. In some instances, although the consumer may be aware of the product itself, they will need information as to where to purchase it (particularly if it is in limited distribution). Advertising will seek to identify stockists of the product.

Many people argue that marketing communications are used to deliberately *persuade* a target audience to *behave* in a particular way. For example, this might be to buy and/or try a product, attend a retailer's sale, telephone for a catalogue, visit a web site or to collect tokens or ring pulls with a view to taking part in a sales promotion event. It could also be argued that communications are used to *persuade* an audience to *think* in a particular way.

From time to time, market research may reveal a dissonance between the stance of the brand and the desired positioning. Perhaps, the image of the brand has become 'old fashioned' or more recently introduced competitor products are seen to have greater relevance to current needs.

Activity 6.3

Identify examples of where advertising has sought to change the product benefit.

How have the images of the brands changed as a result?

Often the role of advertising is to remind consumers (particularly in the case of routine purchases) of the original reasons why they chose the product. In some instances, such advertising will reassert the original values of the brand either to offset competitive pressures or simply to reassure consumers that those brand values have not been changed. Kellogg's, for example, ran a campaign with the broad theme 'If it doesn't say Kellogg's on the box, it isn't Kellogg's in the packet' to reduce the encroachment of retailer products which might otherwise be confused with the leading brand.

All the tools of the promotional mix, with the exception of public relations, are capable of persuading audiences to buy a brand. However, in consumer markets, advertising and sales promotions are the most often used tools and in business-to-business markets, personal selling is the traditional potent force.

The Strong theory of advertising reflects the persuasion view and the Weak theory is reflected in the Remind/Reassurance strategies. It should also be noted that that not only do both these campaign strategies need to inform and make audiences aware but also that a pull strategy may try to differentiate and persuade or inform and persuade or differentiate and inform an audience. Indeed any combination might be applicable, according to the context conditions.

Frequency of purchase

For products and services which are bought routinely, the fundamental role of Marketing Communications are to reinforce the values associated with the brand, and to ensure a high level of pack recognition at the point of purchase. The consumer will not spend a long time evaluating the available alternatives. They will possess adequate information on which to make the purchase decision, and advertising must ensure that the brand values are sufficiently well known and 'front of mind' to ensure that the brand, at the very least, is included on the shortlist of products to be considered.

For products and services which are purchased on a less regular basis, the primary task is to provide the necessary levels of reassurance to the consumer that the purchase is an appropriate one. Since the purchase itself is undertaken less frequently, the advertising will need to remind the consumer of the benefits associated with using the brand, and to establish clear advantages relative to the competition. Sometimes, these will be tangible benefits relating to particular attributes of the brand, such as taste, quality, economy and so on. In other instances, these will be emotional benefits such as good motherhood (caring for the needs of the family), or social values (the type of people who use the product or service).

In the context of products which require more extensive problem solving – as we have seen previously, these are normally expensive and very infrequently purchased items – the role of advertising will be both to establish the specific values of the brand, and to provide much of the necessary information upon which the purchase decision will be made. Sometimes, advertising in such instances will attempt to establish the evaluative criteria which the consumer will use in the making of brand comparisons. It will indicate suggested criteria for choice and, not unreasonably, demonstrate how it performs better than the competition against these given criteria.

Activity 6.4

The role of marketing communications differ when the product is a fast-moving consumer good as opposed to a durable.

It is important to make a distinction between the dimensions of purchasing behaviour. Not all products are purchased for rational reasons, although these may be important in the context of justifying the particular purchase to others.

Push Strategy

The objective with a push strategy is to influence members of the marketing channel (intermediaries). The influence is intended to stimulate demand by encouraging these channel partners to take and hold stock, to allocate scarce resources such as shelf space, and to become advocates of the product. As well as a product purchase orientation, there is also a strong need to provide information, support and encourage participation with a view to building long-term relationships. See Figure 6.2

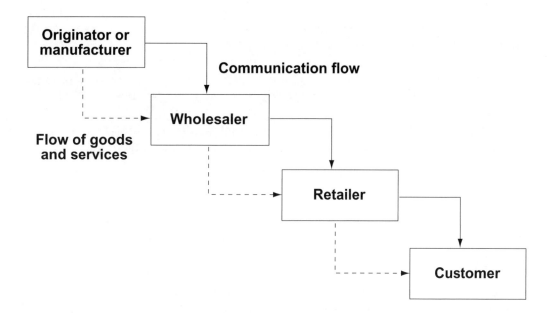

Figure 6.2
Direction of communications in a push strategy

Channel intermediaries include dealers, wholesalers, agents, value-added resellers, distributors and retailers. These organizations must cooperate to achieve their own objectives. Communication within networks serves not only to provide persuasive information and foster participative decision-making, but also enables coordination, the exercise of power and the encouragement of loyalty and commitment, so as to reduce the likelihood of tension and conflict.

The various channel networks have become ever more complex, and the expectations of buyers in these networks have risen in parallel with the significance attached to them by manufacturers. This impacts upon the choice of appropriate marketing communications strategies and tools. Multiple retailers, such as Tesco, have the power to dictate terms to many manufacturers of branded goods. This includes the type and form of promotions.

Communications in marketing channel networks

Communication flows within networks do not usually change radically over the short term. What is more likely is that they become set so that communication becomes standardized. A planned, channel-orientated communications strategy, a push strategy, should contribute to and reinforce the partnerships in the network. There are many factors that can influence channel communication strategy but most notably the following need to be highlighted.

- Power – are some organizations more important than others (including your own organization)?
- Direction – are communications one-way or two-way?
- Frequency – how often should messages be sent?
- Timing – should messages be sent to all members simultaneously or serially?
- Style and content – should messages be formal/informal? What must be included?
- Distortion – will messages be received, stored and acted upon as the originator intends?
- Information sharing – to what degree is there a willingness to share information in the marketing channel?

Activity 6.5

Imagine you are responsible for the marketing communications of a company that manufactures a range of construction plant equipment.

Some of your dealers might be helpful, cooperative and sell a lot of your products. Other dealers might be aloof, aggressive and difficult to do regular business with.

Thinking about the communication and the channel factors write notes outlining how the communications with these different types of dealers might be different.

The development of electronic communications and extranets in particular has helped organizations develop stronger, closer relationships in the marketing channel. These serve to not only bind organizations together but they also represent switching costs which may deter organizations from leaving the channels in which they currently participate.

A push strategy is not complete unless supported by a core message. The DRIP acronym is equally applicable as distributors need to understand how a manufacturer differentiates an offering and why they are different, in other words positioning is equally important. Dealers need to be reminded and often need to be reassured that either the products or the manufacturer are of value to them. Information is constantly required by distributors in order that they provide suitable levels of customer service. Finally persuasion is always necessary to encourage intermediaries to take stock, provide facilities and preference over other suppliers.

Profile strategy

On some occasions it is necessary to communicate with all stakeholders to convey information about the organization itself rather than its products and services. Issues concerning company performance, its stance on particular policies or just to portray the organization in a positive light to encourage investors and attract the best employees. The task here is to project an appropriate corporate identity in order to build and maintain a solid reputation.

Traditionally these activities have been referred to as *corporate communications*, as they deal, more or less exclusively, with the corporate entity or organization. Corporate communications is the process that translates corporate identity into corporate image. It should be noted that the distinction between corporate and Marketing Communications are not always clear. Corporate communications have traditionally been the sole preserve of public relations which has been regarded as separate from the other elements of the marketing communications mix. Integrated marketing communications requires that public relations operates within an overall communication framework and this really needs one very senior person to assume responsibility for the organisation's total communications.

Identifying different stakeholder groups and determining their attitudes and motivations is an important part of stakeholder analysis. Acting on this information to shape stakeholder perceptions of, and involvement with, the organization is a communications function. This shaping is referred to as a profile strategy.

A profile communications strategy is required to address all matters of structure and internal communications and the conflicting needs of different stakeholders so as to produce a set of consistent messages, all within the context of a coherent corporate identity programme. You will recall that Integrated Marketing Communications requires that internal messages to (and from) employees and managers blends with those messages that are sent to (and received from) stakeholders that are external to the organization.

It is possible to identify three central elements to a profile strategy: corporate personality, identity and image.

Corporate personality is determined by the internal culture as well as the strategic purpose. organizational culture reflects the values, beliefs and preferred ways of staff. The degree to which strategy is either formalized and planned or informal and emergent, and whether strategy is well communicated, also plays a major role in shaping the personality of the organization.

Corporate identity is the way the organization presents itself to its stakeholders. It is the outward projection of who and what the organization is, to its various audiences. To do this it uses identity cues, some of which are planned and some of which are unplanned, and of accidental.

Corporate image is in the eye and mind of each stakeholder. It is the audience response and image they form of the organization as a result of interpreting the various identity cues. Image results from interpreting the identity cues. Corporate Reputation develops through the accumulated images and experiences of an organization and its products.

Organizations, like individuals, project their personalities through their identity. The actual perception of identity results in an image formed and retained by stakeholders. organizations can and do have multiple images and must develop strategies that attempt to stabilize, and if possible equalize, them.

There may be a gap between actual and desired perception. The scale and significance of such a corporate perception gap may vary for different stakeholders. If a large number of stakeholders appear to view the organization in ways that are very different from how it perceives itself or wishes to be perceived, then communication strategies must address this large gap and attempt to narrow or close it.

If only a small number of stakeholders perceive a large gap, then a targeted adjustment strategy should aim at those stakeholders while taking care to protect the correct image held by the majority. If a minority of stakeholders see a small gap, a monitoring strategy would be appropriate and resources would be better deployed elsewhere.

If the majority of stakeholders perceived a small difference, a maintenance strategy would be advisable and the good corporate communications continued. The natural extension of this approach is to use it as a base tool in the determination of the communication budget. Funds could be allocated according to the size of the perceived perception gap. These different strategies are depicted in Figure 6.3.

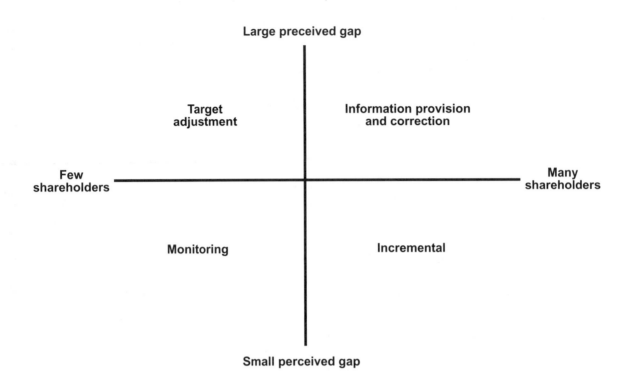

Figure 6.3
Corporate perception grid (Fill, 1999)

Corporate identity is about the management of the corporate personality, corporate identity and corporate image. Corporate Image is managed through the use of the identity cues. It is important that the variety of these cues is understood.

Activity 6.6

Consider an organization with which you are familiar and try to determine the characteristics of the internal culture.

How do you describe the culture and what would you say describes the personality of the organization?

Corporate identity cues

As mentioned earlier identity is conveyed through the use of cues. In addition to the normal cues provided through the promotional mix there are also a range of other cues that can be identified.

- The symbols, e.g. the logo, letterhead, furnishings and uniforms (workwear)
- The behaviour, e.g. how the telephone is answered, how staff interact with customers
- Communication styles, e.g. how media briefings are organized, the tone of communication.

These fall into two main groups. Those that are planned and controlled by management in a predetermined manner and those that are accidental and to a large extent unplanned.

Corporate identity programmes should not be considered as the unique province of major manufacturers, or those involved within the field of fast-moving consumer goods. The process is equally applicable to both profit and non-profit organizations. One only has to look at work carried out by government departments (such as the Department of Trade and Industry), charitable bodies (Barnado's, World Wide Fund for Nature), trade unions (National Union of Teachers) and other organizations (Railtrack, BT) to recognise that their respective identities have all been re-examined and redesigned in order to convey the appropriate desired images to their target audiences.

Key aspects of profile communications

The need for a long-term perspective: In a dynamic and changing environment, corporate communications activities must focus on the longer term aspirations of the organization. They must not inhibit change or potential movement into other operational areas.

Clear statement of objectives: Effective corporate communications, like all other aspects of marketing communications, must be based on a series of clearly stated and quantifiable objectives.

Commitment of management: Corporate communications are the embodiment of the corporate philosophy. The involvement of senior management in the process is imperative if the activities are to achieve the desired objectives.

Involvement of employees: Steps must be taken to ensure the active and positive involvement of staff at all levels. People within the organization must feel a pride of ownership if the activity is to secure their support.

Consistency is paramount: All aspects of the organization and its operations must be examined to ensure that the communications process provides a single unified view. In addition, all aspects of the communications process must be integrated to provide the consistency desired.

People and systems must be in place: Corporate communications demand constant attention. They do not happen on their own. It is important that a process is established to ensure the consistency of approach and application in all areas of the company's operations.

Evaluation: No marketing communications campaign is perfect, and this is no less true of corporate activities. A proper programme of research and assessment must be an integral part of the corporate communications plan. Feedback and revision will be essential components of successful implementation.

Only make changes for good reasons: The oft quoted adage 'if it ain't broke, don't try to fix it' applies here. Changes to the strategy should only be made for solid reasons. Change for its own sake will often result in more problems being caused than resolved.

Activity 6.7

How can a company ensure that it presents a consistent message in its corporate communications campaign?

Crisis management

Crisis management is a further area of corporate communications which is increasingly becoming recognized as a major aspect of the management of corporate identity and image. Perrier in the UK, Tylenol in the USA, and Group 4 in the UK have all faced varying degrees of 'crisis' with which they have had to deal. The nature of their respective responses to their individual problems illustrates the importance of having a positive approach to crisis management. The company that is seen to fail in its response to a disaster, or whose response is deemed to be inadequate, has only itself to blame for the subsequent decline in its perceived persona. Several companies have taken proactive steps in response to situations which have affected their operations. In two instances, Shell ran press advertisements to explain their position following details of their involvement with the regime in Nigeria, and their plan to abandon an oil rig in the North Sea. The company has recently announced a major internal communications campaign intended to boost staff morale.

Activity 6.8

Why do companies need to have a crisis management policy in place even when their business is functioning smoothly and their external relationships are good?

Companies need to be prepared in advance to deal with a crisis – even though it is unlikely that they will know its nature – and have an established system and process to deal with and respond to the issues as they are raised. The process of anticipation is key.

It is important that there are clearly established and identifiable pathways of responsibility within the organization. Ideally, nominated individuals will be in place to deal with enquiries and become the focus for company statements – both internally and externally. Too many people acting on behalf of the company can result in confused or contradictory responses, or responses based on poor information or knowledge of the situation.

Ideally, a company should have some form of plan in place which will be used to identify all areas of potential risk and, importantly, how to deal with them. This will enable a rapid response. As we have seen earlier, the lack of a direct response may itself be inferred by some members of the audience as being intentional.

In any organization, it is possible to ensure that some 'crises' are identified in advance – although they cannot be prevented or eliminated. It may be inherent in the nature of the business that some problems will occur, e.g. deaths in hospitals, or the lay-off of staff during a downturn in the economy. Other crises cannot be so readily foreseen, but the need for a speedy and informed response is the same.

Activity 6.9

Identify an example of a 'crisis' which has befallen a company recently. How did they respond to the problem they faced, and what was the outcome in terms of the organisation's image?

Profile strategies are an important part of an organisation's overall communications programme. The role and significance will vary depending upon individual situations, and each company's branding policy but the need to communicate with a range of stakeholders about non-product matters should not be ignored.

Unit Branding product and corporate branding looks at branding and corporate branding in more detail.

The Media

In order to convey these various messages, whether they be through push, pull or profile approaches, the use of the media will be important, if not vital if the target audience is to receive the message. Selecting the media is strategically important because of the increasing number of media channels and the breakup of the traditional ITV television audience into many disparate groups. These processes are referred to as audience and media fragmentation. It is a major issue as client-side managers become increasingly pressurized to account for their media spend.

Media can be considered against three separate dimensions:

- Does it enable the communication of the advertising message?
- Does it provide cost-effective coverage of the target audience?
- Is it the appropriate environment in which to place the message?

Activity 6.10

You have a media budget of £150,000. Identify the types of media you might use to communicate a charity message to raise funds for famine relief; and a business-to-business campaign for a company involved in mining.

Exam hint

The examiner will not expect you to have a detailed knowledge of the specific costs of advertising media. However, it will be important for you to demonstrate that you understand the appropriate media costs. If, for example, you are asked to deploy a budget across a variety of media, you will need to know (in broad terms only) the allocation of costs to your media recommendations.

Communicating the message

If the nature of the communications message, for example, demands some form of 'live' demonstration of the product or service, then is likely that the media planner will be driven towards the use of television. If the nature of the conversation with the consumer requires a long explanation of product attributes and benefits, then print media uniquely offer that facility. If the purpose of the campaign is simple product or brand recognition, then posters may fulfil that requirement.

However, media planning essentially revolves around two key issues. The balancing of coverage and frequency.

Coverage

Coverage is the percentage of people within the defined audience who will be exposed to the advertising message, in a particular period of time.

Frequency

Frequency is the number of times people within the defined audience will be exposed to the message, in a particular period of time.

However large the budget, there will never be enough money to maximize both elements, and the planner must determine the balance between the two. Inevitably, some form of trade-off will have to be made between a campaign which achieves the maximum level of coverage, but provides few opportunities for the target audience to see or hear the message, and one which narrows the coverage to enable a greater frequency of exposure.

Although a great deal of work has been done to research the balancing of coverage and frequency, there are no definitive answers. Even today, much depends on the skills and experience of the media planner in assembling a media schedule which will achieve the objectives that have been set. This will often be seen in the way in which the media campaign is laid down or scheduled (flighted). In some instances, in order to achieve the maximum level of impact, media expenditure will be concentrated into a relatively short period.

Often associated with awareness objectives, the *burst* campaign compacts media activity into a series of relatively short time frames, with relatively long periods of absence from media activity in between.

An alternative approach, mostly associated with reminder campaigns, is to extend the timescale of the advertising message over a long period. The *drip* campaign provides continuity of the message, although at the cost of impact.

A compromise between the two is the development of a *pulsing* campaign. Here a comparatively low level of media activity is maintained over a long period of time, with periodic increases in the expenditure pattern, often associated with seasonal or other influences on buyer activity.

Activity 6.11

Under what circumstances would it be more desirable to use pulse advertising rather than spreading the available funds evenly over a longer time period?

A third consideration is that of the impact of the message within a given medium. The media environment will be a critical factor in terms of the way the message is received and interpreted by the target audience. In some instances, as noted earlier, the nature of the advertising campaign will, itself, determine the broader issues of media selection – television versus press or radio, and so on. However, it is in the area of the specific selection of the timing of the appearance of the commercial, the press titles or radio stations selected that will have the greatest level of influence on the advertising message.

No media schedule is ever perfect. The aim must be to maximize the effectiveness of the campaign elements by the careful determination of the format in which the schedule is planned and the specific content of the media in which the advertising will appear.

To ensure that the media campaign continues to deliver against its targets, a proper evaluative process must be implemented. Whether this takes the form of periodic *ad hoc research* activity to investigate specific dimensions of the advertising effectiveness, or continuous market research in the form of a *tracking study* is somewhat less important than the fact that appropriate objective measurements are taken.

Interactive Communications

Technological advances now allow participants to conduct marketing communication- based 'conversations' at electronic speeds. The essence of this speed attribute is that it allows for interactive-based communications, where enquiries are responded to more or less instantly. So far in this Coursebook, little specific attention has been given to the emerging area of interactive communications and the role of the Internet in marketing communications. This is not to belittle the subject.

The Internet is, among other things, a medium for communication. The role for Marketing Communications are enormous and currently there is a huge amount of experimentation to determine what works and what does not work on the Internet.

As far as this module is concerned you need to be aware of a number of basic dimensions. The fact that the b2b market is bigger than the b2c market in terms of Internet applications is fundamental.

The benefits of Internet, Extranet and Intranet applications need to be fully understood and their strategic role in the way in which organizations can reduce costs, improve communication effectiveness and provide value-added services to consumers, employees and business partners is highly significant.

At the core of a company's Internet activity is their web site. Web sites are intended to be visited by those browsing the Internet, and once visited the opportunity to interact and form a dialogue becomes more realistic. The commercial attractiveness of a web site is based around the opportunities to display product and company information, often in the form of catalogues, as a corporate identity cue and for internal communications; to generate leads; to provide on-screen order forms and customer support at both pre- and post-purchase points; and to collect customer and prospect information for use within a database or as a feedback link for measurement and evaluative purposes. The principal benefits of an Internet presence at set out in Table 6.1

Table 6.1: Benefits of an Internet presence (Fill, 2001. Used with kind permission)
• Considerably reduced transaction costs • Opportunities for growth and innovation • Improved competitive position • Encouragement of cooperative behaviour • Stimulates review of business and marketing strategies • Enhances communications with customers • Can improve corporate image and reputation • Information about customers improved • Enhanced measurement and evaluation of customer interaction • Customer service developed

The list of benefits is quite extensive and far-ranging. From low barriers to entry for those developing web sites and the attraction of considerably lower transaction costs to improved collaboration and better business relationships and enhanced customer satisfaction, the Internet provides opportunities for considerable development.

The differences between traditional and new media are set out in Table 6.2. The interesting aspect is that the Internet is a medium that provides an opportunity for real dialogue with customers.

Table 6.2: A comparison of new and traditional media (Fill, 2001. Used with kind permission)	
Traditional media	**New media**
One-to-many	One-toone and many-to-many
Greater monologue	Greater dialogue
Active provision	Passive provision
Mass marketing	Individualised
General need	Personalised
Branding	Information
Segmentation	Communities

The development of an Internet presence should be regarded as something that can take place overnight. Experience suggests that organizations develop their Internet facilities according to needs and their preferred business model. For example, a web site can be used as either:

- A shop window – to look at the products and service on offer
- An enquiry facility – to find out more about the products and services on offer
- A fully interactive form of engagement – to buy one or more of the products on offer
- A fully integrated system – to embed business systems and procedures with partner organizations.

In this last phase the transactional activities between organizations are routinised and embedded in the relationship and business processes.

Web sites are the cornerstone of Internet activity for organizations, regardless of whether they are operating in the b2b or b2c sectors and whether the purpose is merely to provide information or provide fully developed embedded ecommerce (transactional) facilities. The characteristics of a web site can be crucial in determining the length of time, activities undertaken and the propensity for a visitor to return to the site at a later time. Should a web site visitor experience a satisfactory visit then both the visitor and the web site owner might begin to take on some of the characteristics associated with relationship marketing.

Summary

In this unit we have seen that:

- Strategy is concerned with the direction and purpose of an organization and can be different to planning. Planning may be regarded as the articulation of strategy.
- Marketing communications strategy is more than a configuration of the marketing communications mix. It should be audience-centred and in that sense it should be regarded as either pull, push or profile.
- Pull and push are product related and profile-related to the organization itself. In reality organizations use these in combination according the prevailing contextual conditions and objectives.
- Corporate identity is made up of three main elements, personality, identity and image. Care needs to be taken not to confuse identity with image.
- Crisis communications are a significant aspect of profile strategies and need to be developed by management in anticipation of a crisis striking.
- The media are an integral part of communications strategy and the development of interactive communications is an additional strategic element that needs to be considered as part of the an organisation's overall communication strategy.

Further study and examination preparation

Try Question 3 of the examination paper for December 1999 following the guidelines provided in Appendix 5.

Question 6.1

The use of planned communications in marketing channels is an important aspect of most communication strategies.

Write brief notes explaining why it is important to communicate with channel members, and suggest what might be the key influences that shape the design and implementation of such communication activities.

See the question guidelines in Appendix 5.

Objectives

In this unit you will:

- Explore different dimensions of branding
- Consider the role marketing communications can play in the development of brands
- Develop your understanding of corporate branding
- Appreciate further the role of branding in integrated marketing communications.

By the end of this unit you will be able to:

- Appraise the way in which marketing communications can be used to develop brands
- Have a clear understanding of the importance of brands, both in the marketing context and that of marketing communications.
- Explain the differences between corporate identity and image
- Discuss the relationships between an organization and its brands.
- Know the principles underlying the development of corporate brand identity and the objectives of corporate communications.

This unit is designed to cover very important issues relating to the brand and the role that marketing communications can play in developing and maintaining strong brands.

The unit is divided into two main parts, product based brands and corporate brands (identity) respectively. This latter topic was first looked at in the unit Marketing communication strategy – the 3 Ps as part of developing a Profile strategy and crisis communications.

This Unit covers syllabus sections 1.1.1, 1.3.9.

Study guide

The topics covered by this unit represent an important aspect of marketing communications, and the Senior Examiner frequently sets questions either explicitly on these areas or within the framework of a broader question to test your understanding. It is important that you attempt to answer the various questions and activities set within the unit before you tackle the example questions which have been extracted from recent examination papers.

Branding

Study tip

Branding is the core of all marketing communications activity, and it is very important that you develop a deep understanding of the issues raised in this unit. You will all have a high degree of familiarity with many brands – both domestic and international – which will underpin your studies in this area.

As with other areas, it is important that you practise applying the principles to real branding issues, and the unit provides a number of key questions and activities to enable you to do that. Make sure that, by the time of the exam, you have identified your own examples with which to illustrate your answers.

Also, make sure that you develop your own examples to use in the examination, rather than simply repeating those covered here. They want to see that you can apply your knowledge to the types of situation described in the questions, rather than simply writing out long lists of points – only some of which may be relevant!

A brand is defined as a name, term, design, symbol, or any other feature that identifies one seller's goods or services from those of other sellers. A brand name may identify one item, a family of items, or all items of that seller.

Activity 7.1

Identify four brands, one from each of the following categories:

- Confectionery
- Services,
- Cars
- and Not-for-profit.

What are their distinguishing characteristics?

Consumers buy brands. Thus, the loyalty which the brand identity can create in the marketplace is fundamental to the ability of a company to offset competitive activities. If the positive values associated with a brand are sufficiently strong, it will enable the owner to overcome major problems with product quality. Both in the UK and elsewhere, some major brands have suffered from such things as contaminants which have required the company to withdraw temporarily from the market. In the very recent past, several products have been removed from supermarket shelves following the disclosure of tampering with the product contents, sometimes with disastrous consequences for the purchaser.

Activity 7.2

What role does branding and packaging play in identifying a product to the consumer?

Branding and packaging are the overt and tangible aspects of a product, and serve to distinguish one manufacturer's product from that of their competitors. In the crowded retail environment, it is these aspects of the product which help the brand to stand out from the crowd. Most brand names are made up of letters and numbers, and in some instances may also include an additional graphic design which is unique to that product. In most instances, manufacturers will register these logo designs to ensure legal protection of their mark, and to avoid the risks of 'passing off'. It is important to remember, however, that in most cases a brand name will only be protected within the specific category of trading, and thus other manufacturers will, potentially, be free to use the same name in another category. In the 1960s, Granada, which had registered the name in the context of television production, rental and associated areas, attempted to preclude its use by Ford in the automotive industry. The legal case decided in favour of Ford and they were able to retain the use of the name for a range of cars. The issue of brand protection is an important one, both in a domestic and an international context, and we will return to the topic throughout this unit.

We have already seen that the core product offered by a manufacturer may, in most instances, be indistinguishable from that of their competitors. Indeed, given the nature of technology, the specific product advantages which one manufacturer has over their competitors will often be readily and rapidly duplicated by them. In countless blind tests, many consumers are unable to distinguish between different manufacturers' products. The key factor, and an area in which marketing communications plays a key role, is the association of other values with the brand name to ensure that the perceptions of the potential consumer may be altered to create a favourable impression of the brand.

Brand image

Brand image is the total impression created in the consumer's mind by a brand and all its associations, functional and non-functional.

If, for one moment, we strip away the brand marks of Levi, Kellogg, Cadbury, Mercedes, and Johnson and Johnson, to name but a few, we are left with commodity products shorn of all of the brand values which are associated with those names. All the investment made by those companies over many years into creating image values through the use of Marketing Communications are lost. It is the latter area which establishes in the minds of consumers, a series of defined images and values which are instantly recalled on exposure to the brand name. The brand values are equally important to the company in terms of its longer term extension of activities. Many brand names have positive values associated with them which extend beyond the particular product with which the name is identified. These intangible values can be used by the company to extend its portfolio into other areas.

Within the soap and detergent markets, two brands stand out as examples of the positive values of branding. Fairy and Persil have both been used as brands which have taken their owners into extended categories by the association of new products with the positive values built up around those names. Mars demonstrated the power of their brands with the moves into the ice-cream market. Despite the fact that the company had no prior representation within the sector, the values associated with the names of Mars, Bounty and others gave an immediate identity to the ice-cream products which bore these logos.

Brand names and identities may also be used in other ways. Once a brand has built up a high level of recognition among consumers, it may be sold or leased to other manufacturers to provide them with an immediate entree into another sector of the market.

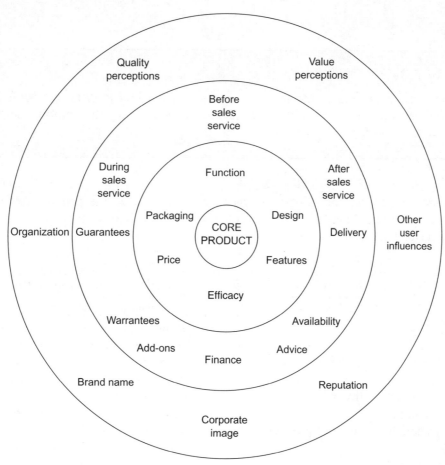

Figure 7.1
The Chernatony and McDonald chart.

The dimensions of a brand can be visually depicted on a Chernatony and McDonald chart (L. de Chernatony and M. McDonald, *Creating Powerful Brands,* Butterworth-Heinemann, 2nd edn, 1998) See Figure 7.1. It must be remembered, of course, that not all of the listed dimensions apply to all products and services. In some instances, the tangible aspects of the proposition will be more important; in others, differentiation may be achieved as a result of the quality of the services – before, during and after sale, guarantees, etc. – which are provided; in yet other instances, it will be the brand image and identity which will assume the greatest level of importance.

Manufacturers, retailers and not-for-profit organizations all realize the benefits that can accrue form successful branding. Many of these are set out in Table 7.1. In order that these be realized it is important to develop a brand strategy.

Table 7.1: Benefits of Branding (Fill, 2002. Used with kind permission)	
Customer benefits	Brand owner benefits
• Easier to identify preferred products • Reduces levels of perceived risk • Improves the quality of the shopping experience • Helps determine levels of product quality • Derivation of psychological rewards status, ownership, etc.)	• Normally allows for premium pricing • Helps differentiate the product from competitors • Enhances cross-product promotion and brand extension opportunities • Encourages customer retention and possibly loyalty • Promotes the development of integrated marketing communications • Contributes to corporate identity programmes • Provides some form of legal protection

Branding strategy

We can discriminate between a series of very different branding strategies adopted by companies.

Manufacturer branding

A key decision to be taken by all manufacturers is the branding policy towards the products which they introduce to the market. In some instances, the manufacturer will choose to adopt a *multi-product* branding strategy. Here, the manufacturer uses the strength of the parent name to communicate a series of common values which 'endorse' all the products which bear that name. Sony and JVC, for example, have both established strong reputations within various sectors of the consumer electronics market. Whether the consumer is intending to purchase a television, a compact disc player, or a video recorder, the endorsement and reputation of the parent company singles out the appropriate product as being worthy of consideration. The name of Kellogg is synonymous with breakfast cereals and Colgate with dental care. The same principle is equally true within the service sector. Similarly, the standing of the Automobile Association lends credibility to its offering of car and other insurance facilities.

Usually, although not always, manufacturers restrict such activity to directly related markets, since it can be reasonably expected that the products all have common values and attributes. If, for example, the consumer perceives the names of Black & Decker and Bosch as being those of manufacturers of quality power tools, those names can reasonably be expected to carry a similar weight within the broader DIY markets. Both those companies have moved into gardening tools, for example.

In many instances, manufacturers maintain several brand names which are used to endorse separate market categories, but the names are kept distinct from each other to avoid the creation of confusion in the minds of the consumer. For example, Gillette maintains its name for the personal care market, but uses the Braun brand for the related electrical appliances market, embracing dry shaving, electric hair dryers, toothbrushes, etc.

Multi-branding is a strategy adopted by those manufacturers who choose to keep the parent name subservient to the end user. For example, the name of Procter & Gamble is little known by consumers, although the brands they produce are all major players in their respective markets. Procter & Gamble manufacture a variety of brands including, among many others, Ariel and Daz in the detergents market, Oil of Olay, Vicks, Pampers and Pantene.

In some instances, the benefit of a multi-branding approach is that it enables the parent manufacturer to have competing products within the same sector of the market. This principle can be seen from the example of Procter & Gamble above, as well as Kraft, Foods International (itself a subsidiary of Philip Morris), which maintains several brands of coffee including Maxwell House, Kenco, Jacobs and Gevalia which variously compete with each other in different markets.

This same principle is adopted in the retail environment where, for example, Dixons, the retail electrical dealer, also owns Currys, PC World and The Link. Similarly, Kingfisher owns the Comet Group, B&Q, Woolworths and Superdrug. An important dimension of multiple branding which deserves mention, is the use of third-party endorsement. Increasingly, manufacturers are recognizing the importance, as underpins to the product message, of names which may be only distantly related to the product category. When Procter & Gamble acquired the name of Vidal Sassoon, it was used to establish major credibility in the hair-care sector, for example. By the same token, the addition of names like Chanel and other couture houses has added a valuable dimension to products which might otherwise not have been distinguishable from their competitors.

In certain instances, typified by the approach of Nestlé, a *combination* approach is taken, where the parent name is used to endorse some products – directly or indirectly – but where others are left to stand alone. In the instant coffee market, for example, the brand name for their main product is a derivation of that of the parent company – Nescafé Gold Blend, their premium quality product, is endorsed with the Nescafé logo; in the cereals, confectionery and other markets, the Nestlé symbol is used alongside that of brand names such as Cheerios and Kit Kat; while in the bottled water market, the name of Perrier is left to stand alone.

Within the retail sector, operators are becoming increasingly concerned with issues relating to branding. For many years they were content to use their operating name on the products which were manufactured on their behalf and sold by them. Consumers derived their perceptions from the support activity which surrounded the store identity. Retailers such as Sainsbury's, Safeway and others developed distinctive positionings within the marketplace in relation to quality, value for money and other dimensions, and the products which bore their logos reflected those values. In recent years, however, the retailers have seen the need to elevate their own (private label) products to brand status. Sainsbury's introduced Novon (a range of washing powder and liquid products) and Gio (a competitor in the soft drinks market) with a distinctive identity. More recently, Tesco have announced a brand called 'Unbelievable' to compete with Unilever's 'I Can't Believe It's Not Butter'. Safeway maintain a comprehensive range of products with distinctive packaging and identities to compete with manufacturers' brands. We will consider other aspects of 'lookalike' brands later in this unit.

Mixed branding

Several manufacturers adopt a *mixed branding* approach to distinguish between products which they manufacture under their own brand names and identities, and those which are supplied to retailers and packaged with their retail identities. Although several manufacturers (including Kellogg) refuse to supply products to private labels, and indeed have used advertising to communicate that fact, others such as Allied Bakeries, United Biscuits, Dalgety and Britvic, to name just a few, simultaneously sell products under their own brand names to compete on-shelf with retail competitors which they have supplied.

Generic branding

In some instances, manufacturers or retailers have been content to sell their products under generic or 'no brand' identities. Often this stance is taken to emphasize dimensions such as value for money. The notion of the 'white pack' originated in France to provide consumers with a range of 'no frills' products at considerable discounts against conventional brands. The approach has been met with mixed success, although there is little doubt that many of those consumers who purchased the products packaged in this way expressed satisfaction and rated them highly in terms of value for money.

Activity 7.4

Why do you think that generic branding has not achieved the anticipated impact on consumers?

Brands and consumer perceptions

Brands continue to maintain a considerable price premium, despite expressions to the contrary. First it was anticipated that pressure on disposable income when the economy turns downwards, second the impact of own label products and third the impact of the Internet would all conspire to reduce prices.

Many companies (e.g. Procter and Gamble) have attempted to change strategy to one which is based on Everyday Low Pricing (EDLP). This worked by reducing the level of marketing communications (P&G by 25%) and the savings were put into lower prices. The policy did not work mainly because the lower prices did not result in higher volumes, they just rewarded regular buyers with lower prices; it did not attract a sufficient number of new customers and so profits fell and they (like others) have returned to a branding policy.

It is not uncommon for brand leaders to charge prices that are 30% to 45% above that of private label products. Indeed, leaders often enjoy a premium of around 10 per cent against their main rival brands, those that are number 2 and 3 in the category.

Importantly, while there has been much talk in the trade press concerning the erosion of the position of brands and while many consumers may say there is little to choose between branded and private label products, there is sufficient and regular evidence to suggest that branded products are important for particular segments and that perceptual values continue to be vitally important.

We have already seen that consumer perceptions are influenced by a variety of internal and external factors. However, we have also seen that marketing communications play an important role in influencing those perceptions and creating images which go far beyond the normal functional factors and may affect the choice of a brand. There are, of course, some areas where these added values may indeed be real and tangible. Virgin Airlines are currently stressing several key attributes of their service delivery in their Club Class advertising – additional seating room, provision of in-air 'lounge facilities', choice of movies, car pick up at destination, and so on.

In most cases, however, especially where there is low involvement, – which include the vast majority of fast-moving consumer goods – it is the combination of the physical attributes of a brand together with the values created by marketing communications, which are important to the creation of perceptual values.

In many instances, the consumer may be more concerned with the intangible benefits delivered by the brand than the physical performance of the product itself. The reputation and lifestyle factors involved in, say, owning a Rolex watch, or wearing a Pierre Cardin suit, have little to do with direct performance comparisons with other watch brands or other clothing manufacturers.

The role of marketing communications

Recalling that one of the prime roles of Marketing Communications are to differentiate (and position) a product or service, it is important to understand that this is paramount when considering how to develop a brand and keep it alive in the minds of the target audience.

Marketing communications can develop and establish key brand values in one of two main ways. These may be considered as the advertising route or the name route. With the advertising route, advertising is used to develop brand related associations for consumers such that they make connections between a brand and its advertising. These associations may be linked to tangible attributes such as taste, colour or price for example. Alternatively, they may be linked to intangible elements such as prestige, status and ego-related aspects of ownership. Therefore branding may be entirely emotional or image-based. For example, the Peugeot 406 'Search for the hero inside yourself' campaign. Alternatively, brands may be based entirely on rational information; e.g. Ronseal's 'It does exactly what it says on the tin'. In many cases a blend of emotive and rational messages may well be required to achieve the objectives and goals of the campaign; e.g. the BT campaign using ET (emotional) plus factual data.

If the naming route is to be adopted then the brand name will be linked to the functionality of the brand itself. The packaging and associated communication devices (often instore/merchandising) will provide further points of brand association reinforcement. All aspects of the promotional mix, if used appropriately, can be used to develop, maintain and extend a brand. Mass media advertising used to be the tried and trusted way of brand development. Times have changed and now integrated marketing communications (IMC) can be used to develop and reinforce brand messages. IMC can be used to establish brand values which consumers then use to understand those brands that are important or significant to them.

Branding, therefore, can augment products in such a way that buyers can understand that it is different to other brands, recognize it quickly and make purchase decisions that exclude competitive products in the consideration set. Premium pricing is permissible, as perceived risk is reduced, and high quality is conveyed through associated trust and experience. Loyalty develops, facilitating opportunities for cross-product promotions and brand extensions. Integrated marketing communications become more feasible as buyers perceive thematic ideas and messages which, in turn, reinforce positioning and values associated with the brand.

Corporate branding – image and identity

Recent years have seen an increasing role for corporate advertising, and an increasing recognition of the importance of developing a corporate identity. When these tasks are carried out effectively and efficiently, they are the epitome of good integrated marketing communications. The process is an important one, and has significant strategic implications. Above all, it is the means by which an organization communicates the very nature of itself to its various publics.

This topic has been considered as part of a profile strategy in Marketing communication strategy – the 3 Ps and so many of the fundamental aspects will not be reconsidered here. If you have not studied that unit yet you are strongly advised to do so before reading the rest of this one.

Activity 7.6

What are the key dimensions of company image?

Corporate Identity is about how an organization chooses to present itself to its target audiences. It does so through planned and unplanned identity cues. Corporate Image is concerned with the way audiences perceive the identity cues and the interpretation and meaning given to the cues. Corporate communication is commonly concerned with the translation of corporate identity into image.

Corporate branding

Corporate branding is the current terminology for what was previously regarded as corporate identity. One of the reasons for this change of name is that many regard identity as visual identity, the logo, the typeface and the signage used by the organization. In the 1980s however, the deeper strategic significance of the subject became apparent and the change of name is supposed to signal the difference. Whether it does or not is immaterial as the Senior Examiner is happy for students to refer to either name, as long as it is the deeper, cultural and strategic view of communications that is taken.

There are sound commercial and communications reasons for this increased level of interest. There has been an increasing recognition that consumers choose between the various products and services available to them for a wide variety of reasons. Not all of these are derived exclusively from the product or service itself. In many purchase situations, company recognition and image are important factors in the decision-making process. Moreover, as the costs of marketing communications increase, the ability of a company to provide support for all the products in its portfolio becomes more remote.

The market segment, while profitable, may be too limited to justify media expenditure. Or the share of market might be too small to fund a marketing communications campaign. Those brands which are embraced by an identifiable and positive corporate identity will tend to be chosen by consumers in a purchasing environment over those which have no identity or which stand alone. This may be exemplified in the purchase of a medicinal product. Whether it is taken to alleviate the symptoms of the common cold or to relieve a headache, the nature of consumption attaches considerable importance to the purchase decision. Familiarity with the corporate name of Smith Kline Beecham or Fisons will help overcome the relative unfamiliarity of names such as Venos Cough Mixture, Ralgex or Opticrom.

Activity 7.8

Look out for some brands which are owned by large companies. Identify how the company image affects your perceptions of their brands.

A further impetus to the process has come from the expanding rate of globalization. Mergers and acquisitions, together with organic growth, have resulted in many corporate operations opening up in different parts of the world. As operations expand and become more dispersed, there is an inherent danger that each operating unit, by retaining responsibility for its own communications programme, produces materials which are inconsistent with other parts of the operation. The development of a cohesive corporate identity programme has the twin benefits of avoiding inconsistencies and of binding the diverse parts of the operation together. The alternative is the lack of a shared identity, with the risk that the operations move apart and the benefits of globalization are lost.

Inherent in this statement, however, is the recognition of the need for corporate identity programmes to work across national divides, and with different languages and cultures. Not only words, but symbols and colours may communicate a different impression from the one intended and desired. There is a need to ensure that companies in competing industries identify a means of differentiating themselves from each other. But it must be remembered that image and identity change are no panacea for other ills. A simple audit of the present identity will establish whether images perceived by the target audiences are positive or negative. In the latter instance work needs to be done to enhance the image. However, if the reality falls short of the image – actual or desired – then it is clear that there is a fundamental problem within the organization which needs to be addressed. The corporate identity can provide the focus for the organization and provide a unique position in the marketplace. In many respects the corporate identity reflects the personalities and values which are associated with a company.

Activity 7.9

Think of some global companies. What image do you have of their organizations?

It is obvious that companies communicate, whether they do so deliberately, or by default. The issue to be addressed is how companies go about the process of communicating to their various publics.

Comparatively few companies have a corporate communications strategy, although the number that do is growing along with the recognition of the importance of the area. The result is that the image and identity which many companies portray 'happens' rather than are deliberately fostered for the overall benefit of the company.

Several years ago, the then Chief Executive of GrandMet saw a refuse disposal lorry bearing the corporate name. As part of its diversification at that time, the company had entered a number of service areas which delivered to the overall income. However, it was recognized that the lorry would be seen by, among others, people in the city or in the media, and that the image conveyed would be contrary to the one desired. It didn't take long before a directive was issued, not only to remove the GrandMet name from the rubbish van, but from all other operating companies that did not have permission to use it. Although this is a long way short of developing a proper corporate identity programme, it was the first step in the appreciation of the fact that all means of communication impact on the various publics who are exposed to them.

Activity 7.10

Why do charities need to be concerned about their image?

Companies which don't communicate – internally or externally – do a great disservice to themselves. A lack of communications may often be interpreted as negative communications, implying that the organization has something to hide. If a company says nothing about an issue, its publics will infer a response. Increasingly, the public is becoming more concerned with how a company relates to it, and the beliefs that it holds or the actions that it takes, than simply with the nature and quality of the products or services it provides.

Activity 7.11

All companies must communicate – but to whom? List the various audiences for a corporate communications message.

There are many lists and some will reflect individual situations. However, the following provide a list of the more critical audiences.

Employees

Many companies tend to forget that their staff and workforce all represent potential ambassadors for the organization. If employees have a positive relationship with their employer, they will tend to communicate a favourable impression. To engender such feelings, it is vitally important that employees feel involved with the company and, wherever possible, are exposed to the company's thinking at regular intervals.

Local community

Companies need to develop positive relationships with the community in which they exist. If, for example, the company is seen to be a contributor to the local economy, they will tend to receive more support for things such as planning applications.

Influential groups

Whether on a local or a national basis, there will be a variety of external bodies which will have an impact on the company's activities. These may consist, among others, of pressure groups and public officials. Their relationships to and perceptions of the organization will have an impact on the way that they respond to the company's activities. Shell, for example, have cultivated a positive relationship over many years with environmental groups who, in turn, have been more supportive than might otherwise have been the case.

The 'trade'

Most companies are dependent on wholesalers, retailers and others who act as the intermediaries between them and their ultimate customers. The cultivation of good relationships and a positive image will be an important factor in gaining their support.

Government

The actions of central government will have a marked impact on company performance. The introduction of unfavourable legislation may well diminish a company's profitability. The support of government agencies who represent companies in overseas markets, for example, may be pivotal in gaining major foreign contracts.

The media

The media, in general, are the recipients of a variety of messages concerning a company. Some messages derive from positive public relations activities, others from impressions received from other sources. The interpretation the media place on stories about the company will have a substantial impact on the way in which those messages are communicated.

Financial

The financial community will require a great deal of information about a company, both regarding its past performance and its prospects for the future. In order to secure a continued flow of investment, these relationships will need to be developed to ensure a positive response to company actions.

Customers

We have already seen that, to an increasing degree, customers are concerned as much about the nature of the company, the actions it takes on important issues, and its general beliefs, as with the quality of the products and services it produces. Because of the recent focus on environmental issues, companies have been able to secure positive images (and negative ones) from the actions they have taken in this area. In turn, this is likely to impact on the sales volume they achieve. Remember, there are always alternatives available, and a company which is received poorly may well find that its customers turn to others to obtain products and services.

The general public

The image of the company to the general public is of similar importance. Ultimately, for many companies, the general public are their consumers. How a company is thought of will often determine whether people purchase from that company or another. Periodic research, such as that carried out by MORI, repeatedly demonstrates that companies with a positive image are expected to produce 'better quality' products.

Activity 7.12

How might a corporate campaign, designed to explain (differentiate and inform) stakeholders about the scope of company activities, affect perceptions of the company?

Many organizations simply assume that they need only communicate when they want to. However, it is inevitable that deliberate and unintended messages get through to audiences all the time. Failure to control all aspects of the communications process may result in the offsetting of those aspects of communications which are more within the company's control, such as advertising and public relations, and result in a confused image.

The adverse publicity associated with Group 4 following its appointment to transport remand prisoners to their court appearances and the subsequent escape of some of their charges had a negative impact on the way people perceived the company and the services it provided.

Activity 7.13

What are the dangers inherent in an organization's failure to adopt a positive approach to corporate communications?

Shell has been consistent, both in its advertising and in its other activities, in identifying itself with environmental issues and concerns. The result , until recently, had been the creation of a very favourable and positive image of an environmentally friendly and caring organization. However, the company image was tarnished by a series of events including its proposal to sink an oil rig in the North Sea, its support of the Nigerian Government and its response to the activities of its shareholders. The recent change of the image of British Airways was designed to provide the company with a more appropriate global identity and to reflect the fact the majority of its passengers originate from countries other than the UK. However, this has now been reversed, as a result of the negative impact on domestic users.

Corporate image

It is important to remember that corporate identity and corporate strategy will be closely related to each other. The strategic direction of an organization will be influenced by its identity, while its identity will be affected by the nature of the strategy.

A core strategic decision which an organization must take is its approach to the market. Wally Olins (*Corporate Identity,* Thames & Hudson, 1989) divides corporate identities into three distinct categories.

Monolithic

The organization uses a single name and visual style throughout all its operations, where each item of communication that the company uses serves to reinforce the identity of the parent company. Examples would be those of IBM, BMW, Shell and Prudential.

Endorsed

The organization maintains a separation between its subsidiary companies and the activities it pursues, but endorses those activities by the addition of the group name and identity alongside that of the operation company. Here, examples would be BAT and P&O. The former has diverse interests in the fields of tobacco, insurance, etc., and uses its corporate name to add stature and credibility. The latter, similarly, owns companies in areas such as housebuilding (Bovis), exhibition halls (Earls Court and Olympia) and others, alongside its more familiar cruise liners and cross-channel ferries. It is only in the last two operations that the P&O name is used directly. Elsewhere, the P&O logo and identity is used alongside the operating name.

Branded

The company operates through a series of brands which may be unrelated to each other. Procter & Gamble owns operating companies in diverse markets such as soap powders, toiletries, perfumes, etc., with brands such as Oil of Ulay, Vidal Sassoon and Pantene. In some cases, the identities are deliberately kept distinct in order to enable products to compete in the same market. Unilever has adopted a similar posture.

Summary

In this unit we have seen that:

- Increasingly, there are few physical differences which serve to enable the consumer to discriminate between competing brands. Many rely on the differences in positioning, image, lifestyle values to provide a reason why the consumer should select one brand in preference to another.
- There are various branding strategies that may be adopted by companies to assist in this process. All aspects of a company's communications to its various publics will serve to create the image of that company. Indeed, the very lack of a communication may well be interpreted negatively by those publics.
- Marketing communications have an important role in the development of brands. Brands can be delivered through advertising which seeks to develop rational attribute related associations or emotional associations that tend to appeal to our social and ego related drives.
- Corporate branding is about the way in which an organization chooses to communicate with a range of stakeholder audiences. The essence of this communication is to communicate about a variety of issues that relate to the organization as a whole rather than to particular products or services.

- Identity is about how the organization wants to be seen, image is about how the organization is actually perceived.
- It is vitally important that all the communications techniques employed are integrated and work together to deliver a cohesive and consistent image of the organization.
- By studying this unit, you should have built up a clearer understanding of the importance and nature of brands and the role marketing communications play in their development. Branding is a strategic issue that all organizations need to address.

Further study and examination preparation

See Question 7 of the examination paper for June 2000 in the appendices.

Objectives

This unit is designed to consolidate your knowledge of marketing communications, and assist you in applying this knowledge in the international context.

In this unit you will:

- Examine the pressures that are resulting in this trend towards globalization.
- Consider the implications of international versus national marketing communications.
- Look at the benefits of standardizing international communications and the needs of the 'international' consumer.
- Consider the role of the international marketing communications agency.

By the end of this unit you will:

- Have a thorough understanding of the international dimensions of marketing communications.
- Be able to debate the merits for both standardized and localized approach to international marketing communications.

This unit covers syllabus sections: 1.5.1 to 1.5.4.

Study guide

The field of international marketing communications is an important one and, in recent years, many of the examination questions have had an international dimension. This particularly applies to the compulsory question which takes the form of a mini-case study.

This unit provides you with the opportunity to reinforce the learning that has taken place since you started on this Coursebook. By now you will have developed a detailed understanding of the major topics of marketing communications strategy. If necessary, refer back to the individual units which cover aspects of the marketing communications process in more detail, in order to remind yourself of the topics covered at that time.

The trend towards globalization

Study tip

We are almost at the end of the programme, and you have done much of the work to cover the ground in readiness for the CIM Integrated Marketing Communications paper. This unit will help you begin the process of revision, which is vital to ensure that you have a good enough command of the subject to approach the examination with confidence.

It is a good idea to re-read all the work units to identify any gaps or weaknesses in your knowledge. If you can identify and rectify any problems now, you will have no problem when it comes to the examination.

Recent years have seen an increasing tendency towards the globalization of brands. As domestic markets have reached positions of virtual saturation, manufacturers have turned to new and often distant markets to ensure a continuation of their growth potential. It is argued by that global marketing is the final phase in a progressive process of this desire for market extension.

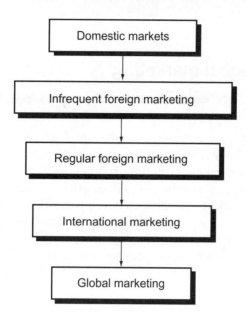

Figure 8.1
Phases of International Marketing Development (From: P. R. Caetora, International Marketing, 8th edn, Irwin, 1993)

Domestic markets	These comprise the first stage of the process, in which companies design products and services to satisfy the identified needs and wants of domestic consumers.
Infrequent foreign marketing	This is often dictated by a short-term need to eliminate production surpluses which cannot be absorbed by the domestic market. However, there is no real desire on the part of the company to exploit these opportunities on a longer term basis, and once the domestic 'problem' of oversupply or low demand has been eliminated overseas sales are curtailed.
Regular foreign marketing	The manufacturer devotes some resources to the exploitation of overseas opportunities on an ongoing basis, but the primary focus remains the need to respond to domestic demand. In these instances, the company often uses middlemen, but may create its own selling operations in important markets.
International marketing	As companies perceive the major opportunity to derive profits from foreign markets, they progressively commit more resources to the development of this potential and, in the process, become more committed to the tasks of international marketing. In general, they perceive their markets as possessing unique characteristics for which individual marketing and marketing communications strategies must be developed.
Global marketing	At this level, companies view the world as a single market. This is accompanied by a tendency towards the standardization of business activities and the adoption of marketing and marketing communications strategies which reflect those elements of commonality throughout the many markets they serve.

Multinational versus global marketing

We can make an important distinction between these two approaches to foreign markets, and these have significant implications for the determination of marketing communications strategies.

The *multinational company* readily perceives the fundamental differences between the various markets it serves. In general, it believes that its success is dependent on the development of individual marketing and marketing communications programmes for each of its territories. As a result, it tends to operate through a number of subsidiaries which, for the most part, act independently of each other. Products are adapted, or developed independently, to meet the needs of the individual markets and the consumers within. By the same token, the other elements of the marketing mix are developed on a local basis. Although there may be some cross-fertilization of ideas through some form of central function, the primary aim is to satisfy the needs of individual country markets, rather than the specific identification of common elements which might allow for the standardization of activities.

The *global organization* strives towards the provision of commonality, both in terms of its products and services, and the propositions which support them. As far as possible, it attempts to standardize its activities on a worldwide basis, although even within this concept there is some recognition of the need for local adaptation to respond to local pressures. The fundamental objective is the identification of groups of buyers within the global market with similar needs, and the development of marketing and marketing communications plans that are as standardized as much as possible within cultural and operational constraints.

The impetus for a more detailed examination of the implications of international marketing was provided by a seminal article by Theodore Levitt (*Harvard Business Review,* 1993, 61, 92-102). The thrust of his argument in 'The globalization of markets' is that a variety of common forces, the most important of which is shared technology, is driving the world towards a 'converging commonality'. The result, he argues, is 'the emergence of global markets for standardized consumer products on a previously unimagined scale.'

It could be argued that it is the convergence of communications which has, and will continue to have, the far greater impact. We know that consumer motivations towards the purchasing of products and services are the result of the influence of a wide range of factors. One central factor which impacts upon many, if not all, of them is the mass media. As the peoples of the world are exposed to the same messages via television, film and other media, it is inevitable that their attitudes towards the products and services depicted will move towards a common central point.

Irrespective of our geographical location, it is likely that most of us will listen to the same music (the bands that top the charts in one country enjoy similar levels of success in others), the same films (which country has not yet been exposed to the film *Titanic*), the same television programmes (note the spread of *Who Wants to be a Millionaire?*) the same computer programmes and games, and even the same articles in the media. While it is undeniable that cultural differences will continue to prevail, at least for some considerable time into the foreseeable future, so too are we witnessing the coming together of many attitudes and beliefs, which enhance the potential for products and services that respond to those common and shared values.

The forces of internationalization

There are many factors that can be cited as contributing to this growth of an international rather than a purely domestic outlook. We have already seen that, from an attitudinal perspective, there are growing similarities between countries. With improved communications, the physical distances between markets matter far less. There is, as mentioned by Levitt, the integrating role of technology. The capacity to produce similar or even identical products in dispersed markets is enhanced as the technological base of manufacturers becomes similar. At the same time, we are witnessing the progressive removal of the former barriers to international trade – tariffs. Most regions of the world are joining together in supra-national groupings for their mutual economic benefit. among others, these include the EU (European Union), NAFTA (North-American Free Trade Agreement), ASEAN (the Association of South East Asian Nations), CARICOM (the Caribbean Community and Common Market), and CACM (the Central American Common Market).

With slowing domestic economic growth in many areas, manufacturers are being forced to seek potential markets away from their home base. Indeed, specific government actions are being taken to incentivize foreign trade. A similar impetus comes from the recognition that, as products reach the maturity or decline phase of the product life cycle, they will need to identify new markets which are in a different stage of development.

The intensity of domestic competition may also force companies to look elsewhere, where perhaps the costs of market entry are lower or their offerings appear to be more innovatory and exciting. Of course, there is the opportunity for manufacturers to secure the benefits of differential pricing. A product sold for a premium price in one market can be sold in another for a lower price and still make a profit contribution, so long as the marginal costs are covered. The changing base of competitive advantage and the emergence of global competitors is forcing other manufacturers to seek joint ventures and coalitions, often with foreign partners. Apart from the benefits of shared technologies, the participants in such deals obtain 'ready-made' set-ups which enable them to access other markets in return for a comparatively low investment.

The forces restraining standardization

As much as there are many forces driving the move towards internationalization, so too there are a number of factors which preclude, or at least slow down, the rate at which manufacturers from one country can introduce their products directly into another. National and cultural characteristics remain a fundamental point of difference. Although, as many have argued, there is a progressive convergence of attitudes and behaviours, many such patterns are sufficiently ingrained to be unchangeable in the mid-term. We will discuss these factors in more detail later in this unit, as they have important implications for the determination of marketing communications strategies.

The different levels of economic growth and national living standards will, similarly, act as restraints in some areas. However attractive a particular offering may be, if the individual is on a low income or unemployed, he or she will not be able to make the desired purchase.

There will be fundamental differences between markets which cannot be altered in the short term. While some will relate to the ingrained behavioural patterns mentioned above, others will be a direct consequence of environmental factors – the comparative penetration of such items as fridges and freezers, the availability of domestic storage space, distribution factors, and so on.

There may be a more basic resistance to change which will inhibit the acceptance of products and services which are commonly accepted in other markets. Also, there remain a number of legal and regulatory factors which may preclude the penetration of particular markets where the sale of individual products may be limited or even banned. Finally, there is the political environment which may discourage foreign trade in general, or that from individual companies in particular. At the same time, manufacturers may be wary of making substantial investments in markets with unstable economic or political environments where they do not have sufficient confidence of being able to secure an adequate level of return because of underlying changes.

Activity 8.4

How does the information required for the development of an international communications campaign differ from that required for domestic planning?

Activity 8.5

Find three examples of brands which have adopted a global communications strategy and three which have adopted a multinational communications strategy. In what ways are their communications strategies different from each other?

The development of global brands

It is inevitable that the progressive standardization of products results in significant economies of manufacture which, potentially, lead to lower prices and a more competitive positioning for the brand. The high investment in product development will be rapidly amortized if the market for the resulting product is global and enormous rather than domestic and limited. Such developments, however, will not obviate the need in many instances to adapt the product to meet 'special' local needs, however these are occasioned.

Some manufacturers perceive the world of the future to be one in which global brands dominate. The perceived benefits of a single worldwide brand identification outweigh those of country-specific products with separate brand identities. However, it is important to remember that, even here, it is not essential that the product delivered in each market is identical – only that the branding and the imagery associated with it are the same. Nestlé, for example, have adopted the same packaging and style for their leading brand of instant coffee across most international markets. However, the specific product may well be different in many of those markets to reflect local taste characteristics.

Activity 8.6

Locate examples of some products sold in your market but originated elsewhere. How have they been adapted to suit local needs? Consider product, packaging, advertising, etc.

Even where it is necessary to subjugate the current brand identity in favour of a single consistent worldwide brand mark, major manufacturers have determined that the long-term benefits are likely to outweigh the short-term losses. Despite enjoying considerable consumer acceptance in the UK with their Marathon brand, Mars opted for a standardization of the brand under the name of Snickers across all markets. In 2001 the household cleaner Jif was renamed as CIF to provide consistency across the markets the brand was offered.

Activity 8.7

In what ways does the construction of a marketing communications campaign differ in an international context?

The move to global marketing communications

In the same way that we have seen a progressive move towards the standardization of brands, so too has there been a movement towards the development of standardized marketing communications programmes. The rapidly accelerating costs of producing separate campaigns for individual markets, the difficulties of co-ordinating separate campaigns in physically close markets, together with the desire for the establishment of a single world-wide identity for its brands, have induced many companies to explore the potential of single campaign development across many, if not all, markets. Inevitably, there are polarized views on the merits of such moves.

At one extreme, as a response to the pressures indicated above, some companies have developed central campaigns which provide the core of all of their marketing communications activity in all markets. For a number of years, Coca-Cola have run essentially similar campaigns in many markets, with all or most of the elements being constantly applied in all of the territories in which they operate. Promotional activities and sponsorships, wherever possible operate globally. Similarly, identical advertising, save only for the language of the voice-over, has been run by the brand across all territories.

At the other end of the spectrum are a wide range of international brands for which 'local' advertising propositions have continued to be developed and which, in their producers' view, enable them to reflect more readily the needs and desires of the individual markets in which they operate.

Between these two positions are those brands which adopt a common communications strategy, but allow for the local development of specific executions. In these instances, there is a cohesion in the underlying message of the brand in all of its markets, but room for the development of tightly focused and tailored propositions which reflect the subtleties and nuances of the local marketplace. Some manufacturers have developed this approach to the position where they develop 'pattern book' communications campaigns. An overall stance for the brand will be taken centrally, with semi-finished examples of advertising and sales promotion approaches laid down centrally. These, however, provide the 'shell' of activity and the local operations have the flexibility to adjust the specific content to meet their local requirements. It is this latter area which has witnessed the greatest growth over recent years. Indeed, even the ubiquitous Coca-Cola have recognized the need to develop specific messages for individual markets to respond to pressures on the brand's position.

Activity 8.8

The emergent 'new Europe' – the old Eastern European nations – represents a major market opportunity for many manufacturers' products and services. To what extent should they plan to use existing marketing communications campaigns to support the introduction of their products to these markets?

The merits and demerits of standardized communications

We have already seen that the proponents of standardized communications campaigns cite the cost savings to be accrued from the development of a single campaign, together with the comparative ease of co-ordination, as partial justifications for the move towards common global marketing communications activities.

It cannot be denied that the cost savings may be enormous. For example, the average cost of production of a television commercial is of the order of £300,000 to £500,000 and, very often, very much more than that. Moreover, if several creative teams are working in different parts of the globe to resolve the communications needs, the time involved and the associated costs will be considerable. As we have seen, there may be an underlying commonality of requirements, and thus much of that time will be spent covering the same ground as others in the search for the communications message.

Not only does a standardized process eliminate the problems of conflict arising from dissimilar messages being communicated in adjacent territories, it also saves a considerable amount of management time involved in resolving such difficulties. Similarly, management would otherwise need to be involved – within each market – in the briefing and approval of creative work, the development of separate sales p romotion campaigns, public relations activity and even packaging changes.

Ultimately, the key benefit results in the creation of a single consistent image for the brand across all markets. The management and monitoring of the campaign can be more consistent, and the implementation process simplified. Against these, however, it can be argued that there are a number of significant disadvantages.

Inevitably, if the brand is at a different stage in its development, it may be less responsive to a marketing communications campaign developed for all markets, than to one specifically designed to deal with its own particular needs. We have already seen that different objectives, such as creating awareness, stimulating repeat purchase, and so on, will require different motivations and, hence, different messages. Similarly, in order to ensure universal appeal and comprehension, the resultant execution may be bland and boring and satisfy none of the individual requirements satisfactorily. This may, in turn, inhibit the opportunity to generate sales volume and result in management frustration.

Indeed, the problem is often one of motivation for staff, both within the company and the agencies it uses. As they may not be involved with the development of the marketing communications programme, they may perceive it as being irrelevant to their needs. And they will often feel no commitment to its successful implementation. As multinational campaigns take a long time to create and produce, this may reduce the ability, on a local level, to respond rapidly to local pressures.

Understanding the international consumer

If marketing communications demand a thorough understanding of the consumer and the environmental factors which surround them, this is even more true of marketing communications in an international context. Where we can reasonably expect to understand important facets of consumer behaviour in a domestic context, this is far less likely to be the case in different and separate markets where culture, tradition, and other factors may result in vastly different meanings being attached to the communications message. Market research will play an important part in identifying areas of similarity in order to allow for the development of a single consistent message, if that is the objective.

Activity 8.9

What are the key issues to be addressed in the development of an international marketing communications programme?

What approaches should be used to minimize the potential difficulties?

It should be clear that, in order to develop an effective multinational or global communications strategy, a number of 'new' dimensions will have to be considered, beyond those which would be appropriate for a single-market communications strategy.

- Language
- Culture and tradition
- Legal and regulatory requirements
- Buying habits and motivational factors
- Standards of living
- Media availability and usage
- The competitive environment.

Language

Multinational communications campaigns often fail because the message is simply translated rather than *reinterpreted*. This is not merely a semantic diff e rence. Not only is it true that specific words often will not have a corresponding word in another language, sometimes the true translation will have a negative impact on the target audience. Furthermore, the same principles apply equally to body language and gestures. As we move increasingly towards non-verbal communications, it is vitally important to ensure that the visual imagery we employ communicates positively rather than negatively.

Culture and tradition

Arguably, this is one of the most difficult areas of multinational communications. Perceptions which are based on tradition and culture are extremely difficult to overcome. Fundamental areas, such as pack colours or symbols, may have totally different meanings resulting from cultural interpretation. White may indicate purity in many markets, but in others it is a symbol of death. Certain numbers may be symbols of good luck in some countries, but have opposite meanings in others. More significantly, the cultural values, sometimes derived from religious views, result in markedly different attitudes towards products and services. For example, it would be an anathema to show pork or shellfish ingredients in a product intended for a predominantly Jewish market, the same would apply to beef in Hindu communities, or alcohol for Muslims.

While the specific advertising message might avoid such obvious errors, it is important to remember that the surroundings in which the message is set (a home, a retail outlet, etc.) may, similarly, contradict existing cultural beliefs in some markets. In some markets, for example, it would be inappropriate to depict a woman wearing Western clothes; in others, a commonly used motif of a man stroking a woman's skin to connote smoothness would be regarded as taboo.

Legal and regulatory requirements

There are few common standards for marketing communications across all markets – although there are progressive moves towards harmonization is some areas, such as the EU. Yet tobacco advertising, for example, is still commonplace in many parts of Europe, while limited or totally prohibited in others. Most countries now see condom advertising as part of the global campaign to control AIDS. However, in certain countries, such advertising would be unthinkable due to strong religious beliefs. Sales promotion techniques which are commonly accepted and widely used in some markets are not allowed in others.

Buying habits and motivational factors

The patterns of purchasing frequency differ markedly between countries, sometimes resulting from differences in income levels and on other occasions being the results of patterns of usage. In some parts of the East, for example, fresh produce is bought on a daily basis, whereas in the West shopping, even for fresh ingredients, may be carried out weekly and the purchases stored in the fridge or freezer. Motivational factors and aspirations are, similarly, different from one country to another, leading to difficulties in communicating aspirational 'norms' where such values either do not exist or have different parameters.

Standards of living

Products which are consumed on a daily basis may be considered as luxuries in others, particularly if the relative cost is high. Cigarettes, for many purchased in packets of 20, are sold singly in some African markets, with the resultant difficulties of the lack of packaging to communicate brand values. Elsewhere, the incidence of fridges may preclude the sale of some packaged convenience foods, and so on.

Media availability and usage

A primary consideration, especially in the context of global campaigns, is the need to access constant media outlets. After all, if a major aim of standardization is to eliminate costly production, then the same media must be available in all markets. However, not only are certain media not available to the marketer in some areas – certain countries, for example, have only limited television penetration, while others do not allow advertising – the patterns of usage may also differ. In some countries, spot advertising throughout the day is commonplace. In others, all advertising is grouped together and broadcast at set times of the day.

Other aspects of media are equally important. In different markets, different media have a different status, such that advertising placed in them have greater or lesser credibility. This is particularly the case in those markets where media have a distinct religious or political orientation.

The competitive environment

Just as consumers differ between markets, so do the brands available to them. Identifying the aspirational values of a brand, in order to define a unique positioning, becomes more difficult as the number of markets increases and the competitors differ in their stances. Often, a desired positioning is already occupied by another brand in a particular market. As we have seen, the relative position of a brand – leader or follower – will have important implications for communications strategy determination. It is extremely unlikely that all but a very few brands will occupy the same position in all of the markets in which they are available.

It is clear from the above that the task of developing a singular marketing communications strategy, while not impossible, is an extremely difficult one. Many companies have accepted that, in order to achieve their communications objectives, they must adopt a somewhat different stance. Indeed, such consensus as exists suggests that the policy towards multinational marketing communications campaigns should be based on the statement: 'Think globally, act locally.' Inherent in this statement is the acceptance of the fact that common communications strategies can be developed across all markets, but that their implementation must be effected on a local basis, in order to reflect the multitude of differences which, despite convergency, continue to exist.

The development of multinational communications agencies

In the same way that companies have become international, so too have advertising agencies, public relations and sales promotion consultancies, etc. Two important and parallel trends have occurred.

There has been a progressive 'internationalization' of the service companies to the point where few do not have representation in all of the key markets. As a result of mergers, acquisitions and alignments, the major practitioners in the fields of marketing communications have subsidiaries or associates in all the major countries of the world. In addition, global clients are increasingly appointing global agencies to handle and co-ordinate their marketing communications business across all their territories.

Cisco Systems announced in April 2001 that it was in talks about its £120 million world-wide creative account and the possibility of reducing the number of agencies on its roster. This and a large number of similar moves by other major organizations, are typical of the process of global re-alignment. Indeed, the key requirement to inclusion on the shortlist for many such accounts is the extent to which a company has the ability to service the business on a multinational basis.

Often, companies will maintain a roster of agencies to handle their business, particularly where they have multiple brands. In most cases, the same agency will be used across the brand in all markets. Examples of this practice may be seen with Procter & Gamble, Mars and others.

The selection of an agency for international business

The principles underlying the selection of an agency to handle business across a number of markets are essentially the same as those involved in the appointment of an agency to handle an account within a single market.

Activity 8.12

What skills would be required by an international marketing communications agency as opposed to one dealing exclusively with domestic business?

These principles are:

1. Determine the overall nature of the service you require:
   a. Full service
   b. A la carte.
2. Decide which services you will require:
   a. Creative
   b. Planning
   c. Media
   d. Market research
   e. New product development
   f. Public relations
   g. Sales promotion. etc.
3. Define the quantitative criteria:
   a. Should the agency be large, small or medium?
   b. Should the agency be independent or part of an international network?
   c. Is previous experience in the category relevant or essential?
   d. What are the desired terms of business – billings/fee/combination?
4. Define the qualitative criteria:
   a. What sort of agency style are you looking for?
   b. What sort of creative work do you require?
   c. Should your agency have won creative awards?
   d. Do you require direct access to the various departments (e.g. creative, media, planning)?
   e. Do you want a formal or informal relationship? etc.

In the case of the appointment of an agency to an international account, item (3b) will take on special importance.

Obviously, the decision as to agency selection will, to a large degree, be governed by the strategic direction of the company. As such, there are a number of separate options to be considered:

- The appointment of a single, multinational agency.
- The appointment of an international agency network.
- The appointment of a series of local agencies.

Multinational agencies

As noted above, the trend has been for the large agencies either to acquire or establish branches in all those markets in which they might reasonably expect to generate international client opportunities. Indeed, some of this process has been client inspired, in the sense that the agency is encouraged to establish an office in a country in which the client is intending to operate. Over the past two decades, led originally by US agencies, but more recently by British and Japanese agencies, groupings have been assembled to respond to client needs.

Independent networks

To offset the competitive threat posed by the multinational agencies, networks and confederations have been formed to provide the global coverage demanded by some client companies. CDP Europe, Alliance International and ELAN (European Local Advertising Network) are three examples of such groups. From the agency perspective, these associations meet clients' needs to operate on a global basis, while preserving their own independence. Usually, these groupings are based on 'like-minded' philosophies, with agencies of similar views of the marketing-communications process (creative style, media prowess, the role of planning, and so on) coming together.

Local independent agencies

In many countries, newly emergent agencies remain bitterly jealous of their independence and, at least in the short term, are prepared to forgo some international accounts. Indeed, many such agencies remain independent in the longer term as a means of offering their own unique positioning in a crowded market.

Criteria to be considered in selection of an agency

Before deciding on its agency, any client must consider a set of important criteria in the international context.

To what extent is it planned to implement a single communications strategy in all markets?

For those companies wishing to pursue a global communications strategy, it is sensible to consider only the first and second options i.e. a multinational agency or an independent network. The benefits of already established links will ensure the speedy transfer of knowledge and understanding which, in turn, should facilitate the process of implementation in the variety of countries in which the campaign will run.

To what extent will the intended agency be precluded from operating in other market areas?

Some companies adopt a strict policy whereby the incumbent agency is not only precluded from handling directly competitive business, but also from those other areas in which the client company has an interest. This, it has to be said, is becoming an increasingly untenable situation. As multinational companies expand their businesses, both horizontally and vertically, they embrace increasingly diverse market segments.

Acquisitions of companies and brands result in their taking an interest in markets far beyond their original businesses. For example, Procter & Gamble have interests in diverse fields including hair-care preparations, sanitary protection, cough and cold remedies, soap powders and toothpaste, to name just a few. Apart from their coffee interests, Nestlé operate in the following markets: confectionery, bottled waters, cereals, tinned soups and yoghurts and mousses. Here again, the list is only a partial one.

Clearly, to function profitably, the multinational agencies have to think carefully about client conflicts, both current and in the future, before taking on a new account. Though the short-term increase in billings might be attractive, their tenure of a particular client might inhibit their growth potential in the future. In turn, therefore, some agencies with otherwise desirable credentials may be precluded from consideration.

Do the multinational or network agencies possess all the appropriate skills in all markets?

Often, a multinational agency may have relatively weak representation in one or more of the markets considered important to the company. The same is equally true of agency networks, where not all of the participants may have the same reputation and skills.

Are there specific local skills which need to be accessed?

In some instances, a local independent agency may have a far greater in-depth knowledge or understanding of the market, the consumers or the general environment which it may be important to access. Indeed, the independent local agency may have greater prowess, for example, in media planning or creativity. It should not be assumed that simply because an agency is part of a wider international grouping it will possess all the skills required.

Where co-ordination is not a requirement, some companies have taken the decision to locate the creative development with one agency – usually referred to as the 'lead' agency – and to appoint several local agencies to handle the implementation. In other instances, they have chosen to appoint the 'best' agency in each market, to ensure access to the necessary skills in all areas.

How will the company cope with co-ordinating the campaign globally?

Deploying company personnel to the co-ordinating task may be one solution to this requirement. An alternative, particularly where a multinational agency is appointed, is to devolve that responsibility to the agency. Usually, a senior member of the agency structure is appointed to the specific role of ensuring consistency, both of creative work and implementation, throughout all markets. It will be his or her role to ensure cohesion between all aspects of the campaign in all markets, although ultimately it will be the client's responsibility to determine whether the role has been fulfilled adequately.

Activity 8.13

What are the benefits of using a local marketing communications agency to launch a new product rather than the branch office of an international network?

This internal agency role is often of considerable importance to other aspects of the smooth running of the campaign. The task involves overcoming the 'not invented here' syndrome, whereby the local brand responsible for the implementation of the activity may feel detached from it, since it was created elsewhere.

Similarly, the international co-ordinator may have the responsibility for allocating funds between branches to ensure that such tasks as market research are carried out adequately. In many cases, although the work is an important aspect of the understanding of the communications task in the market, the branch office may not generate sufficient income to afford their contribution.

Activity 8.14

Coca-Cola was a major sponsor of the 1998 World Cup. To what extent should they, and sponsors of other global events, integrate this activity with the other aspects of their marketing communications programmes?

A final point to consider concerns the degree to which clients seek effective integration of their marketing communications and the necessity to have the best people in each application area, working on their account. Some research suggests that because of their structure, agencies (normally advertising) are unable to provide both integration and expertise. As a result there has to be a trade off between the degree of integration and the availability of expertise. A loose consortium of independent agencies allows for high levels of expertise (and poor integration) while centralized multinational agencies are better able to provide for integration but cannot always provide the very best expert in each promotional area.

Exam tip

Increasingly, marketing communications takes on an international dimension. Many companies operate globally or internationally. Brands are available in a wide diversity of markets. To reflect this growing reality, many of the examination questions take on an international dimension.

It is therefore important that students prepare themselves fully to deal with the international aspects of marketing communications. At times, specific questions will be present in the second part of the examination paper. At other times, the mini-case study will have an international flavour. It may be set in a specific country or the question may ask you to adopt the role of marketing communications manager for a particular product, for a country of your choice.

Summary

In this unit we have seen that:

- Although there is some evidence of a progressive move towards international standardization, the bulk of marketing communications activity is developed either locally or across only a few of the total number of markets in which a company operates. There are many reasons for this situation.
- Certain cultural factors may present barriers to the effective communication of a single message across all markets.
- As individual markets may have developed in different ways, and to varying degrees, the needs of the brand may well be different. The same brand may be well established in some markets, in others, while representing a comparatively new proposition to its prospective consumers. It may be the brand leader in some areas, while only a minor brand in others.
- In addition to the brand strategy being different, therefore, there will also be a need to develop marketing communications strategies which are responsive to the localized requirements.

Further study and examination preparation

See Question 2 of the examination paper for December 2000 in the appendices.

Objectives

In this unit you will:

- Familiarise yourself with the need to set budgets
- Examine the various methods which are used to determine marketing communications budgets.
- Consider aspects of budgetary allocation.

By the end of this unit you will:

- Have examined the major approaches to budgeting and will be in a position to appreciate their respective benefits and drawbacks.
- Be able to apply the principles to practical situations.
- Discuss the strategic significance of budget setting and investment.

This unit covers syllabus sections: 1.3.7 and 1.3.8.

Study guide

There are many important and, at first sight, potentially complicated issues covered in this unit. With careful study, the task will be far less daunting and you will rapidly grasp the principles established.

Take care to study the various elements of the unit and to consider each of the issues carefully. Where possible, carry out the various exercises at different times in order to reinforce your learning of the key aspects of the budgeting process.

Determining the marketing communications budget

Study tip

This unit is much more about application than the simple ability to state information. Often you will be given some of the financial dimensions of a brand scenario and asked to develop a marketing communications budget.

Practice with the tasks provided in this unit will ensure that you are far more able to cope with the requirements of the examination on the day.

This unit is designed to introduce you to issues and techniques associated with the management of marketing communication budgets.

Introduction

A key task within the framework of marketing communications is the appropriate determination of the levels of expenditure required to fulfil the task established. The amount of money spent on marketing communications differs widely among companies, even within the same industry.

The annual brand survey published by *Marketing Magazine* in conjunction with AC Nielsen (the worldwide market research organization) which is the source of the following figures, provides a comprehensive analysis of many consumer goods markets. For example:

In the fabric care market, the largest brand, Persil, spent approximately £23.1 million defending sales of between £240-245 million. This contrasts with Ariel spending £9.6 million against sales of between £185-190 million and Daz spending around £4.2 million against sales of between £75-80 million.

In the breakfast cereals market Kelloggs spent £5.7 supporting their Corn Flakes brand which had sales of between £85-£90 million. In contrast they spent £7.7 million on advertising support for their Special K brand where sales are around £40 million. Shreddies is a brand of similar size in the same market, offered by Nestlé, but advertising support was reported to be just £2.8 million in the same period.

In the confectionery market, the Nestlé brand KitKat received around £9 million of advertising support against sales of approximately £180 million. Its competitor, the Mars Bar, spent slightly less than Kit Kat – £8 million against sales of about £115 million. In the instant coffee market, the brand leader, Nescafé, spent £22.6 million on sales of between £335-340 million while Kenco spent almost exactly half – £11.3 million on sales of between £80-85 million which represent just a quarter of Nestle's turnover.

In the snacks market, Walkers spent £7.6 million defending sales in excess of £460 million while Pringles spent over £4 million on sales of between £135 and £140 million.

The data for these examples was reported by Jane Bainbridge in the 10 August 2000 issue of *Marketing*.

The primary issue is that of identifying the reasons for this wide variation in expenditure patterns, and of determining an effective approach to the setting of a budgetary level. It should be clear that the determination of the correct level of expenditure must depend on a proper analysis of the context, rather than the use of 'norms', rule of thumb, or 'gut-feel'. According to Simon Broadbent, author of *The Advertising Budget,* the amount to spend is determined by a process, not a formula. Hence, there is no simple solution. Various methods of budget determination have been suggested and the issue is one of deciding which approach is right for the situation.

In the course of this unit, we will examine some of the most important approaches that have been suggested and consider their application to the real environment. The following list gives most of the ways used to determine the budget:

- Percentage of previous year's turnover (sales)
- Percentage of product gross margin
- Residue of last year's surplus
- Percentage of anticipated turnover
- Unit or case/sales ratio method
- Competitive expenditure/parity
- Share of voice
- Media inflation
- Objective-and-task method
- Experimentation
- What we can afford
- New products.

Marginal analysis

Several attempts have been made to transfer the learning from the principles of economic theory to that of budget determination. In essence, the principles of marginal analysis suggest that a company should continue to increase its marketing communications expenditure until the point where the increase in expenditure matches, but does not exceed, the increase in income which those expenditures generate. This can be shown graphically, as illustrated in Figure 9.1.

Unfortunately, the application of the theory of marginal analysis does not transfer readily into the real-world situation. The first problem to deal with is the fact that the theory assumes sales are a direct function of marketing communications expenditures. While it is possible to postulate situations in which this might be the case – for example, in the area of direct marketing – this may be somewhat wide of the mark.

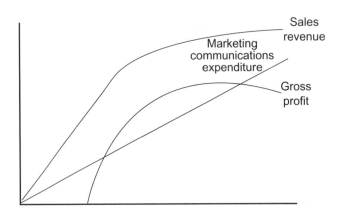

Figure 9.1
Marginal Analysis

The level of expenditure is only one of the variables which needs to be considered. The theory makes no attempt to consider, for example, the location of the activity in terms, say, of media placement, or of the copy content of the advertisement or sales promotion tool. It simply assumes that every pound spent is likely to achieve the same impact on the market. Clearly, other marketing activities will have an impact on the level of achievement which will render the formula almost incalculable. Importantly, most marketing communications activities rely on a built-in time lag. Even in the area of direct marketing, where a more precise correlation can be established between patterns of expenditure and achievement, it will be necessary to make an allowance for other indirect variables.

The nature of the message, its placement, the competitive environment and other factors will all have to be allowed for if the theory is to stand up in practice. Certainly, until the advent of rapid response computer programmes, the amount of detail which would need to be built into such a calculation proved unwieldy at best. Several attempts have been made to build econometric models against which to 'test' different levels of expenditure. Suffice it to say that, at best, they only provide some *guidance* as to the likely impact of the proposals in the real world.

Percentage of sales

Probably the most widely used method of budget determination is the calculation of a ratio between past expenditure and sales. The calculation itself is quite straightforward. The previous year's expenditures are calculated as a percentage of total sales, and the resultant figure is used to calculate the budget for the coming year. Thus, if £12 million worth of sales was achieved against a communications budget of £300,000, the percentage would be 2.5%. Assuming that the sales forecast for the coming year was £15 million, this would yield a budget of £375,000.

While the process is a quick and easy one, there are flaws in the argument. In the first place, the data used will be considerably out of date by the time that it is implemented. As we do not have a full picture of the current year's sales, we must rely on, at best, the latest 12 months for which we have information on which to base our calculations for next year's activity. Second, the model creates a situation in which the budget only increases against an expectation of higher sales. If sales are expected to decline, then the future communications budget must be reduced to bring it into line with the defined ratio. The inherent danger is that a brand that is under threat – and losing volume – actually has a reduced budget rather than an increased one. Thirdly, the model fails to recognize that marketing communications activity can create sales volume for a brand. The application of the principle in fact operates in reverse – with sales being the determinant of expenditure levels.

Percentage of product gross margin

This approach is, essentially, similar to the previous one, except that the gross margin rather than the level of sales is used as the basis for calculating the future level of expenditure. Here, a percentage of either the past or expected gross margin – net sales less the cost of goods – is used.

Activity 9.1

Given that your objective is to increase your share of the £550 million pet food market from 10 per cent to 15 per cent, and the leading brands spend approximately £7-9 million on advertising, discuss what marketing communications budget you would recommend, and how would you support your argument.

Residue of previous year's surplus

This method is entirely based on prior performance, whereby the excess of income over costs in the previous year is designated as the budget for the following year. Although simple in principle, it clearly demands that a surplus is achieved in order for monies to be spent in any future period. It fails to recognize the need for investment in growth brands or, for that matter, the impact of competitive activities.

Percentage of anticipated turnover

This approach is based on the allocation of a fixed percentage of future turnover to the marketing communications budget.

Unit or case/sales ratio method

This method, sometimes referred to as the case rate, requires that brand volumes for the next year are estimated and a fixed sum per unit is allocated towards marketing communications expenditure. It is then a simple process of multiplying the expected sales volume (in units or cases) by the fixed allocation to arrive at a total communications budget.

Activity 9.2

After several years of growth, your market has begun to decline at a rate of approximately 5 per cent per annum. Although your share has held up, the volume has begun to decline.

What recommendations would you make, as brand leader, for the setting of next year's marketing communications budget?

In some instances comparisons are made between the company's own case rate and those of its competitors in order to explore the relationships between them. Obviously the approach is a simple one, but it begs the question as to how the case rate itself is calculated. In some instances it may be based on past experience. Usually it is a company or industry norm.

Here again, as with other ratio-based approaches, expenditure patterns reflect past achievement or anticipated sales. As such, the method tends to benefit growth brands and disadvantage those which are declining. It ignores the fact that a brand which is suffering in the marketplace may need increased levels of expenditure in order to arrest the decline, rather than a reduced budget which would be the automatic result of applying the method.

Competitive expenditure

Another frequently used approach is to base a brand's expenditure levels on an assessment of competitors' expenditures. Often a calculation is made of the level of category expenditure and a percentage – usually related to a brand's share of market – is chosen as the basis of calculating the expenditure levels for the brand. In other instances, an attempt is made to achieve parity with a nominated competitor by setting a similar level of expenditure to theirs.

At the very least, this approach has the benefit of ensuring that brand expenditure levels are maintained in line with those of the competition. However, it suffers from the obvious difficulty of being able to make an accurate assessment of the level of competitors' spends. While it is obviously possible to obtain a reasonable fix on advertising spend from published information (from *Register MEAL*), the same is not true of sales promotional spend and other categories of marketing communications. Figures for the latter are rarely published. Moreover, the model fails to recognize that the expenditure patterns of a competitor may well be dictated by a totally different set of problems and objectives.

Activity 9.3

You are attempting to introduce a new product to the £670 million hot beverage market and are targeting a share of 5 per cent in year 1. Describe what factors you would consider to help you determine the budget for marketing communications?

Share of voice

This approach is an extension of the previous one, where management relates the volume share of the product category to expenditure within the category as a whole, and is primarily related to advertising expenditure. Thus, if a brand has a 15 per cent share of the market in which it competes, and total advertising expenditure for the category is £8 million, in order to retain a proportional share of voice a budget of £1.2 million would need to be set. By the same token, the company would have a benchmark against which to establish the levels of expenditure required to drive a brand forward. Hence, it might decide to increase its share of voice to, say, 20 or even 25 per cent in an attempt to gain a greater level of visibility for its brand and a greater share of the overall category. Conversely it may decide to underspend relative to its competitors and market share. This may due to profit taking motives or sheer economies of scale that large brands in particular, are able to generate through their overall communication effort.

These issues of relative spend are very important as they indicate not only competitive but also strategic communication intention.

Activity 9.4

Set out your arguments in favour of adopting a share-of-voice approach to budget determination.

Media inflation

This approach makes the simple assumption that a budget – usually the previous year's – should be increased in line with the growth in media costs to ensure a similar delivery of the message to the target audience. At the lowest level, this approach ensures that the real level of advertising expenditure is maintained. However, it fails to acknowledge any of the other variables which will have an impact on the achievement of marketing objectives.

Objective-and-task method

This method is based on a more realistic examination of the specific objectives which the marketing plan needs to meet, and was established as an attempt to apply a more scientific approach to budget determination. The basis of the approach was a paper commissioned by the American Association of National Advertisers and published in 1961. In the paper 'Defining advertising goals for measuring advertising results' (DAGMAR) the author, Russell Coley, proposed that advertising should be specifically budgeted to accomplish defined goals or objectives.

The DAGMAR approach – also known as the objective-and-task method – requires that specific objectives for the campaign are defined at the outset. These may be expressed in terms of, for example, increasing brand awareness, encouraging sampling and trial, promoting repeat purchase and so on. In each case a finite numerical target is given, and the costs of achieving this target are calculated. The resultant budget is thus based on a series of goals rather than on past or future results, and is thus the most realistic in marketing terms.

The method offers the benefit of being able to monitor the campaign achievement against the targets set, and provides a more accurate guide to budgetary determination for the future. The limitation on the accuracy of the method is the ability to access sufficient information to ensure that all relevant variables can be considered.

Although the original paper dealt specifically with the task of establishing advertising budgets, the method is equally applicable to other areas of marketing communications.

Activity 9.5

Why is the objective-and-task method of budget determination increasingly preferred over other approaches?

Experimentation

A guiding principle for budget determination, as with other aspects of marketing, is the need to, on the one hand, protect the company investment, while, on the other, ensuring that sufficient new and innovatory approaches are taken to drive the brand forward. It is for this reason that most major marketing companies use an experimental approach at various times.

Having established the overall marketing communications budget by the normal or most appropriate means, it is possible to create a 'mini-test market' for the purposes of experimenting with a variation. By isolating, say, one region of the country, it is possible to experiment with alternative budget constructions. In many cases, and in the absence of definitive data, it is useful to determine the impact of, for example, an increased level of media expenditure or of a particular sales promotion technique.

The benefit of this approach is that the main sources of business are 'protected', in the sense that they receive the 'normal' support levels. Hence, the position of the brand is not unduly prejudiced. By 'hot housing' a different approach, real experience can be gained and the budgetary process enhanced with the additional knowledge.

The method thus represents an attempt to apply an empirical approach and, therefore, a more scientific method to the process of budget determination. However, it is important to restrict the number of 'experiments' in order to ensure that the data are readable against the norm, and that the individual variables can be properly assessed within a real market environment.

Activity 9.6

Write a short note to your managing director justifying the adoption of a more scientific approach towards budgeting as opposed to its arbitrary determination.

What we can afford

This approach is based on a management assessment of either the brand itself or the overall company position. In effect, management determines the level of profit desired, or the return on investment, and the marketing communications budget is the amount that remains after calculating that level. Of course, the approach fails to recognize the contribution of marketing communications itself, and ignores other environmental factors, such as competitive pressure, which might mitigate against the profit level being achieved.

Although this is a somewhat arbitrary approach to the budgetary process, it should be recognized that the issue of affordability plays an important part in any financial procedure. There will always be competing demands for funds within a company – to support the activities of other brands within the portfolio, to fund areas such as production capability, to finance research and development, and so on. It is a fundamental role of management to determine company priorities and to allocate funds accordingly.

Budgets for new products

One area that demands a separate mention is that of developing a marketing-communications budget for a new product. Clearly, past data will be unavailable and hence many of the usual budgeting approaches cannot be applied.

At the simplest level, the approach to new products is similar to the objective-and-task method described above. Calculations must be made of the amount of money required to achieve the objectives established for the brand.

It must be recognized that, in most instances, new products require investment in advance of sales performance. Indeed, without the appropriate levels of investment in marketing communications, most new products are unlikely to succeed. A realistic time frame for achieving the goals set must be established at the outset. It is unrealistic to expect a new product to make a major contribution in the short term.

It is important to restate that there is no hard and fast formula for defining a marketing communications budget. It is important to experiment with a number of the methods described above, and to ensure that appropriate use is made of previous company experience, industry data and experimentation. The imperative for all companies is to ensure that a database of information (both within-company information and information on competitors) is built up, which can be used to enhance the process.

The process of budget determination

Whichever method, or methods, of budget determination is adopted, however, the task must be to consider the process of budget determination itself. Broadbent suggests that the process is made up of six separate stages as dipicted in Figure 9.2.

Figure 9.2
Stages of budget generation

Stage 1 – brand objectives

Here we must consider the role of the brand within the company and the importance of the brand to the achievement of the overall objectives. The consideration should encompass both the short-term time frame of the plan, e.g. the year ahead, as well as longer term considerations, e.g. over the next 3-5 years. It is also important to examine the relationship between volume and profit contribution. At this stage also the source of the brand's sales should be identified. The larger the audience, the greater the likely budget requirement. By the same token, by adopting a more concentrated approach, the media budget may be lowered.

Activity 9.9

Why are long-term brand objectives important in budgetary determination?

Stage 2 – review the brand budgets

It is important to consider how the brand has performed in the past, as this will have significant implications on its ability to perform in the future. If a brand has been in decline, then the previous budget will need to be increased if the decline is to be arrested or reversed.

Stage 3 – marketing history and forecasts

As well as a consideration of the brand itself, it is important to consider the market category which will help place the brand in context. This will reveal a number of important factors which will assist in the brand planning process. Although volume sales may be increasing, it is important to determine whether they are keeping pace with the category as a whole. In fact, the brand may be losing share of market which, in the longer term, could endanger its position.

Stage 4 – assess expenditure effects

It is important to examine the effects of previous advertising and promotional expenditure in order to determine the level of brand responsiveness to marketing communications activity. Previous experience is a valuable guide to likely future performance. And remember that, in this respect, it is possible to learn as much from competitor performance as from that of your own brand.

Stage 5 – set budgets

When setting budgets consider the application of a number of the standard approaches to budget determination (these are set out in detail above). This is very much a preliminary exercise in budget determination, as it will suggest a range of possible amounts to be spent, with affordability and feasibility being checked in the final stage.

Stage 6 – check feasibility

The final stage of this proposed process is to ensure that the budget determined is feasible and practical within the context of the established objectives.

Allocating the promotional budget

Having established how the overall budget is to be calculated, the allocation of funds within the budget must be addressed. Again, the emphasis must rest with integrated marketing communications and the identification of the most appropriate and cost-effective communications channels for achieving the specific task. That having been said, however, it must be recognized that there are no set formulae for allocating budgets between competing communications approaches.

In many instances, the appropriate channels will be easily identified by carefully examining the objectives and the techniques which can best meet them. Since all marketing communications tools have identified roles in the communications process, it will be apparent that a careful consideration of the needs will, similarly, identify the areas likely to be most appropriate. If the task is defined as generating high levels of awareness among a wide target audience, then it is probable that advertising will absorb a substantial proportion of the communications budget. If the task is to generate trial and sampling, the budget will need to be apportioned primarily between sales promotion and advertising. If the need is to promote the corporate identity, the budget is likely to be spent on corporate advertising and public relations. If the task is to reach a narrowly defined and readily identified group of consumers, direct marketing techniques will come to the fore. The imperative in all cases is the need for integrated marketing communications.

We have seen, from the beginning of this Coursebook, that the consumer does not discriminate as to the source of the message. Our fundamental objective is to deliver the brand proposition in the most cost-effective manner to the defined target audience. As such, we need to identify and integrate those marketing communications techniques that best achieve this goal.

The budget contingency

It may be an axiom, but it remains true that if anything that can go wrong, it will! It is, therefore, both sound practice and prudent to identify a sum of money (usually expressed as a proportion of the overall budget) to be used to remedy deficiencies in the performance of the marketing communications plan. Inevitably, much of the planning process takes place in advance of the implementation of the details of the plan.

Activity 9.13

During the recent economic recession, many major manufacturers cut back on the expenditure on marketing communications. How would you suggest that adopting the opposite approach, i.e. increasing spend, might have benefited a company?

It is important to understand the budgetary implications of marketing communications. On the one hand, candidates will often be required to identify the approach they would adopt towards budget determination within the case study contained in the first part of the exam paper. Indeed, the ability to demonstrate how and why a particular level of expenditure should be allocated will mark out a better candidate. In many of the recent papers, the Senior Examiner has asked students to identify the key communications issues facing the company set out in the mini-case. Invariably the communication budget is going to be a central point and students need to be able to understand the significance and relationship between communication investment and the need for profit, efficiency and competitiveness. Very often aspects of Share of Voice are important as well as competitive parity. In some papers, where total budgets are indicated, candidates are expected to indicate the allocation to the proposed areas of marketing communications and justify their recommendations.

Summary

In this unit we have seen that:

- The determination of the marketing communications budget is of strategic importance.
- The sums spent on advertising to support fmcg brands is counted in millions so any saving that might be made can be diverted into other forms of marketing communications or taken as profit.

- There are a variety of methods available to work out the budget. These vary in complexity and value. Most organizations use a number of different methods with objective and task and share of voice approaches of particular significance and utility.
- The marketing communications budget is normally determined without account taken of sales force costs (where present). If integrated marketing communications is to be achieved then it is important to account for the range of communication tools and associated media. Increasingly, the use of the Internet to support brands is regarded as an important part of the communication programme and these costs need to be accommodated.

Further study and examination preparation

Try this question from the June 1999 paper following the guidelines below.

Question 9.1

You are a newly appointed Marketing Manager for a company that makes hair care products which are sold through supermarkets and major national distributors. You have identified the need to review the process by which the marketing communications budgets are determined each year.

Prepare an internal paper for the Marketing and Sales departments reviewing the available methods and outline your proposals by which these budgets should be set in the future.

See the question guidelines in Appendix 5.

Objectives

In this unit we will:

- Consider the requirements of the business-to-business sector and the objectives of marketing communications in this area.
- Examine the dimensions of services marketing and the differences with the communications of products.
- Be introduced to low-budget campaigns.

By the end of this unit you will be able to:

- Explain the principles of marketing communications in the business-to-business sector
- Argue why services based marketing communications needs to be different to that for product-based communications.
- Answer examination questions that ask specifically about either the b2b, services or low-cost campaigns.

This unit covers syllabus section 1.4.1.

Study guide

This unit contains a number of important topics for you to study. They will enable you to fill in any gaps which remain in your understanding of the principles relating to marketing communications, and the strategic issues which remain.

Business-to-business marketing communications are a very important part of the syllabus and you may be asked questions that are specific to this topic.

Do not assume that because the topics are shorter they are any less important than those which we have covered previously.

The development of marketing communications activity

Study tip

Now is the time to start thinking about the examination itself. Make sure that your notes are all in order and that you have everything to hand so that you can begin the process of revision. If you find any gaps (missing examples, articles which you would like to re-read) make sure that you get everything in place in readiness for the last stage in the process.

Revision will ensure that by the time of the examination you will have the knowledge to pass. Be sure to take note of the guidelines for answering the questions. They may make the difference.

Much of the material contained in this Coursebook deals specifically with the area of consumer goods and services, although there are equally a number of specific examples taken from the important areas of business-to-business and non-profit marketing.

In many respects, the initiatives which are now broadly applied to all marketing communications had their origins in the highly competitive nature of fast-moving consumer goods. This reflected the need to develop progressively better techniques for communicating with the identified target groups. However, it must be recognized that some of the marketing communications techniques, used frequently in fast-moving consumer goods may not be available to other areas, either for strategic reasons, budgetary reasons or both. Candidates for the CIM Diploma will need to be able to apply their thinking to all aspects of marketing communications, not just the area of fast moving consumer goods.

The sections which follow immediately deal with specific issues relating to other areas of marketing communications.

Business-to-business communications

Business-to-business (b2b) communications is the promotion of goods and services to businesses rather than individuals.

Traditionally referred to as 'industrial marketing communications', this term fails to recognize the diversity of the products and buyers involved within this area. It is now more usual to refer to this as b2b marketing communications. The importance of the sector is underpinned by the extraordinary development of Internet-based marketing communications in this sector, compared with the relatively sluggish growth in business-to-consumer (b2c) market.

It is also a reflection of the fact that many business-to-business markets are larger than most consumer goods markets. There are, of course, a number of similarities and differences between consumer markets and those involved in the business-to-business area, as can be seen from the Table 10.1 (reproduced from T. Yeshin (ed.), *Inside Advertising,* Institute of Advertising Practitioners, 1993).

Table 10.1: Business-to-business markets	
The differences	Consumer markets
Use company money	Use own money
Small number of buyers	Large number of buyers
Group buying decision	Individual or family decision
Extended buying timescales	Often short timescales
The similarities	
All buying decisions are taken by people	

It is often believed that, whereas consumers often make irrational buying decisions – based on the image dimensions of a brand, businesses base their decisions on a rational consideration of the variables. This, to say the least, is something of an oversimplification. Companies, as such, take no decisions at all. The decision to purchase or not to purchase a particular good or service on behalf of the company is taken by one or more individuals. These, in other circumstances, are the same people who are responsible for buying goods and services on their own behalf or for the benefit of their families. Whatever role they fulfil, they are influenced by the same demographics, personalities, aspirations, lifestyles and so on. Both consumer purchases and business-to-business purchase decisions are, therefore, influenced by a complicated array of factors, some rational and some irrational.

However, it is important to recognize some key differences between the two types of market. First, in the business context, buyers are using the *company's money* not their own, and this fact may have ramifications for the way in which they consider the purchase.

Not only is it important that they spend the company's money in a way that delivers value for money, it must be perceived as achieving that. For many years, the litany of 'Nobody ever got fired for specifying IBM' dimensionalized this factor. So long as IBM was perceived as the primary source of computing equipment, the purchase decision was unlikely to be challenged, even if it failed to deliver the best value.

A second consideration is, in many instances, the relatively *small number* of potential buyers in business-to-business markets. Often, the target audience for a company's products or services may be numbered in the hundreds, rather than the many millions of potential consumers in the vast majority of retail markets.

The most important difference, however, is that with only a few exceptions business buying decisions are taken by *groups* of people rather than individuals. A key strategic issue may, therefore, relate to the identification of the individuals who comprise the decision-making unit rather than any one person.

Most business decisions are taken as a result of the interaction of a number of different individuals who fulfil different roles within the organization. These may include specifiers (responsible for identifying the specific goods or services), users, purchasers and authorizers. Any or all of these may be able to exert an influence over the ultimate purchase decision. A successful sale can only be achieved following the identification of all members of the decision-making unit, and the key factors which will affect the part they play in the decision-making process.

Another important distinction between business-to-business and consumer goods marketing is that the product itself may be *modified* to suit the needs of the individual user, as indeed can other aspects of the specification. Despite the fact that the product is often more complex than its consumer equivalent, the nature of satisfying the consumer's needs may be dealt with by adaptation to the specific requirements of the customer. Adjustments may be made in the terms of trade, delivery, training of the user's staff, repairs and spare parts to ensure that the offer matches the individual needs of the customer.

Moreover, because the typical business-to-business market is comparatively small, *personal contact* is the most widely used method of promotion. Often the scale of the order, the length of the negotiations, and the technical nature of the purchase will demand that the supplier maintains in-depth contact on a regular basis with the potential customer. The role of other forms of marketing communications is often to provide the essential support to the personal selling effort.

Activity 10.4

What are the important strategic issues to be addressed in business-to-business marketing?

In the business-to-business sector, marketing communications can fulfil a variety of specific objectives which will vary according to the circumstances:

- To create awareness
- To generate sales leads
- To pre-sell sales calls
- To contact minor members of the decision-making unit
- To build corporate and product images
- To communicate technical information
- To support the promotional effort.

While personal selling is often the most motivating form of communications, it is also the most expensive technique, and other forms of marketing communications must be used to ensure maximum cost-effectiveness. As with consumer goods marketing, business-to-business communications will depend on the successful identification of the appropriate mix of communications tools to achieve the objectives.

The *planning process* is, essentially, the same as that for other forms of marketing communications, and it is important to identify the key objectives of the activity at the outset. Inevitably, however, given both the nature of the objectives and the scale of the budgets available, the planning considerations may be somewhat different.

Activity 10.5

Prepare an outline marketing communications plan for a company involved in industrial cleaning. You have a marketing communications budget of £75,000.

Integrated marketing communications is no less important here than in other areas of business. Indeed, it might be argued that the relative sizes of budgets require an even more careful consideration of the dimensions of integration to ensure that every element of the marketing communications campaign reinforces the others.

In his book on *Integrated Marketing Communications* (Butterworth-Heinemann, 1995), Ian Linton cites the example of ICL, a major player in the computer industry. At the time of the launch of their customer services division, ICL sought to ensure that every element of their external and internal material presented the same series of core messages. Product literature, direct marketing activity, exhibitions, videos, and internal materials reinforced the proposition that customer services were strategically important, and underpinned the statement that customer services contribute to corporate efficiency. Over a three-year campaign period, these messages were reinforced and, where appropriate, altered to reflect the changing perceptions of the organization.

Although direct marketing techniques are increasingly being applied to consumer goods and services, they are especially relevant to the business-to-business area. Indeed, to a far greater degree, business-to-business marketing relies on the underlying mechanics of direct marketing as a key platform for marketing communications. There are a number of reasons which serve to explain this situation.

Identification of contacts

In many instances, the sales universe for business products is comparatively small. Often, we are talking about thousands of potential customers (or even hundreds) against multiple millions for most consumer goods. It is thus relatively easy to identify – by name and title, in many cases – the individual targets for a business-to-business proposition.

Sales-force size

Few business-to-business organizations maintain large sales forces. In some cases, the number of representatives is in low single figures. Accordingly, some mechanism is required to maximize their effective strike rate. Maintaining conventional contact with potential purchasers would otherwise be extremely hit and miss, or over a very extended time frame.

The need to create/reinforce awareness

The interval between purchases may be extremely long and relationships with alternative suppliers may be quite strong. In this context, organizations need to ensure cost-effective contact with potential purchasers over an extended time period in order to maintain an awareness of their company and its products at a reasonable level.

The decision-making unit

In many company purchasing decisions, it is unusual that a single person will have the necessary authority to arrange the purchase. Often there will be several people, fulfilling different functions within the organization, who will all contribute to the decision-making unit. Each of them will need to be exposed to the product or service proposition, and it is quite likely that they will require different aspects of the offering to be detailed. Some, for example, will be interested in the performance of the product itself; others in the financial aspects of the proposition; yet others in the technical aspects of integration with existing machinery or materials; and so on.

For many organizations, direct marketing represents the most cost-effective solution to their marketing communications requirements. In this context, direct marketing can ensure:

- Cost-effective lead generation by maintaining regular contact with potential purchasers and prospects
- Corporate and product awareness, by targeting specific messages which are 'tailored' to the needs of named individuals or job functions
- A more effective sales visit, by ensuring that prospects have pre-awareness of the proposition – and may be motivated to request a sales call.

Managing and maintaining a sales force is extremely expensive. Direct marketing and the use of interactive communications enables organizations to focus the sales force on face-to-face opportunities and allow low value accounts and maintenance operations to be managed via these other facilities. Figure 10.1 sets out some ideas about how this might be accomplished.

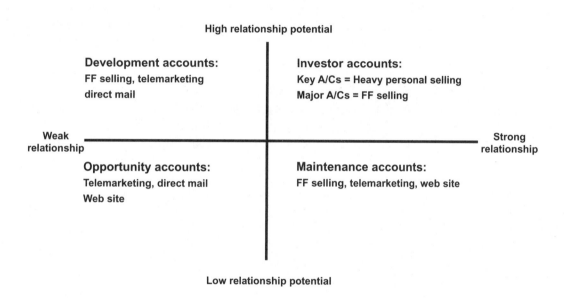

High relationship potential

Development accounts:
FF selling, telemarketing
direct mail

Investor accounts:
Key A/Cs = Heavy personal selling
Major A/Cs = FF selling

Weak relationship — Strong relationship

Opportunity accounts:
Telemarketing, direct mail
Web site

Maintenance accounts:
FF selling, telemarketing, web site

Low relationship potential

Figure 10.1
Use of direct marketing to supplement field sales force selling (Fill, 2002, used with kind permission)
FF = Field Force

Key Account Management

One prime area for personal selling is key account management. Some customers are strategically significant not just because of size of turnover or level of activity but also as a function of their market position, the technology they use, or are developing, or their access to technology or markets.

Whatever the reason, these key accounts (house accounts, major accounts) require marketing communications with a strong bias towards personal selling and a high orientation towards developing relationships. Marketing communications play an important role in nurturing and developing these relationships. Table 10.1 sets out some of the stages key account relationships pass through.

Table 10.2: Main stages in the development of key accounts	
Relationship stage	Main characteristics
Search	The identification of potential key accounts
Agreement & Understanding	A period when both parties learn about each other's needs and agree contractual offerings
Development and maintenance	The relationship develops, becomes established and settled
Commitment	The relationship assumes the status of a partnership and parties share sensitive information and try to resolve problems jointly.
Dissolution	When both parties perceive no further value in the relationship the relationship begins to dissolve. This might be because goals have been achieved, technology moves on or the status of one of the parties changes (takeover, merger) or the channel network alters.

Marketing communications in the b2b sector have been transformed by technological advances and the Internet in particular. Through the use of extranets and intranets organizations are able to work together more closely, build relationships and free other resources for more effective work.

Services campaigns

The promotion of services, which has been referred to throughout this Coursebook, is similar to that of goods, although the application of the principles may differ to take account of the intangible nature of the service offering. As a result, the *objectives* of promotional activity are substantially the same. They may be expressed as:

- The building of awareness of the service or the company that provides it
- Communicating the benefits of the service
- Persuading the consumer to sample the service
- To induce re-purchase of the service
- Differentiating the service from that of competitors
- Building an image and reputation for the service company. etc.

Activity 10.7

Find an example of a service-based campaign and evaluate its success and main characteristics.

However, it is equally important to recognize that there are also fundamental differences in terms of services marketing that must be considered when developing marketing communications programmes. In the first place, unlike consumer goods, many *service provisions* differ in both form and quality to the end consumer. Ultimately, the delivery of the service is dependent on the performance of some intermediary. Even though efforts may be taken to ensure that certain standards of consistency are applied, the reality may be that the end result differs widely. An example might be in the field of fast food. The quality of the hamburger purchased from a chain of restaurants will, despite the consistency of the ingredients, be dependent on the performance of the staff who prepare it at the point of purchase.

Personal involvement is often a key dimension of quality perceptions of service provision. Unlike products which take on a constant tangible form, the provider of the service is synonymous with the quality of provision. Often, marketing communications will be used both internally and externally to reinforce this aspect of the service.

Internally, it may be used to motivate staff to deliver to a high standard; externally, it may be used to convince potential purchasers that the service provider understands the needs of the consumer.

Activity 10.8

How should marketing communications activity respond to an inconsistent delivery of a service at the point of purchase?

Second, there may be *sector constraints* which limit the nature of promotion within the category. The medical professions are restricted from actively promoting the services they provide because of codes of practice imposed by their professional bodies.

Third, in many instances, the *scale of service provision* may limit the type of promotional activity. In the determination of the promotional campaign designed to support a service company, the available budgets may restrict the use of all but a limited range of marketing communications tools.

Activity 10.9

How do airlines and other travel operators promote their services?

What techniques do they use to differentiate themselves from their competitors?

Low-budget campaigns

There may be instances where candidates are asked to consider the implications of marketing communications planning in the context of low budgets. Although the access to financial resources will, inevitably, limit the scale of the communications activity, this should not be interpreted as a reason for ignoring the basic precepts of the role of planning. The same rigour as that applied to the planning of large-scale marketing communications plans must be applied to the planning of small budget activity.

Activity 10.10

How does the process of marketing communications planning differ when applied to a small business?

Indeed, it can be argued that the significance of following a series of set procedures assumes greater importance because of the scarcity of the financial resource. Having said that, it must be recognized that some dimensions of planning will not be available to small-scale campaigns.

Market research procedures, for example, may be innately too expensive to be affordable on a small budget. Nonetheless, this is no excuse for a failure to gather as much information as possible to complete the situational analysis. Much relevant material is available from published sources and will be available at limited cost. At the minimum it will ensure that the subsequent campaign is developed against reliable data. Similarly, it will be immediately apparent that specific forms of activity will be precluded from consideration. It is important, however, to ensure that you give appropriate consideration to the relevant methods of communication which are affordable on a low budget.

Activity 10.11

What marketing communications techniques are likely to be used by a charitable organization?

Low budget campaigns need to focus on exact tasks (just like other campaigns) but incorporate a marketing communications mix that makes increased use of public relations, direct marketing and Internet related media. Advertising is normally not cost-effective and an emphasis needs to be placed upon building a word of mouth (WoM) campaign and enhancing the corporate reputation as quickly as possible.

Word-of-mouth communications are loaded with credibility because, as we saw earlier, we are more prepared to believe someone who we perceive to be objective rather than a biased advertisement or media related information.

WoM can be stimulated through astute use of public relations or increasingly through e-mail and viral marketing programmes. Whatever the techniques used low budget programmes need to be versatile and accurate.

Activity 10.12

Find an example of a low budget campaign and prepare notes evaluating its success and main characteristics.

Summary

In this unit we have seen that:

- Marketing communications is an important part of the business-to-business sector. The principle component of the marketing communications mix is normally personal selling with close support from direct marketing. However, Internet related technologies are helping to provide more efficient communication mixes.
- Similar principles apply to the area of services marketing where we are dealing with intangible rather than tangible dimensions of the proposition. Here the role of service delivery plays an important part in the overall execution of the proposition and care must be taken to ensure that those responsible for service delivery reflect the desired image dimensions.

- When developing limited budget campaigns, the same guiding principles must be applied, although you must be careful to ensure that the chosen strategy is capable of being fulfilled within the financial constraints. The integration of communications activity is important to ensure that the desired message is reinforced to the target audience.
- There are a number of ethical factors within the context of marketing communications. Most societies have established effective controls to ensure that the interests of the consumer are adequately protected but, ultimately, it remains the responsibility of producers to ensure that their activities are consistent with the general good. Indeed, the increasing power of consumer groups makes the acceptance of the principles even more important.

Further study and examination preparation

See Question 3 of the examination paper for June 2000 in the appendices.

Preparing for your examination

You are now nearing the final phase of your studies and it is time to start the hard work of exam preparation.

During your period of study you have been used to absorbing massive loads of information, trying to understand and apply aspects of knowledge that are very new to you, while information provided may be more familiar. You may even have undertaken many of the activities that are positioned frequently throughout your text, which have enabled you to apply your learning in practical situations. Whatever the position is of your knowledge and understanding and level of knowledge application, do not allow yourself to fall into the trap of thinking you know enough, you understand enough or even worse, thinking you can wing in on the day.

Never underestimate the pressure of the CIM examination, getting into the examination hall, and wishing it had all been different, that indeed you had revised and prepared for this big moment, where all of a sudden the Senior Examiner becomes an unrelenting question master!

The whole point of preparing this unit for you is to ensure that you never take the examination for granted, and that you do not go into the exam completely unprepared for what you find what might come your way for three hours at a time.

One thing for sure, is that there is no quick fix, no easy route, no waving a magic wand and finding you know it all.

Whether you have studied alone, in a CIM study centre, or through distance learning, you now need to ensure that this final phase of your learning process is tightly managed, highly structured and objective.

As a candidate in the examination, your role will be to convince the Senior Examiner for this subject that you have credibility. You need to demonstrate to the examiner that you can be trusted to undertake a range of challenges in the context of marketing, that you are able to capitalize on opportunities and manage your way through threats.

You should prove to the Senior Examiner, that you able to apply knowledge, make decisions, respond to situations and solve problems. Above all else, you must demonstrate a **strategic** perspective. The list of solutions you will need to provide to prove your credibility could be endless.

Very shortly we are going to look at a range of particular revision and exam preparation techniques, methods, time management issues and encourage you towards developing and implementing your own revision plan, but before that, lets look a little bit a the role of the Senior Examiner.

A bit about the Senior Examiners!

You might be quite shocked to read this, or even find it hard to understand, but while it might appear that the examiners are 'relentless question masters', but they actually want you to be able to answer the questions and pass the exams. In fact they would derive no satisfaction or benefits from failing candidates, quite the contrary, they develop the syllabus and exam papers in order that you can learn and utilize that learning effectively in order to pass your examinations. Many of the examiners have said in the past that it is indeed psychologically more difficult to fail students than pass them.

Many of the hints and tips you find within this unit have been suggested by the Senior Examiners and authors of the Coursebook series, therefore you should consider them carefully and resolve to undertake as many of the elements suggested where possible.

The Chartered Institute of Marketing has a range of processes and systems in place within the Examinations Division to help to ensure that fairness and consistency prevail across the team of examiners, and to ensure that the academic and vocational standards that are set and defined are indeed maintained. In doing this, CIM ensures that those who gain the CIM Certificate, Advanced Certificate and Postgraduate Diploma, are worthy of the qualification and perceived as such in the view of employers, actual and potential.

Part of what you will need to do within the examination is be 'examiner friendly' and you will need to ensure that they get what they ask for, doing this will make life easier for you and for them.

Hints and tips for 'examiner friendly' actions are as follows:

- Show them that you understand the basis of the question, by answering precisely the question asked, and not including just about everything you can remember about the subject area.
- Read their needs – how many points is the question asking you to address?
- Is the question asking you to take on a role? If so, take on the role and answer the question in respect of the role. If you are asked to be a Marketing Manager, then respond in that way. For example, you could be positioned as follows:

  'You are working as a Marketing Assistant at Nike UK' or 'You are a Marketing Manager for an Engineering Company' or 'As Marketing Manager write a report to the Managing Partner'.

  These are actually taken from questions in past papers, so ensure you take on board role-play requirements.

- Deliver the answer in the format requested. If the examiner asks for a memo, then provide a memo, likewise if the examiner asks for a report, then provide a report. If you do not do this, in some instances you will fail to gain the necessary marks required to pass.
- Take a business-like approach to your answers. This enhances your credibility. Badly-ordered work, untidy work, lack of structure, headings and subheadings can be off-putting. This would be unacceptable in work, likewise it would be unacceptable in the eyes of the Senior Examiners and their marking teams.
- Ensure the examiner has something to mark, give them substance, relevance, definitions, illustration and demonstration of your knowledge and understanding of the subject area.
- See the examiner as your potential employer, or ultimate consumer/customer. The whole purpose and culture of marketing is about meeting customers' needs. Try doing this, it works wonders.
- Provide a strong sense of enthusiasm and professionalism in your answers, support them with relevant up-to-date examples and apply them where appropriate.
- Try to differentiate your exam paper, make it stand out in the crowd.

All of these points might seem quite logical to you, but often in the panic of the examination they 'go out of the window', indeed out of our minds, therefore it is beneficial to remind ourselves of the importance of the examiner. They are the 'ultimate customer' – and we all know customers hate to be disappointed.

As we move on some of these points will be revisited, and developed further.

About the examination

In all examinations, with the exception of Marketing in Practice at Certificate Level and Analysis and Decision at Diploma level, the paper is divided into two parts.

- Part A – the Mini-case study = 40 per cent of the marks
- Part B – Option choice questions – choice of three questions from seven = 60 per cent of the marks.

Let's look at the basis of each element.

The mini-case study

This is based on a mini-case or scenario with one question possibly subdivided into between two and four points, but totalling 40 per cent overall.

In essence, you, the candidate, are placed in a problem-solving role through the medium of a short scenario. On occasions, the scenario may consist of an article from a journal in relation to a well-known organization, for example in the past, Interflora, EasyJet, Philips, among others, have been used as the basis of the mini-case. Alternatively they will be based upon a fictional company, which the examiner has prepared in order that the right balance of knowledge; understanding, applications and skills are used.

Look at the examination papers at the end of this book and see the mini-case.

Approaches to the mini-case study

When undertaking the mini-case study there are a number of key areas you should consider.

Structure/content

The mini-case that you will be presented with will vary slightly from paper to paper and of course from one examination to the next. Normally the scenario presented will be between 500–700 words long and sometimes will centre on a particular organization and its problems or may even specifically relate to a particular industry.

The length of the mini-case study means that usually only a brief outline is provided of the situation and the organization and its marketing problems, and you must therefore learn to cope with analysis information and preparing your answer on the basis of very limited amounts of information.

Time management

Your paper is designed in order that you are assessed over a three-hour period. With 40 per cent of the marks being allocated to the mini-case, it means that you should dedicate somewhere around 70-75 minutes of your time to write up the answer, on this mini-case, plus allowing yourself approximately 20 minutes reading and analysis time. This takes you to around 95 minutes, which is almost half of your time in the exam room.

Do not forget that while there is only one question within the mini-case it can have a number of components. You must answer all the components in that question, which is where the balance of times comes in to play.

Knowledge/skills tested

Throughout all the CIM papers, your knowledge, skills and ability to apply those skills will be tested. However, the mini-cases are used particularly to test application, i.e. your ability to take you knowledge and apply it in a structured way to a given scenario. The examiners will be looking at your decision-making ability, your analytical and communication skills and depending on the level, your ability as a manager to solve particular marketing problems.

When the examiner is marking your paper, he/she will be looking to see how you really differentiate yourself, looking at your own individual 'unique selling points' and to see if you can personally apply the knowledge or whether you are only able to repeat the textbook materials.

Format of answers

On many occasions, and within all examinations, you will most likely be given a particular communication method to use. If this is the case please ensure that you adhere to the requirements of the examiner. This is all part of meeting customer needs.

The likely communication tools you will be expected to use are as follows:

- A memorandum
- A memorandum/report
- A report
- Briefing notes
- Presentation
- Press release
- Advertisement
- Plan

Make sure that you familiarize yourself with these particular communication tools and practise using them to ensure that on the day you will be able to respond confidently to the communication requests of the examiner. You may look back at the Customer Communications Text at Certificate level to familiarize yourself with the potential requirements of these methods.

By the same token, while communication methods are important, so is the meeting the specific requirements of the question. **Note the following carefully.**

- **Identify** – select key issues, point out key learning points, establish clearly what the examiner expects you to identify
- **Illustrate** – this means the examiner expects you to provide examples, scenarios, and key concepts that illustrate your learning.
- **Compare and contrast** – look at the range of similarities between the two situations, contexts or even organizations. Then compare them, i.e. ascertain and list how activities, features, etc. agree or disagree. Contrasting means highlighting the differences between the two.
- **Discuss** – questions that have 'discuss' in them offer a tremendous opportunity for you to debate, argue, justify your approach or understanding of the subject area- *caution* it is not an opportunity to waffle.
- **Briefly explain** – This means being succinct, structured and concise in your explanation, within the answer. Make your points clear and transparent and relevant.
- **State** – present in a clear, brief format
- **Interpret** – expound the meaning of, make clear and explicit what it is you see and understand within the data provided
- **Outline** – provide the examiner with the main concepts and features being asked for and avoid minor technical details. A structure will be critical here; or else you could find it difficult to contain your answer.
- **Relate** – show how different aspects of the syllabus connect together.
- **Evaluate** – This means review and reflect upon an area of the syllabus, a particular practice, an article, etc, and consider its overall worth in respect of its use as a tool or a model and its overall effectiveness in the role it plays.

Your approach to mini-cases

There is no one right way to approach and tackle a mini-case study, indeed it will be down to each individual to use their own creative minds and approaches to the tasks which are presented. What you will have to do is use your initiative and discretion about how to best approach the mini-case. However having said this, there are some basic steps you can take.

- Ensure that you read through the case study at least twice before making any judgements, starting to analyse the information provided, or indeed writing the answers.
- On the third occasion read through the mini-case and, using a highlighter, start marking the essential and relevant information critical to the content and context. Then turn your attention to the question again, this time reading slowly and to carefully assess what it is you are expected to do. Note any instructions that the examiner gives you, and then start to plan how you might answer the question. Whatever the question ensure there is a structure: a beginning, structured central part of the answer and finally, always closing with a conclusion.
- Always keep in mind the specifics of the case and the role which you might be performing, and keep these contexts continually in mind.
- Because there is limited materials available, you will sometimes need to make assumptions. Don't be afraid to do this, it will show initiative on your part. Assumptions are an important part of dealing with case studies and it can help you to be quite creative with your answer. However, if you do use assumptions, please explain the basis of them within your answer so that the examiner understands the nature of them, and why you have arrived at your particular outcome. **Always ensure that those assumptions are realistic.**
- Now you are approaching the stage where it is time to answer the question, tackling the problems, making decisions and recommendations on the case scenario set before you. As mentioned previously, these will often be best set out in a report or memo type format, particular if the examiner does not specify a communication method.
- Ensure that your writing is succinct, avoids waffle and responds directly to the questions asked.

Part B

Again, with the exception of the Analysis and Decision case study, each Part B is comprised of six or seven, more traditional questions, each worth 20 per cent. You will be expected to choose three of those questions, to make up the remainder of the 100 per cent of available marks.

Realistically, the same principles apply for these questions, as in the case study. Communication formats, reading through the questions, structure, role-play, context, etc. everything is the same.

Part B will cover a number of broader issues from within the syllabus and will be taken from any element of it, the examiner makes the choice, and no prior direction is given to students or tutors on what that might be.

As regards time management in this area, you should have approximately one and a half hours left, i.e. 90 minutes. If you do have, this means you should give yourself seven minutes to read the question and plan out your answers, with 22 minutes to write and review what you have put within your answer.

Keep practising – use a cooker timer, alarm clock or mobile phone alarm as your timer and work hard at answering questions within the timeframe given.

Specimen examination papers and answers

To help you prepare and understand the nature of the paper, you will find that the last two CIM examination papers and specimen answers are included at the end of this unit. During your study, the author of your book may have on occasions asked you to refer to these papers and answer the questions, providing you with a specimen answer for guidance. Please utilize every opportunity to undertake and meet their requirements.

These are vital tools to your learning. The specimen answers are not always perfect, as they are answers written by students and annotated by the Senior Examiners, but they will give you a good indication of the approaches you could take, and the examiners provide annotation to suggest how these answers might be improved in the future. Please use them. You can also access this type of information through the Virtual Institute on the CIM web site using your student registration number as an access code.

Other sources of information to support your learning through the Virtual Institute are 'Hot Topics'. These give you scope to undertake a range of associated activities related to the syllabus, and study areas, but will also be very useful to you when you are revising.

Key elements of learning

According to one Senior Examiner, there are three elements involve in preparing for your examination.

- Learning
- Memory
- Revision

We are going to look at what the Senior Examiner suggests, by examining each point in turn.

Learning

Quite often, as students, we can find it difficult to learn. We passively read books, look at some of the materials, perhaps revise a little and regurgitate it in the examination. In the main this is rather an unsatisfactory method of learning. It is meaningless, useless and ultimately leaves us mindless of all that we could have learned had we applied ourselves in our studies.

For learning to be truly effective it must be active and applied. You must involve yourself in the learning process by thinking about what you have read, testing it against your experience by reflecting on how you use particular aspects of marketing, and how you could perhaps improve your own performance by implementing particular aspects of your learning into your everyday life. The old adage goes something like 'learning by doing'. If you do this, you will find that passive learning does not have a place in your study life.

Below are some suggestions that have been prepared to assist you with the learning pathway throughout your revision.

- Always make your own notes, in words you understand and ensure that you combine all the sources of information and activities within them.
- Always try to relate your learning back to your own organization
- Make sure you define key terms concisely, wherever possible
- Do not try to memorize your ideas, but work on the basis of understanding and most important, applying them.
- Think about the relevant and topical questions that might be set – use the questions and answers at the back of each of your Coursebooks to identify typical questions that might be asked in the future.
- Attempt all of the questions within each of your Coursebooks since these are vital tests of your active learning and understanding.

Memory

If you are prepared to undertake an active learning programme then your knowledge will very probably be considerably enhanced, as understanding and application of knowledge does tend to stay in your 'long-term' memory. It is likely that passive learning will only stay in your 'short-term' memory.

Do not try to memorize parrot fashion, it is not helpful and even more important, examiners are experienced in identifying various memorizing techniques and therefore, will identify them as such.

Having said this, it is quite useful to memorize various acronyms such as SWOT, PEST, PESTLE, STEEPLE, or indeed various models such as Ansoff, GE Matrix, Shell Directional, etc., as in some of the questions you may be required to use illustrations of these to assist your answer.

Revision

The third and final stage to consider is 'revision', which is what we are now going to concentrate on.

Revision should be an ongoing process rather than a panic measure that you decide to undertake just before the examination. You should be preparing notes throughout your course, with the view to using them as part of your revision process. Therefore ensure that your notes are sufficiently comprehensive that you can reuse them successfully.

For each concept you learn about, you should identify, through your reading and your own personal experience at least two or three examples that you could use; this then gives you some scope to broaden your perspective during the examination. It will of course, help gain you some brownie points with the examiners.

Knowledge is not something you will gain overnight, as we saw earlier, it is not a quick fix; it involves a process of learning that enables you to lay solid foundations upon which to build your long-term understanding and application. This will benefit you significantly in the future, not just in the examination.

In essence you should ensure that you do the following prior to the real intensive revision process commencing.

- Ensure that you keep your study file well organized, updated and full of newspaper and journal cuttings that may assist you formulate examples in your mind for use during the examination.
- Practise defining key terms and acronyms from memory
- Prepare topic outlines and essay answer plans
- Read your concentrated notes the night before the examination.

Revision planning

You are now on a critical path, hopefully not too critical at this time, with somewhere in the region of between four and six weeks to go to the examination. Hopefully the following hints and tips will help you plan out your studies.

- You will, as already explained, need to ensure that you are very organized and therefore before doing anything else, put your files, examples, reading material in good order, so that you are able to work with them in the future and of course, make sense of them.
- Ensure that you have a quiet area within which to work. It is very easy to get distracted when preparing for the examination.
- Give up your social life for a short period of time, as the saying goes 'no pain – no gain'.
- Take out your file along with your syllabus and make a list of key topic areas that you have studied and which you now need to revise. You could use the basis of this book to do that, by taking each unit a step at a time.
- Plan the use of your time carefully. Ideally you should start you revision at least six weeks prior to the exam, so therefore work out how many spare hours you could give to the revision process and then start to allocate time in your diary, and do not double-book with anything else.
- Looking at each of the subject areas in turn, identify which are your strengths and which are your weaknesses. Which areas have you really grasped and understood, and what are the areas that you have really struggled with. Split you page in two and make a list on each side of the page. For example:

Planning and control

Strengths	Weaknesses
Audit – PEST, SWOT, Models	Ratio analysis
Portfolio analysis	Market sensing
	Productivity analysis
	Trend extrapolation
	Forecasting

- However many weeks you have left, break down your list again and divide the points of weaknesses, giving priority in the first instance to your weakest areas and even prioritizing them by giving them a number. This will enable you to master the more difficult areas. Up to 60 per cent of your revision time should be given over to that, as you may find you have to undertake a range of additional reading and also potentially gaining tutor support, if you are studying at a CIM Accredited Study Centre.
- The remaining time should be spent reinforcing your knowledge and understanding of the stronger areas, spending time testing yourself on how much you really know.
- Should you be taking two examinations or more at any one time, then the breakdown of your time and managing of your time will be critical.
- Taking a subject at a time, work through your notes and starts breaking them down in to subsections of learning, and ultimately down into key learning points, items that you can refer to time and time again, that are meaningful and that your mind will absorb. You yourself will know how you best remember key points. Some people try to develop acronyms, or flowcharts or matrices, mind maps, fishbone diagrams, etc. or various connection diagrams that help them recall certain aspects of models. You could also develop processes with that enable you remember approaches to various options.

(But remember what we said earlier about regurgitating stuff, parrot fashion.)

You could use the type of bomb-burst in Figure X.1 as a way of remembering how the key components of STEEPLE break down in your learning process.

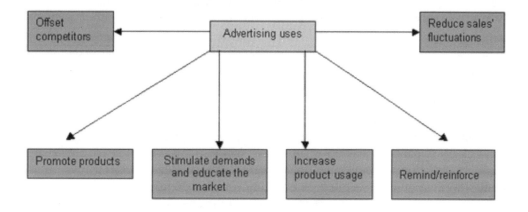

Figure X.1

Figure X. 1 is just a brief example of how you could use a flow chart diagram which, in this case, highlights the uses of advertising. It could be a very helpful approach to memorizing key elements of learning.

- Eventually you should reduce your key learning to bullet points, from which you can revise. For example: imagine you were looking at the key concepts of Time Management - you could eventually break them down into a bullet list which contains the following key points in relation to 'Effective Prioritization:'
    1. Organize
    2. Take time
    3. Delegate
    4. Review

Each of these headings would then remind you that you need to discuss elements associated with the subject area.

- You should avoid getting involved in reading too many textbooks at this stage, as you may start to find that you are getting a little confused overall.
- Now refer to the end of this book and look at some of the exam questions listed, and start to observe closely the various roles and tasks they expect you to undertake, but more importantly the context in which they are set.
- Without exception, find an associated examination question for the areas that you have studied and revised, and undertake it, more than once if necessary.
- Without referring to notes or books, see if you can draft a answer plan with the key concepts, knowledge, models, information, that are needed for you to successfully complete this answer and list them. Then refer to the specimen answer to see how close you are to the actual outline presented. Planning your answer, and ensuring that key components are included, and that the question has a meaningful structure is one of the most beneficial activities that you can undertake.
- Having done this, now write the answer out in full, time constrained and in hand written not with the use of IT. At this stage, you are still expected to be the scribe for the examination and present your hand-written work. Many of use find this increasingly difficult as we spend more and more time using our computers to present information. Spidery handwriting is often offputting to the examiner.

When you are ready to write your answer in full - ensure you do the following.

- **Identify and use the communication method** requested by the examiner
- **Always have three key parts to the paper** - an introduction, middle section where you will develop your answer in full, and finally a conclusion. Where appropriate ensure that you have an introduction, main section, summary/conclusion and if requested or helpful - recommendations.
- **Never forget to answer your question in the context or role set.** If you answer the question void of either of these, then you will fail to gain marks.
- **Always comply with the nature and terms of the question**
- **White Space** do not overcrowd your page - make sure there is white space. There is always plenty of paper available for you to use. Make sure you leave space between paragraphs, and that your sentences do not merge into one blur.
- **Count** how many actions the question is asking you to undertake and double-check at the end that you have met the full range of demands of the question.
- **Use Examples** - to demonstrate your knowledge and understanding of the particular syllabus area. These can be from journals, the Internet, the press, or your own experience - this really helps you add value to your answer.
- **The Senior Examiner is your customer** - or indeed future employer, as we have previously said. Consider carefully what is wanted to satisfy their needs and do your best to deliver. Impress them and show them how you are a 'cut above the rest'. Let them see your vigour and enthusiasm for marketing.

- **Use the specimen exam papers and specimen answers** to support your learning and see how you could actually improve upon them.

Practical actions

The critical path is becoming even more critical now as the exam looms. The following are vital points.

- Have you registered with CIM?
- Do you know where you are taking you examination - CIM should let you know approximately one month in advance.
- Do you know where your examination centre is? If not find out, take a drive, time it - whatever you do don't be late!
- Make sure you have all the tools of the examination with you. A dictionary, calculator, pens, pencils, ruler, etc. Try not to use multiple shades of pens, but at the same time make your work look professional. *Avoid using red and green as these are the colours that will be used for marking.*

Summary

Many of the hints and tips here are very generic and will work across most of the CIM. However we have tried to select those that are most helpful, in order that you take a sensible planned approach to your study and revision.

The key to your success is being prepared to give it the time and effort required, planning your revision, and equally important, planning and answering your questions in a way that will ensure that you pass your examination on the day.

The hints and tips presented are there to guide you from a practical perspective, the syllabus content guidance and developments associated to your learning will become clear to you while you work through this coursebook. Each of the authors have given subject specific guidance on the approach to the examination and how to ensure that you meet the content requirements of the question, in addition to the structuring issues we have been discussing throughout this unit.

Each of the authors and Senior Examiners will guide you on their preferred approach to questions and answers as they go. Therefore where you are presented with an opportunity to be involved in some activity or exam question either during or at the end of your study units, do take it, as it helps you learn in an applied way, but also prepares you for the examination.

Finally as a reminder

- Ensure you make the most of your learning process throughout
- Keep structured and orderly notes from which to revise
- Plan your revision - don't let it just happen
- Provide examples to enhance your answers
- Practise your writing skills in order that you present your work well and your writing is readable
- Take as many opportunities to test you knowledge and measure your progress as possible
- Plan and structure your answers
- Always take on the role and context of the question and answer in that context
- Adhere to the communication method selected by the examiner
- Always do as the question ask you
- **Do not leave it until the last minute!**

The writers and editorial team at Butterworth Heinemann would like to take this opportunity to wish you every continuing success as you endeavour to study, revise and pass your examinations.

Introduction

These specimen answers are indicative of the type of answer that students can use to gauge the style and approach they should adopt in their forthcoming examinations.

These answers are not necessarily the very best. The answers all achieved pass marks, and all show areas in which they could be improved.

Chris Fill

Senior Examiner

The copyright of all The Chartered Institute of Marketing examination material is held by the Institute. No Case Study or Questions may be reproduced without its prior permission which must be obtained in writing.

Exam material

Woodstock Furniture

Woodstock Furniture is a privately owned company located in a fashionable area in London. The company makes bespoke, high quality kitchen and bathroom furniture. Kitchens account for 80% of sales and the average order value is £25,000.

The general kitchen furniture market in the UK is worth over £800 million but of this the bespoke market is only worth a static 1%. Woodstock's sales have fluctuated over its 22 years of trading and currently stand at £1.7 million per annum with net profit at 6.9%. However, the balance sheet is weak and there is little opportunity to attract finance for promotional investment. Staff are very supportive of the company, appear to identify strongly with the customized approach and many have been with the company since its start up. However, many of the internal systems and procedures are old, slow and in need of updating - perhaps a reflection of the slower, detailed craftsmanlike culture that identifies the Woodstock Furniture Company.

In recognition of some of the problems facing the company, the management has developed a marketing plan which seeks growth of 15% per annum to be achieved by market penetration and in particular, the attraction of new customers. It now needs a marketing communication programme to develop a strong corporate brand. The problem is that profit margins are small and there is little to invest in developing the brand and competing with well known high street outlets.

The competition, as Woodstock see it, have huge resources which can be used to invest in promotional campaigns to drive awareness and action. For example, these companies have authentic web sites, unlike Woodstock's site which is little more than an on-line brochure. Many of the large national standardized companies can produce promotional literature in large production runs and are happy to ignore wastage. Using expert photography of 'pretend' kitchens, the quality and impact of the literature is high. Woodstock's smaller budgets dictate that photographs of real customers' kitchens are required, which seldom look perfect and can even appear amateurish. It costs £4 to produce each of the Woodstock brochures so vetting of each request for literature is important to avoid those people who ask for brochures but buy nothing. A high conversion rate is necessary and although 50% of quotations are converted into sales, Woodstock cannot afford this figure to be lowered.

Woodstock's customers do not want the standardized kitchen units provided by the larger, more dominant players in the market. They want kitchens made to measure and which complement the character of their homes. They look for attention to detail, design, craftsmanship and support when commissioning bespoke companies such as Woodstock. The target market is affluent, often has more than one home and relies on word of mouth recommendation when drawing up a shortlist of possible providers. For many, price is not the key issue - rather it is the capability to craft suitable furniture to match the required decor and house style. This requires a high degree of trust, which successful companies in this market are able to reciprocate and in turn generate commitment. Many of Woodstock's customers are celebrities but because discretion and privacy is important to them, they often refuse to allow their names (and kitchens) to be used for Woodstock publicity. However, customer loyalty is extremely important with over 60% of new business being driven from existing customers.

In recognition of this, Woodstock now believes that it is in the business of craftsmanship and the design and construction of customised furniture rather than the business of making and installing kitchen and bathroom furniture. It has improved levels of support and service (having, for example, introduced annual maintenance contracts) and has high levels of customer satisfaction. The marketing plan states that prices are to be raised to capitalise on premium pricing opportunities and the high levels of demand inelasticity. The marketing plan involves forming relationships with architects and developers and creating cross promotions and alliances with firms operating in similar markets, such as conservatories, studies and staircases.

Source: Adapted from an article in the Sunday Times, 15th August 1999.

PART A

Question 1

As a Marketing Adviser you have been asked to help the company achieve its objectives. In particular you are to prepare an Integrated Marketing Communications Plan for Woodstock Furniture covering the next two years. It is important to justify your recommendations and state any assumptions made in order to prepare the plan.

(40 marks)

Answer - Question 1

Report

To: The Marketing Director

From: Marketing Adviser

Date: 13th June, 2000

Re: Marketing Communications Plan for Woodstock Furniture

1. Introduction

Woodstock Furniture is a company with enormous potential for growth. The following plan will show how growth may be achieved in the next two years, in line with corporate objectives of 15% per annum.

2. Contextual Analysis

I have already detailed my analysis in a previous report, examining the business, external, organizational, stakeholder and customer contexts. To summarize, the main points that should be recognized are:

- Business: The market has potential for growth, and bespoke products have little interest for the big furniture manufacturers.
- Customer: Customer trends are that luxury at home is worth more than expensive holidays which offer ephemeral benefits. Customers like the prestige of bespoke products.
- Internal: It is essential that we maintain workforce loyalty and pride in the company; at the same time systems must be updated. It looks as if financial resources are limited and this will restrict the type of campaign we can use.
- Stakeholders: Not a critical element in this situation.
- External: Recycling and environmental concerns are important at all levels.

3. Marketing Objectives

1. Trade relationships and alliances - to establish alliances with five trading partners in 2 years.
2. To gain 15% new customers per year for the next 2 years.
3. To maintain workforce confidence and allegiance during systems changeovers.

4. Marketing Communications Objectives

1. Trade
   o To obtain 40% interest in Woodstock's bespoke products by architects in the local and semi-local area by mid-2002.
   o To have 80% awareness of Woodstock as a source of bespoke furniture in firms operating in similar markets by mid-2002.
2. Customer
   o 100% customer delight after every installation - in place by end of 2001.
   o 80% awareness of Woodstock in the target market of affluent homeowners by mid-2002.
3. Internal
   o To have 100% of employees recommend Woodstock as a good company to work for, producing top-quality items.

5. Marketing Communications Strategies

Our positioning has already been clarified - we want to be perceived as top quality and supportive of both trade partners and customers. 'Woodstock is expensive, but it is the best' is our positioning statement.

To reach the three main audiences, a mixture of 'pull', 'push' and 'profile' strategies will be used. Because the budget is extremely limited, and we have very strong word of mouth new business, I recommend that we concentrate in Year 1 of this plan on a 'push' strategy, to drive trade alliances and cross-promotions. We should also be completely consistent in all communications from the company, in order to drive branding, which will be the main thrust of promotions in Year 2.

Branding will strengthen our communications and secure our place against cost-cutting competitors. By having everything we do (vehicles, staff uniforms, letterheads, invoices, literature, and promotional activity) carry the same message of quality, we will consistently be placed in the minds of consumers and partners, and all promotional activity will be more efficient, effective and give more value for money.

6. Tactics

The Internet is an inexpensive way of reaching many targets, both trade and consumer. Upgrading the site will enable us to suggest that prospective customers visit the web site instead of ordering expensive brochures. We must also use the web site to communicate with trade partners - for example offering information about different types of wood, about our recycling and environmental policies (which will also concern customers). Our target customers are likely to be computer literate, and will expect a good site. Making the web site a communications channel (answering questions, arranging site visits) will also make us more customer friendly, and extend office hours without incurring too many staff overheads.

PR will also be very important - the public's awareness of environmental concerns is high, and favourable publicity will be important. I recommend retaining a small PR agency for the next 2 years at least.

Advertising is expensive and should be carefully assessed. I recommend drip campaigns in selected trade and consumer magazines.

Personal selling is very important, and training is essential for all our salespeople.

Direct marketing will enable us to target potential trade partners, and build a database of the best prospects, whom we can mail regularly with suggestions and product ideas. We can use limited direct marketing - telesales is recommended - to target prospective customers, but this must be done with care. Direct mail to customers is not recommended - we do not want to be associated with 'junk mail' in any way.

	2000 Q3	2000 Q4	2001 Q1	2001 Q2	2001 Q3	2001 Q4	2002 Q1	2002 Q2
TRADE								
Advertising (Drip for awareness)	x		x		x		x	
Personal Selling (to build relationships)	x	x	x	x	x	x	x	x
Web Site	x	x	x	x	x	x	x	x
Direct Marketing (to keep partners informed)	x		x		x		x	
CONSUMER								
Advertising (Glossy magazines and possibly broadsheets)		x		x			x	
Personal Selling	x	x	x	x	x	x	x	x
Internet	x	x	x	x	x	x	x	x
PR	x	x		x		x		x
Direct Marketing (To support sales and for research and product development)		x		x			x	
Research	x		x		x		x	

7. Budget

STRATEGY	2000	2001	2002
£s	£42,000	£10,000	£6,000
Push	60%	50%	40%
Pull	27%	40%	50%
Profile	10%	5%	5%
Contingency	3%	5%	5%

8. Control and Evaluation
Quantitative

- Sales.
- (Return on investment).

- Leads generated.

Qualitative

- Awareness by consumers and trade partners.
- Workforce confidence in the company.

9. Conclusion

I believe that the plan set out above will enable us to meet our marketing communications objectives, which in turn will, with other marketing strategies (product, price, distribution, people) allow us to meet the corporate objectives of 15% growth.

Senior Examiner's Comments

It is always sensible to start with a general introduction. Sometimes an Executive Summary is included, obviously written after the plan has been completed.

The introduction is a little too brief and suggests that the plan alone will achieve the required growth. The objective of this plan is to develop Woodstock's corporate brand and this should have been mentioned at this point as it is the purpose of the whole exercise.

That approach to the context analysis is not fully recommended as it fails on two levels. The first is that it is too brief and provides little insight. The second is that the content does not analyze the communications issues.

This student should have examined each of the contexts with a view to establishing how they impact on the communications. For example, the Customer context needs to consider levels of risk, privacy, involvement and the implications each has for the communications strategy. How is the brand currently perceived and how should it be perceived?

The Business context must refer to the new mission and strategic orientation of Woodstock. The repositioning intention, clearly flagged in the case, is the main focus or the raison d'être for the plan.

Whilst the Stakeholder context is limited, reference could have been made to the need to develop relationships with architects and the media.

Overall, it is NOT the way to write a context analysis as it does not provide any significant inputs to the marketing communications plan.

The objectives are quite good. They clearly set out the various elements (customers, trade and internal) and have been written in SMART format.

To be complete, they objectives should have referred to Corporate Objectives and the repositioning to a craftsman orientation.

There is a good attempt at the strategic aspects. It reveals that the student is aware of the different audiences and their different communication needs. The positioning aspect is well signalled as is the branding aspect.

I also like the reference to the timing and the way in which the strategy is to be implemented. Too many students failed to recognize the importance of the Specifiers as part of the strategy. A little more reference to the needs of the customer segment and a reasoning for the word of mouth campaign would be necessary in real life.

The use of a Gantt chart to depict the scheduling of the promotional tools is well established. This chart shows the differences between the needs of the trade and the consumers, which is important.

I like the short note that provides the justification but the chart tends to show that all the tools are to be used all the time (generally).

The budget is realistic and if anything is a little under what could be allocated to marketing communications, especially over a 2 year period. That answer could have been improved had it stated how this financial resource was determined, and which methods were used to deduce it.

The evaluation aspect is good in that it highlights both the qualitative and quantitative aspects. However, it is too short, fails to relate directly to the objectives and makes no reference to the overall goal of developing the corporate brand.

PART B

Answer THREE Questions Only

Question 2

Many marketing communication campaigns make use of opinion leaders and opinion formers. Using examples to illustrate your points, explain how and why these personal influencers might be used.

(20 marks)

Guideline answer

Introduction

Outline of what constitutes the wider external environment and the structure of the answer.

Political

Explanation and example of impact on marketing communications.

Economic

Explanation and example of impact on marketing communications.

Social

Explanation and example of impact on marketing communications.

Technological

Explanation and example of impact on marketing communications.

Competitive

Explanation and example of impact on marketing communications.

Evaluation

Comment about how useful is it appraising the external environment, possibly ranking competitive elements higher than the PEST factors in terms of significance.

Conclusion

General short conclusion making a final few comments.

Answer - Question 2

Introduction

Opinion leaders and opinion formers are the names given to a type of characteristic portrayed by the different personalities of consumers and customers. Opinion leaders are the 'Innovators' and 'Early Adopters' as described when using a model to illustrate the adoption process when comparing these models to the product life cycle:

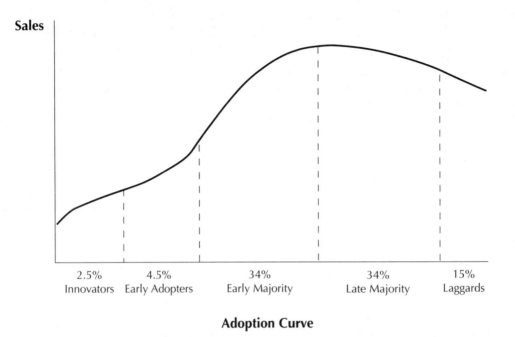

Sales

2.5%
Innovators

4.5%
Early Adopters

34%
Early Majority

34%
Late Majority

15%
Laggards

Adoption Curve

Figure 1
Process of Adoption

These early adopters and innovators play a crucial part in either the success or failure of a new product launch. After they have trialled or used the product, they will make recommendations and can influence other buyers towards believing that the product is good and lives up to its expectations - or not, as the case may be. This process of recommendation or negative opinion can play a vital part in whether the rest of the market buys the product. It is therefore crucial that these 'personal influencers' are happy with the product and thus initiate public demand and allow the product to be pulled through its life cycle.

How Marketing Communication Campaigns can make Use of Personal Influencers

Product acceptance from these opinion/personal influencers is vital and the marketing communications campaign must be utilized to maximize the opportunity to ensure acceptance is achieved.

Selecting the correct promotional tools at this launch stage of the product, such as exhibitions, trade fairs and press releases in trade journals and the quality press, will ensure a positive stance from these opinion/personal influencers.

Using the DRIP model (Differentiate, Remind/Reassure, Inform, Persuade) to plan communication techniques, and being aware of the adoption process, e.g. AIDA model, the campaign can be tailored at each stage of the product's life cycle.

The effects the opinion leaders (OL) and formers (OF) can have on the rest of the market is as follows:

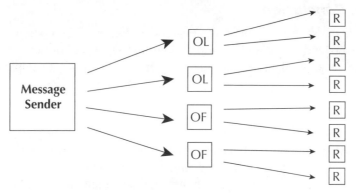

Two-Step Communication Flow

Figure 2

Effects of OL and OF

i.e. the opinion leader will inform many of the audience. The opinion leader is someone the public will listen to as a reference point. *[Senior Examiner's Comment: Not well defined]*. The opinion former is usually an expert in the field that will give a professional opinion on the product and is looked to as an expert by the public. *[Senior Examiner's Comment: Correct.]*

Examples

The Sony Mini Disc and the compact disc (CD) are two formats for reproducing recorded music using a similar technology, but the CD has become the product that has established itself as the norm over cassettes and vinyl records. The same idea can be illustrated using the Betamax video versus VHS video format to reproduce transmissions from television. The VHS format became the norm and is the direct result of the influence of opinion leaders and formers. *[Senior Examiner's Comment: This example is not very convincing.]*

In the pharmaceuticals industry, the doctors and chemists would be targeted to ensure they prescribed and stocked a new drug. The public accepts the advice of the GP/pharmacist as the expert. *[Senior Examiner's Comment: This is a better example but again lacks detail and any critical evaluation.]*

Conclusion

Personal influencers are key to ensuring the acceptance of a new product in a market and therefore the communications campaign must pay particular attention to this segment to win their approval and acceptance first.

Senior Examiner's Comments

How Marketing Communication Campaigns Can Make Use of Personal Influencers

This answer could have been improved by reference to word of mouth communications and reasons why people like to talk about the product purchases.

Two Step Communication Flow

This answer would have been improved had the student set out their definitions (or understanding) of the opinion leader concept much earlier. Indeed this should have been clarified at the outset of the answer.

An opinion leader is someone who has a lay (unprofessional) interest or particular expertise/knowledge in a topic area. They are part of a peer group whom other people (opinion followers) refer to for information because they are accessible, the service is free and they are just one of the group. People are normally only opinion leaders in a particular subject area.

Examples and Conclusions

The strengths of this answer lie in the quite discursive nature of the content and the fact that this student clearly understands what an Opinion Leader and Opinion Former are and what their main characteristics are. The weaknesses in this answer are the poor examples and the rambling structure.

Question 3

For many organizations, business to business marketing communications have been transformed by the development of the Internet and related digital technologies. Prepare notes for a meeting at which you are expected to argue the case for the development of Internet based marketing communications for a business or company of your choice.

(20 marks)

Guideline answer

Introduction

Short outline of answer structure and the business for which the argument is to be made. What is the problem that is to be addressed?

Traditional/Established Forms of Communication

Brief explanation of what Internet based marketing communications is, strengths/weaknesses and opportunities. A comparison of current and new forms of communication might be useful.

Internet and Digital Technologies

Introduction to the new technology and the various formats and opportunities available. Comment on the general potential impact they may have on an organization's communications.

Internet based Opportunities

Distribution/Communication impacts, efficiency and effectiveness, personal/impersonal issues, Internet, intranets and extranets, impact on the buying process, impact on current communication mix.

Benefits

Faster communication, more information, lower costs, more effective, reduction in sales force personnel costs, improved relationships with intermediaries, new/revised types of intermediary, potential for improved levels of customer satisfaction, speedier problem resolution, greater accuracy and less noise in the communication system, provision of exit barriers for intermediaries etc. etc.

Evaluation

Short appraisal of Internet based marketing communications and impact it might make on your chosen business sector.

Conclusion

General short conclusion about the need to develop such communication facilities and mix off-line with on-line marketing communications.

Answer - Question 3

Meeting Notes: Development of Internet based Marketing Communications for Oce UK Ltd - Business Equipment Suppliers

Introduction

The advent of the Internet brings business to business marketing communications to a new playing field. *[Senior Examiner's Comment: This is slang - not to be used.]* The Internet presents opportunities in speed in accessing information. It also offers new levels of market research where our products can be viewed by customers we don't even know exist, but have found our business through the Internet. It can be a means of transacting business without the time and paperwork associated with paper transactions. In addition, the medium of the Internet can be used for capturing data from prospective clients - for example, if they want further information they can fill out an on-line form with name, job title, address details and company statistics. This is information we currently pay an agency for!

So, the Internet is a powerful business tool but how will Oce UK Ltd utilize this medium to aid the sales of business equipment such as photocopiers, printers and paper supplies?

Development of Internet Use

1. Brochureware.
2. Channel of distribution.
3. Integrated marketing communications on the Internet.

Brochureware

Nearly all businesses of any size have the facility to look up information on the company, performance, size, range of products and services. This is use of the Internet at its most basic level and ensures a presence on the Internet which seems a 'must' these days. Brochures on products/services/company infrastructure - service and call centres etc.

Channel of Distribution

The Internet could be utilized to enable customers to purchase equipment and supplies. This could be relatively easy for current customers as their details are already on our database. We could allow access to an account via a password and they could order more toner for their printer, or paper, or another photocopier and the invoice would automatically be generated and sent on to the customer. For brand new clients, an application would be sorted first, then after credit checking the business, they could also be set up to purchase on-line.

Integrated Marketing Communications

Use of the Extranet. This facility could be utilized to allow customers access to their own accounts with Oce so they know at any time what their monthly billing for toner/maintenance is, where customers have contracts for 'cost per copy' or rented reprographics equipment.

This could be developed further to warn the customer that their toner/paper levels are low and they should re-order. The annual maintenance price increase could be foretold on information stored on their account. And, when the device is at the end of its life, the customer could be informed of the newer products that could replace what they have in good time. Customers could have discounts incorporated in their accounts for volume purchases - visibility of these could encourage the customer to buy more to utilize the discount.

These are all things our marketing department does. It has to take data from reports manually. It then briefs the salesperson, who then spends time with the customer informing them of all the things they are entitled to. This prevents the salesperson concentrating on generating new business, and stops the marketing department concentrating on marketing. Both end up doing account management.

Benefits of Using the Internet

- Company image can be transformed by having a modern, easy-to-use Internet service.

- Cost reductions in time and resources where the customer administration departments respond to requests from clients or prospects on product information and pricing information.
- Events, exhibitions could be advertised with a complementary ticket or free merchandise (pen, key ring) if exhibition tickets are ordered over the Internet.
- Personal selling time greatly reduced and emphasis of account management role eliminated to allow more time for actual selling.
- Cost reduction in postage and brochureware where the information can be downloaded by any prospect.
- Lead generation from enquiries on the Internet.
- Intranet for internal selling and marketing communications.

Considerations

- Infrastructure - expertise needed to develop the Internet pages and maintain them.
- Image of company goes down if there are problems with the web site.

Conclusion

The benefits and opportunities outweigh the considerations and the opportunities in new leads. Reductions in cost mean that the development of marketing communications over the Internet must not be delayed.

Senior Examiner's Comments

Introduction and Development of Internet Use

This is a useful way of setting out the benefit areas.

Brochureware and Channel of Distribution

The points made here relate to marketing and business issues, not communication. The point that could have been made is about the propensity and technological ability to share information with channel partners and in doing so build stronger relationships.

Integrated Marketing Communications

This combination of an example and setting out some of the benefits works well. Perhaps the student could have written a little more under each section but on the whole this is a good approach.

Benefits of Using the Internet, Considerations and Conclusions

The content of this answer is quite good and it is reasonably clear to the Examiner that the student understands this part of the syllabus. However, the student lost marks because the end of the answer tended to run off into a series of points that were not justified or supported by any discussion or validation. Bullet points on their own are not acceptable and should be avoided.

Question 4

Write a report for your Senior Managers, explaining how marketing communications can contribute to the development of **EITHER** a consumer **OR** business to business brand. Use examples to illustrate your points.

(20 marks)

Answer - Question 4

How Marketing Communications can Contribute to the Development of the Consumer Brand

Introduction

What is a brand? I feel that it is important first to elaborate on what a brand is and the role it can play.

Essentially a brand has two aspects - a brand name (either a person such as Estée Lauder, a location e.g. United Airlines, artificial such as Exxon, or level of quality) and a brand mark or logo. Both of these aspects involve recognition by all levels of stakeholders and ownership by the company. The added benefit is that brands, names and logos can be protected through legislation such as trademark and copyright so that they become unique to a company and a possible source of competitive advantage.

Elements of the Brand

Brands can be seen as having up to six different levels. They reflect:

- Benefits.
- Attributes.
- Values.
- Culture.
- Personality.
- User.

These relate to the brand offering - i.e. what it stands for in the minds of those who come into contact with it, in terms of the basic or core aspects of the brand.

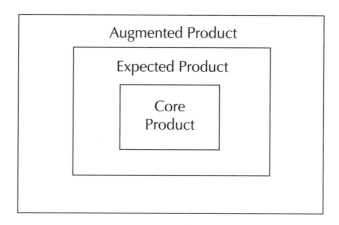

Three Parts of a Brand

Figure 3
Three Parts of a Brand

If for example we think of Estée Lauder, the core aspect of the brand is beauty products of a high quality and the expected elements of the brand are high level of customer service and quality products that will make us look and feel good. The augmented aspect is the additional quality - the unexpected bonus offers and the self-esteem the brand creates for its very specific user.

So, if we refer back to the six levels of the brand, the brand has to portray the benefits that the consumer is seeking (in this case high quality beauty products) so that it has relevance to the target audience. Its attributes are the physical elements such as the trademark or distinctive packaging.

Values are the values that the brand stands for in relation to its customers and stakeholders - in this case, quality and above average customer service. The personality reflects the type of people who are expected to be associated with the brand - in this case, glamorous and beautiful people. Similarly, it reflects the user's status as someone who looks after their appearance and takes pride in it.

Why is a Brand Important?

Having looked at what a brand is, we need to consider why it is important. Aaker identified the concept of brand equity - brand as a value to the bottom line of the business. The brand is more than just a physical or psychological entity: when Nestlé took over Rowntree's, brand equity was calculated at £1.4 billion, whereas the company itself was worth just £1 billion. *[Senior Examiner's Comment: Good example, incorrect figures.]* The reason is that brand identity means something to the consumer: they know the level of quality and service they can expect. It reduces risk in the purchase and leads them to become brand loyal, so that they repeatedly buy the brand. The brand has an element of perceived quality for which consumers will often pay a premium. *[Senior Examiner's Comment: Good points, well made.]*

What Role can Marketing Communications Play in Building a Brand?

The concept of the brand has to be communicated otherwise it is useless. The fundamental principle of the brand is that consumers are aware of it and then understand it: marketing communication is vital in this role.

Marketing communication through its various media - advertising, sales promotions, public relations, personal selling and direct marketing *[Senior Examiner's Comment: incorrect understanding of media, methods and promotional tools]* - communicates the meaning of the consumer brand: of products and overall corporate brands. These two are likely to have similar meanings and at least 'fit' with each other, but they may be different and have very specific messages, requiring communication through very different media.

Communication relates to the brand by building the brand image, brand awareness and association.

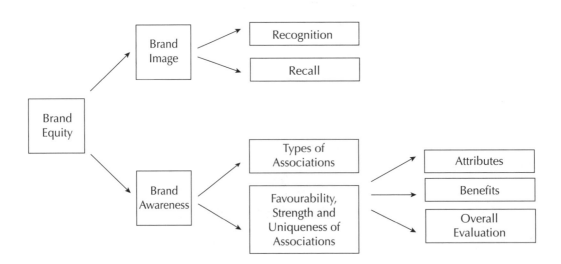

Brand Equity/Attribute Relationship

Figure 4
Brand Equity/Attribute Relationship

Communication is intended to provide brand recognition and recall. For example, integrative communication using similar messages and imagery - such as the red Coca-Cola brand - is then recreated at the point-of-purchase with the famous red Coca-Cola bottles and cans. Consumers then remember the images when they see these cues and reminders and are persuaded again to buy the brand, remembering a favourable feeling. Marketing communication is intended to create a specific positioning of the brand by providing messages that leave consumers with strong, favourable and unique impressions of the brand, giving them an edge over competitors.

Communications' creative strategy highlights the benefit of brand focusing - functional needs, experiential (pleasurable) needs or symbolic (such as the status of Estée Lauder). The aim is to leave the consumer with a positive overall evaluation and a favourable attitude towards the brand.

The power of the brand can be such that it actually makes marketing communications more effective: you have to spend less because you are more likely to reach consumers who are already familiar with, and hopefully possess favourable attitudes towards, the brand.

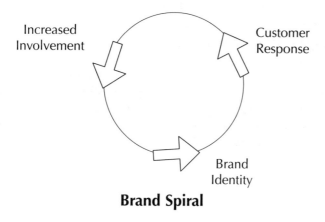

Brand Spiral

Figure 5
Brand Spiral

This brand spiral arises as a result of the favourableness of the brand, leading to increased customer loyalty, which leads to increased sales and more money to invest in marketing communications and brand building activity.

Marketing communications, as well as having a day-to-day brand awareness role, can also play several key strategic roles relating to brand. The power of brand means that well known, popular brands are likely to have more chance of success if they are extended - marketing communications can communicate similar messages through packaging and advertising as the original brand. Take, for example, the now highly successful KitKat Chunky which features the same brand mark and colours as the original KitKat.

Marketing communications can increase the use and take-up of a new brand, by promoting its relative advantage in promotional literature, the compatibility or fit with consumers, reducing the complexity, and providing methods of trial through coupons, sampling and direct mail.

Marketing communications can play a vital part in repositioning a brand, should that become necessary due to a change in customer attitudes or unfavourable consumer opinions. Think of the Skoda advertising campaign and its cheeky but effective 'It's a Skoda. Honest' strapline. This promoted humour and the fact the brand can laugh at itself, but also the image of quality at the same time. Finally, marketing communications has the potential to communicate the brand to its internal audiences. A brand is not just communicated by products and publications, but by the whole performance of a company, which includes its staff. Marketing communications through internal marketing can communicate the brand values, using internal newsletters or staff Intranets.

Conclusion

As consumers become more demanding and accept more than just care or expected elements of the brand, it is vital to portray the augmented aspects of what the brand stands for to all stakeholders, be they customers, employees, internal, referral, distributor or supplier markets. The company that fails to invest properly in its marketing communications or brand is the company likely to be facing problems tomorrow. Look no further than Marks & Spencer for an example.

Senior Examiner's Comments

Introduction

This represents a good understanding of what a brand is. It is also a good example of building in an example to the theoretical point being made. Extra marks could have been earned by passing an opinion of the relevance, usefulness or general applicability of the theoretical points.

The rest of the answer demonstrates good knowledge and depth of understanding (note the length of the answer). It tries to integrate examples, and rather than just tell the Examiner what a brand is, it makes a good attempt to answer the question. The key to answering this question is to focus on differentiation and added value. Although these words were not expressly used it is clear through the combination of theory and examples that the student understands these points.

Question 5

Many marketing communication campaigns are influenced and shaped by competitive and wider external environmental forces. Using examples, explain how such forces might influence and shape the marketing communications for a brand (or brands) of your choice.

(20 marks)

Answer guidelines

Introduction

Purpose, structure and intent of the answer

The Communication Process

One Step and Two Step models of communication.

Understanding Opinion Leader/Formers

Explanation of the difference, the role they perform in the communication process, the people they interact with, reasons why they like to talk about product purchases/experiences, characteristics, adoption and diffusion.

Examples

At least two examples should be used to demonstrate understanding.

These can be drawn from any market.

Evaluation

Appraisal of the usefulness of using personal influencers in the communication process.

Conclusion

General short conclusion making a final few comments.

Answer - Question 5

Notes on Lecture to Marketing Students: External Forces and their Influences on Communications Campaigns

1. Greeting and Introduction

Explain present job and role.

2. Background

Marketing communications do not operate in a vacuum. It is essential to examine the context in which they occur.

Slide 1: Forces that Affect an organization

1. Organizational
2. Stakeholder
3. Competitor
4. Business
5. Environmental

Today we are concerned with points 3. and 5.

3. Competitors

Unless a company operates in a tiny niche - possibly a new start-up - there will be competitors. They may be the main players with the biggest market share, in which case your concern is to take market share from them; or they may be smaller, in which case you must watch carefully.

For example, Marks & Spencer stopped watching its competitors, and suddenly realized that Next, Gap and other traders had taken part of its market share.

Companies compete on price, quality and service.

Slide 2:

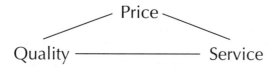

Figure 6

You can provide two of the three, but not all three, or you will go bankrupt. *[Senior Examiner's Comment: This is rather questionable.]* Assess competitors - would it be better to copy their strategy (e.g. the way Go copied EasyJet) or to use an alternative? (e.g. Tapley offers service and quality, MFI offers low price with appropriate, lesser quality).

4. Environmental Forces

i) Political

To try to gain popularity, the UK government is moving to implement the EU ban on tobacco advertising early. This has implications for tobacco companies' communications. Other forms than advertising are needed - B.A.T. has launched a web site informing people of the debate and providing data about smoking.

ii) Ecological

Packaging laws and EU concern for recycling mean companies must design packs carefully. Direct mail carries connotations of 'junk' and wastage of paper, so must be targeted very carefully. For example, Rover sent very selected mailshots to potential buyers and increased not only sales, but awareness and approval as well.

iii) Legal

The Data Protection Act has been updated. You may not fax a private individual, nor a company which has requested to be removed from your fax list. Other direct marketing has laws to be aware of too.

Competitions and other promotions have strict laws - the local raffle run by an amateur dramatic society is actually breaking the law. Why? It is a random draw but paid for. However, prize draws run by car manufacturers where your entry is just your name and address are legal, because that is not considered 'a consideration', such as money.

iv) Social

Society is changing rapidly. Communications which reflect this are more likely to be successful. For example, the Oxo family is moving away from the traditional grouping round the family dinner table to more modern situations. *[Senior Examiner's Comment: Good example]*. Society also has a concern for truth; the recent Iceland booklet on genetically modified foods has been challenged by a scientist who says it contains untruths and inaccuracies.

v) Technological

Technological developments are shaping communications to a great extent. The Internet is becoming more and more important, both to consumers and for business to business communications. Iceland has just rebranded itself Iceland.co.uk. DRTV offers new interactive direct marketing opportunities - Chicken Tonight is taking advantage. *[Senior Examiner's Comment: How?]*

The new WAP technology will also have an effect - instant communications will become more and more the norm. *[Senior Examiner's Comment: This is descriptive and quite brief. Greater depth is required]*.

5. Conclusions

First, the rapid pace of change means that marketers must be flexible and prepared to respond quickly to any changes. For example, Virgin's 'BA couldn't give a shiatsu' was a very quick response to British Airways' massage offer which was only given to first class passengers.

Secondly, rapid changes mean that it is more important than ever to integrate all communications, thus gaining effective and efficient co-ordinated campaigns, and maintaining brand values.

6. Questions

Time for questions.

Handouts.

Senior Examiner's Comments

Points 1,2 and 3

This is a poor response as it says nothing about the communication elements. How do competitors affect marketing communications? Well, there are plenty of areas to consider, such as the attributes used to position (and deposition) organizations, comparative advertising, use of a different promotional mix, message or media schedule.

Environmental forces

Political

A rather predictable example. Students should be familiar with EU issues, and should certainly know more up to date examples from their home government about changes in television advertising, direct marketing and privacy regulations, laws on sales promotion and personal selling. Use of lobbying should also be presented.

Ecological

Can you see the relationship between ecological issues and the Rover example?

Social

This is an even better example but unfortunately this student has not really provided any real depth of analysis.

Final comments

There are some good parts to this answer. The structure is fine and the base constituents of the answer are correct.

What is not good about this answer is its failure to understand the competitive impact on communications (a common mistake). A further problem is the lack of depth in the examples. Greater depth, clarity and analysis are required.

This student has used the Iceland case to illustrate one point. However, this case could have been used to demonstrate competitive issues, political, legal, ecological, social and technological impacts and how they all impact on the strategy and the positioning of the organization.

This is not a good quality answer and I hope you can see this for yourself.

Question 6

As Marketing Communication Manager for a global financial services organization, you have decided to ask your assistant to attend a meeting with your full service agency. Prepare a briefing note advising your assistant of the key media concepts to be considered when developing media strategy.

(20 marks)

Answer - Question 6

Developing Media Strategy

Media strategy must be developed as part of the total Marketing Communications (Marcoms) strategy. Therefore it is useful to consider Shimp's planning process before we look at media strategy in detail.

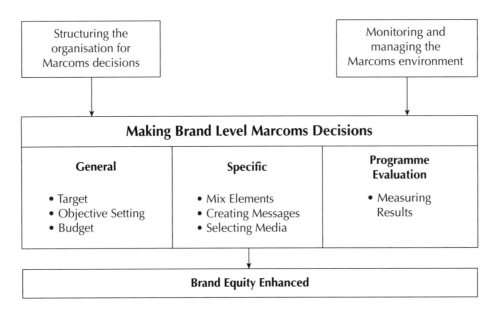

Shimp's Planning Process

Figure 7
Shimp's planning process

This provides the context in which to consider media strategy.

For example, in order to select the best elements of media to use and the messages to employ, you need first to have the professional skills in place within the organization. The pressure may be from customers, competitors and consumers in general for category management as opposed to brand management, for example.

You need to be aware of the environmental factors affecting your business - Davidson's macro-, micro- and direct influences - such as political, economic, social/cultural and technological. These may affect the messages or the media you need to use. For example, taking political/legal aspects, the recent news that the DTI has scrapped 'wealth warnings' on radio advertisements may be an incentive to consider using this medium, which previously had a poor take-up among financial services because warnings about payments were considered off-putting to customers.

In terms of general choices, you need to be very aware of who the target audience is. This will determine:

- Who you speak to.
- What you say.
- How you say it.
- When you say it.

Traditional segmentation techniques such as profile (demographic, geographic, geo-demographic), behavioural (benefits, user, purchase occasion, usage, loyalty status, buyer readiness stage and attitude) and psychographic (values and lifestyles, attitudes, interests and opinions) will have been used to select the most appropriate target audience. From this, image analysis may have been undertaken, such as familiarity, favourability, and variance analysis to assess the level of awareness, positive feeling and any gaps in terms of what the brand communicates. A mental map from the consumer's point of view will enable marketers to decide what they need to communicate.

The level of budget available will also determine the media strategy that can be planned, having taken into consideration elements such as the task to be done, the method to be employed and media, the nature of the product, the level of sales and extent of the competition.

Then can the marketer move to consider media strategy itself.

It is important to decide on the **mix of elements**.

Before deciding upon the major media vehicles to use, you need to consider the:

- Type of product.
- Information to be disseminated.
- Product nature.
- Persons to whom you communicate.
- The location of the buying decision (for example, if this is made at home, you need to communicate at home - direct mail etc.)
- Extent of competitive activity.

If you want to communicate product samples, direct mail may be the most appropriate medium. For general awareness, it may be that advertising, for example in the Financial Times, is more appropriate. You need to consider the nature of the competition in terms of their Marcoms activity: if they are dominating 'share of voice' in the market, perhaps you need to increase the level of your marketing communication activity.

You also need to consider the mix of elements that best complement each other - there needs to be integration, so that the multiple media and multiple messages speak with the same voice and achieve synergy.

In determining the specific media elements to use, you need to consider the advantages and disadvantages of each specific medium.

Kotler talks about considering the stage in the **product life cycle**, where growth, maturity, and decline sections can determine the objectives of media strategy:

- Whether to raise awareness.
- Build relationships.
- Reposition brand.
- Influence target audiences.
- Build loyalty.

There needs to be consideration of whether, for example, a push or pull strategy is employed, or whether advertising or sales promotion may be more effective.

Advertising has the power of mass communication, whereas direct mail has the power of personalization and mass customization. Magazines have the advantage of quality reproduction as opposed to the poor print quality of newspapers. Digital TV offers the benefits of demonstration and interaction: it is about considering the trade-offs and a cost/benefit analysis based on what you want to achieve.

In detail you need to consider:

Reach, Frequency, Impact

Essentially, how many people you need to reach, and how often you want them to see (or hear) the messages. Considering Gross Rating Points of different media available, looking at media packs or media research available.

Timing

Considering the timing of the campaign - whether you want to achieve **continuity** (which is expensive), **concentration** (putting promotions in one time period to achieve maximum impact), **flighting** (some months of concentration, some months of activity) or **pulsing** (whereby there is activity all year round but more so in some months). You need to consider buyer carry-over (of brand awareness) and buyer habitual behaviour (in purchasing) regardless of brand advertising/media activity. Consider the macro- scheduling problem - pressures of seasonal/cyclical trends - in context with the micro-scheduling problem - the temptation to put all the money into a few months to achieve maximum impact.

Erwin Ephron's shelf space model advocates trying to have an almost continuous presence focusing on reach rather than frequency to reach as many people as possible with the first powerful exposure. This is one option, though Krugman's three exposure hypothesis has traditionally been seen to be that you should concentrate on three exposures to advert messages, not vehicles, to attain maximum impact and comprehending.

Creating Messages

Consider the messages you need to provide in terms of the objectives of the communication, methods being used and the target audience. Essentially, there are seven generic creative strategies:

- Generic (dominance, benefit).
- Prescriptive (benefit, authority).
- Unique selling points (preference).
- Brand image (personality).
- Positioning (mental niche).
- Resonance (patterning life).
- Emotional (emotional selling point).

Once you have decided on the creative strategy you wish to use you need to:

- Specify the key fact - what the target audience is looking for.
- State the primary marketing problem - what you are trying to achieve.
- Develop creative strategy.
- Establish measurement of effectiveness.

A useful tactic is Bernstein's double funnel theory which asks you to consider what the key facts are (the benefits of the product), what the proposition should be, the idea (or stimulus of purchase) then the media method, which amplifies the message and the audience.

Finally you need to consider the structure, format and type of the advertising.

Measuring Results

A vital part of media strategy is considering how results will be measured, to ensure objectives set at the start have been achieved and whether there is a need to change the message, the media used, the frequency of media schedule and so on. It also increases accountability of the marketing function. Techniques include: recognition and recall, purchase intention, familiarity and favourability research surveys, laboratory testing of messages/media, take-up and sales of products, enquiries/consumer panels.

Senior Examiner's Comments

All the material presented in the first part of the answer is generally correct but not specific to the question. What follows is question specific, and if you do not know this material then you should familiarize yourself with these concepts and issues about media planning.

Timing

These last two paragraphs are the real crux of the answer to this question. This student has a broad and useful knowledge of a wide range of influences but this question specifies media concepts and so the main part of the answer should be focused on reach (coverage), frequency, duplication, impacts, OTSs, CPT and ratings.

Creating messages

This section of the answer has degenerated into a list format, which is not acceptable.

Final comments

Overall this answer demonstrates that the student has a good general knowledge of media planning and associated concepts. Notice the amount the student has written; quite impressive considering it was written under real examination conditions.

This answer was awarded a high mark even though it did not go into any depth on the real issues. The breadth of issues covered compensated for this failure of focus.

Question 7

In 1999 British Airways decided to reverse a decision concerning the design of their corporate identity used on the tail fins of many of their aircraft. The controversial designs were said to be disliked by overseas customers. At the same time, the redesign had been criticized by many staff who had been in conflict with the organization about a cost cutting campaign introduced previously by management at the airline.

Prepare a report in which you identify the main theoretical elements of corporate identity/branding and use examples to illustrate how corporate communications can be used to reach important internal and external audiences. Use organizations of your choice to answer this question.

(20 marks)

Guideline answer

Introduction

Purpose, structure and intentions of the report.

Corporate Branding

To reach multiple audiences (stakeholders), reasons for the increased attention given to this area of communications, key concepts of personality, identity and image (and reputation as a separate area), ability to differentiate between image and identity, the importance of internal audiences as part of IMC.

Methods used to project the corporate brand

Corporate identity cues (planned and unplanned) through symbolism, behaviour and communication. (e.g. video conferencing, intranets, extranets, Internet, email, noticeboards, conferences, reports, advertising, signage, architecture, dress codes, letterheads, personal greeting and the promotional mix etc. etc.)

Examples

At least two examples to illustrate the use of corporate identity/branding cues to reach one internal and one external audience.

Evaluation

Short appraisal of corporate identity and its use by organizations.

Conclusion

General short conclusion making a final few comments.

Answer - Question 7

Report

Prepared for: Marketing Director

Prepared by: Marketing Manager

Date: 13th June, 2000

Title: Developing Corporate Identity/Branding

Contents:

1. Introduction.
2. Audiences and Stakeholders.
3. Objectives of Corporate Communications.
4. Implementing Corporate Communications.
5. Conclusion.

Introduction

The increasing number of stakeholders interacting with an organization, and the increasing visibility of the corporate identity, has led to recognition of the importance of communicating consistent messages to all stakeholders. In this report I shall seek to address the theoretical concepts of corporate identity, and illustrate how corporate communications can reach internal and external audiences.

1. Theory of Corporate Identity

1. Corporate identity is like the badge that a company wears. The perception of this by stakeholders is known as corporate image.
2. The difference between the intention of corporate identity and image is known as the corporate perception gap.
3. It is the reduction of the 'perception gap' that the planned communication with all stakeholders seeks to achieve.
4. Corporate image is communicated to give credibility to all its stakeholders in an attempt to gain buy in, loyalty and motivation of the organization's corporate objectives.
5. Corporate reputation is an extension of the theory of corporate identity. It is deep-rooted over time and is of benefit to an organization as it signals:
   o Credibility.
   o Responsibility.
   o Trustworthiness.
   o Reliability.
6. In line with corporate identity is another dimension: that of ethical behaviour and social responsibility, to all stakeholders. This is the notion of corporate citizenship, and is embedded in corporate identity.

2. Audiences for Corporate Identity Development

There is an increasing number of stakeholders that an organization needs to communicate with, with differing needs.

Stakeholders include: financial community, employees, customers, local community, distributors, suppliers, press.

It is important that messages are consistent to all these stakeholders, that communications add value, and that they are perceived as timely, likeable and co-ordinated.

3. Objectives of Corporate Communications

Corporate communications aim to build the positive corporate identity of the organization to all its stakeholders. These communications should aim to present the company as one with strategic credibility, and thus strengthen the commitment and loyalty of its stakeholders.

Specifically, the objectives are to:

1. Motivate and gain support from employees.
2. Gain support and financial backing from the financial community.
3. Gain loyalty from the support network.
4. Be perceived as credible by customers.

4. Implementing Corporate Communications

There are many activities to support this. It is important that they are positioned as appropriate, credible, and proactive, and that they are consistent with each other.

Methods include:

Logo:

As with the BA tailfins, organizations use the logo as a tangible form of communicating consistently. The logo must be appropriate to the organization and stakeholders and desired positioning. BT spent millions on its logo redesign and launch when it became a privatized company.

Employees:

'Internal customers' are increasingly recognized as a key market in their own right. They have needs which require satisfying. Hence, they are a key target in their own right for communications by the organization. Once satisfied, this leads to the development of:

- Motivated employees committed to implementing the corporate objectives, in an efficient and productive way.
- They become brand ambassadors delivering improved customer service; and hence become an important delivery mechanism for corporate communications, e.g. delivering improved customer service in Burger King.

Views/preference of CEO

CEOs are a way to gain visibility and credibility. Anita Roddick was a leading spokesperson for the Body Shop. Richard Branson 'fits' and pushes the 'challenge the establishment' brand for Virgin. Peter Davis provided the reassuring face for the Prudential.

Marketing Budget

The level of SOV vs. SOM communicates a certain image. Internet start-ups advertising by TV, such as Egg, clearly communicate that they are serious organizations.

Unintended Behaviour and Transport

The Eddie Stobart haulage company has made itself a cult through the use of its transport facilities and drivers wearing tie and jacket.

Strategic Intent

Communicating the credible strategic intent is a key means, particularly to reach the financial and stakeholder communities. The intention stated, e.g. for expansion by Bookers has increased its share price.

The Ethical Stance

The idea of corporate citizenship is increasingly important to stakeholders. Corporate communications is the interface between an organization and its stakeholders, and is responsible for communicating an ethical stance. The Co-operative Bank, the NatWest Community Bond, and the Body Shop have all used this means.

Sales Literature and Internet Sites

Both communicate clearly the strategic interest, credibility, ethical stance and position of an organization. Orange has used this particularly well. The Durex web site scores over 80,000 hits per week.

5. Summary

Communicating to all stakeholders in a consistent manner is increasingly important. Corporate identity and reputation take years to build, and seconds to destroy. It is important that all stakeholders feel committed to an organization, and this can lead to significant competitive advantage.

Senior Examiner's Comments

A sensible, appropriately sized introduction, setting out clearly the direction and content of the answer. Writing these introductions is a useful exercise as they serve to focus attention on what needs to be addressed in the answer.

The point 1 is on the right lines. The answer would be much improved if it referred to both Corporate Personality and Corporate Image. A really high mark would be awarded if the difference between identity and image were examined. All students should know this material.

The implementation points are really corporate identity cues. The range is good and there are some excellent strategic observations. In addition, workwear, architecture, letterheads and employee behaviour are other important cues.

The corporate identity mix (behaviour, communication and symbolism) should have been the base from which to answer this question.

This student has a reasonable knowledge about corporate identity but has not really answered the question. The question calls for an understanding of how internal and external audiences can be reached (with corporate communications). The answer does not explicitly address this question.

One way in which students could answer this question is to discuss (yes discuss) how internal communications can be used to reinforce externally oriented corporate identity cues and then explore issues of integrated marketing communications. Always a favourite with the Senior Examiner.

Introduction

The secret of success when taking any examination is preparation. With this important thought in mind, The Chartered Institute of Marketing has asked the Senior Examiners to produce these specimen answers to the actual questions set.

The answers are for your guidance and should not be seen as perfect solutions. In marketing, there is never one entirely correct solution. Whatever the style adopted, the format and the content of these answers should be indicative of what the examiners want to see.

It is hoped that you will find these specimen answers, and the examiners' comments, useful and informative. However, it is regretted that no correspondence can be entered into regarding the subject matter. We advise students to practise past questions and to use their tutors for guidance and feedback.

The copyright of all The Chartered Institute of Marketing examination material is held by the Institute. No Case Study or Questions may be reproduced without its prior permission which must be obtained in writing.

Exam material

Apollo Data Loggers

Apollo Data Loggers manufactures and distributes a range of equipment (both hardware and software) designed to monitor and capture data concerning temperature, humidity, damp, and shock. For example, growers of fresh produce need an accurate record of temperatures experienced during the growth, preparation and transportation of their produce. For freight carriers and transporters, data logging provides a means of verifying the conditions in which their customers' products are carried.

Apollo has established itself in the market partly through superior technology which, unlike its competitors, is capable of downloading data whilst it continues to record. Sales revenues have grown to approximately £3m but profitability, whilst respectable, remains unexciting at around 6%. The market is becoming more competitive which in turn impacts on price. To avoid price competition and discounting which eventually leads to an erosion of profitability, Apollo's marketing strategy requires a move to niche markets where premium pricing can be sustained.

To reach its markets Apollo has developed a global network of over 40 distributors. These channel intermediaries provide their customers with solutions but the decision making is often complex involving all three parties; Apollo, the distributor and the client. This network can require vast amounts of information and the development of customized products to meet client requirements. For example, Apollo's distributors need information about the range of 42 mainstream products and the product revisions which occur with increased frequency. These revisions can be caused by customers buying equipment to support their own businesses which is not compatible with the data logging equipment. Apollo is required therefore, to update its own equipment constantly and communicate information about the revisions more frequently.

In order to communicate with and support its distributors Apollo produces sales literature, manuals, product specifications, brochures and data sheets. In addition, data capture software needs to be made available and updated as necessary. Contact with the distributors is maintained by telephone, fax, email and through visits by members of the sales force. Apollo is also well represented at leading exhibitions, either directly or indirectly through agents and distributors. There is little advertising apart from some in the trade press and public relations has been largely ignored.

In order to retain clients, build longer term relationships and reduce costs, many manufacturers are looking to develop positive life-long relationships with their distributors. One way in the past has been to increase the switching costs for distributors. However, this is difficult unless there is some distinct and sustainable competitive advantage or reason to be aligned with a particular manufacturer. Correspondingly, distributors are looking for improved reliability, manufacturer commitment and integrity as well as product expertise. To meet these requirements a shift in the form of the relationship between Apollo and its distributors is necessary and to do this a more effective and efficient communication system needs to be introduced.

To date, Apollo's marketing communications strategy has been to use its distributors to present Apollo's products to their markets. This has often resulted in a fragmented and varied set of messages which are largely product oriented and based on the provision of information, product attributes and benefits. The strategy is now being questioned as some people claim that the current approach is slow and inefficient due to duplication and repetition which drives up communication costs. With increasing competition, a requirement for faster information flows and a need to present a more unified and focused identity to clients and distributors means that the marketing communications strategy is in need of review.

Source: The information provided in this case is based on a case in Bickerton, Bickerton and Simpson-Holley 1998, Cyberstrategy, Butterworth-Heinemann. Information has also been provided by the company, whose name has been disguised. Some of the material has been adapted in order to provide a suitable context for the mini-case study and in no way is intended to imply good or bad management or even actual situations or current practice.

PART A

Question 1

As Marketing Manager for Apollo you have embarked upon the process of reviewing the company's marketing communications. You are required to make a report to the Directors about the following points.

It is important to answer both these questions separately and **NOT** write a marketing communications plan.

Identify and prioritize the key strategic issues concerning the communications between Apollo and its distributors and clients.

(20 marks)

In view of the issues you have identified, recommend and justify a means by which technology might be used to develop Apollo's marketing communications strategy.

(20 marks)

(40 marks in total)

Answer - Question 1a

Report

To: Board of Directors, Apollo Data Loggers

From: Richard Biranne

Date: 5th December, 2000

It has been acknowledged that Apollo Data Loggers' (ADL's) present position in the data logging market is one of superior technology and products. However, increased competition and price consciousness is eroding margins.

Key to ADL's survival and continued development in this market is a move to niche markets, where premium pricing can be maintained.

Fundamental to this move are several key strategic issues concerning our marketing communications strategy. These are, in order of importance:

- A dissonance currently present within various messages the company provides to the market. There is a lack of any integration within our current marketing communications.
- A lack of any strong brand characteristic by which our company and its products can be recognized.
- A need for faster, more efficient communication with our distributors and customers than we presently achieve.
- Present communication with our customers is linear, via our distributors, whereas in many cases a 3-way communication is required. At present this is only achieved at exhibitions and technical seminars, during sales visits from head office and during occasional customer visits to ADL.

Integrated Marketing Mix

With the corporate objectives and strategy established, it is necessary to establish a series of marketing objectives, and derived from these, a series of marketing communications objectives.

These should integrate not only the different elements of the promotional mix (advertising, sales promotion, direct marketing, sales force and PR) but should also integrate these with the rest of the marketing mix (product/customer, price/cost, place/convenience to buy, people, physical evidence and process).

In all of the areas except marketing communications there is the risk of our messages and qualities being confused with those of our competitors. Our research clearly identifies that superior technology is no longer sufficient and that quality of service and an understanding of our customers' needs will be at the heart of future activity and branding.

It is necessary to create a strong brand which reflects the high technology and service oriented positioning we wish to project. This must be projected in a cost-effective manner to the key customers and personnel within our target niches.

In developing such an integrated marketing strategy, all stakeholders, including manufacturing, new product development, finance and distributors must be fundamentally involved. The strategy is also to present a seamless, consistent image of the company and its products and services, reflected in reality.

Senior Examiner's Comments

Note how this student has prioritized their strategic communication issues. This was asked for in the question but many students failed to accomplish this task and consequently failed to collect easy marks.

If in doubt what the priority should be, leave a space and return to fill it in once you have completed Question 1a.

Simple presentation of what IMC is, not just the promotional mix.

This section conveyed the points in a succinct manner. However, this student could have elaborated a little more by highlighting issues such as positioning and corporate branding as these are indeed serious issues facing ADL.

Answer - Question 1b.

In developing the integrated communications strategy referred to earlier, it is necessary to consider again two significant points:

- The need for speed.
- The need for 3-way communication involving distributors and customers.

Clearly there is modern technology available, some of which we are already using in the form of email, which can be instrumental in addressing these needs.

However, other factors also need to be considered:

- The international dimension, with over 40 distributors.
- Our own continued growth and the implications for our own infrastructure.

In considering the use of technology it is useful to consider the model for take-up elaborated by CISCO systems, which indicates that new technology is adopted in the following stages:

1. 1. Email.
2. 2. Web site.
3. 3. E-commerce/trading.
4. 4. E-service/interaction.
5. 5. 'Eco-system'.

Email and web sites we are already familiar with. E-commerce is the widest known next step, involving trading through the Internet. However, e-service/interaction offers our company significant extra opportunities. With e-service customers can access their own order records, observing progress as it takes place, can engage company personnel on-line if necessary, and technical monitoring of customers' software and hardware in live time can be achieved. This enables problem diagnosis and solution in addition to the benefits already highlighted.

The 'eco-system' stage may be too early for us, in that it involves extensive partnering and sharing of information between companies within the same supply chain. It is more suited at this time for large companies and is particularly useful where large purchasing savings can be made.

I am therefore proposing a move towards a full e-commerce and e-service technology based system. This would be the vehicle for ADL's marketing communications strategy, but would be integrated with other aspects of the marketing mix.

Key elements would include:

- Mobile communications, enabling sales people and distributors to communicate and access company information.
- Web site reflecting ADL's chosen positioning.
- Interactive facilities enabling on-line ordering.
- Modem linked communications allowing ADL's technicians to monitor and service customer software and hardware remotely.
- Video conferencing enabling virtual meetings. For instance these meetings might be set up by distributors, at customers' premises, involving video link-up with ADL personnel via laptops, which the ADL people themselves are using.

- Intervention assisted web site activity, whereby an ADL operative assists with web site navigation via an integrated voice link. The web site www.landsend.com is a good example of such a site.
- Interactive sales configurations for use by sales personnel and distributors, whereby product information and pricing may be obtained online. Several examples of such systems exist.

These moves can be considered an extension of our present sales automation and order entry systems, extending their present focus.

A conscious development must be that of a sophisticated Customer Relationship Management System, whereby information on our customers and their behaviour is put at the heart of our differentiation.

Clearly, such moves must embrace the whole company, and must be made in the context of an Integrated Marketing Communications strategy involving all elements of the marketing and promotional mixes, and all stakeholders.

Senior Examiner's Comments

An interesting approach to the question and not necessarily one that all students could utilize. However, what the student makes clear is the range of technology that can be used and s/he recognizes that such a strategy has to be implemented in stages. To some extent this answer to Question 1b. is more tactical than strategic and hence did not achieve the very top marks.

The answer would have gained more marks if the student had tried to address the positioning and overall strategy problem. Namely, how is communication with customers to be undertaken - through distributors where corporate branding will be dominant, or direct to customers where an approach focused more on product branding would be more appropriate?

General Comments

Although there was a lot involved in this question, simplification was a route to success. Students who recognized what the strategic marketing communications issues were, scored well. Some students did not know what this meant and unfortunately resorted to writing a marketing communications plan, despite the advice not to do so. These students received fail marks for the question.

My advice to **all** students preparing for this examination is to be absolutely sure they understand what Strategic Marketing Communications issues are - and how to recognize them.

PART B

Answer THREE Questions Only

Question 2

Determine and explain the key issues that an international advertising agency might advise a client about when discussing the development of an integrated marketing communications strategy for consumer products across several countries.

(20 marks)

Guideline answer

Introduction

Establishing the agency perspective and structure of the answer.

The Role of the Agency

Brief outline of an agency's role with respect to Clients and the need to provide expertise, integration and results across borders.

Understanding of IMC

Brief explanation of what IMC means (not just promotional mix) and the role an agency has in contributing to integration.

Issues

- Depth and significance of IMC
- Client and Agency structures
- Access to relevant expertise
- Quality of relationships - propensity to share information
- Need to involve employees
- Standardization/Adaptation issues
- Use of promotional mix
- Media buying
- Budgets
- etc.

Evaluation

Short appraisal and prioritization of the issues and how some agencies try to help their clients.

Conclusion

General short conclusion about the problems of international client/agency relationships.

Answer - Question 2

Report

To: Marketing Manager

From: Accounts Manager

Date: 5th December, 2000

Subject: Integrated Marketing Communications Strategy

1. Introduction

1.1 We at Murdoch & Murdoch International Advertising Agency have shifted our focus from full advertising services to integrated advertising services because it has become a new concept with a lot of benefits. It is of great concern that we discuss and advise you on this new concept, as you are our valued client.

2. Definition

2.1 Integrated Marketing (Communications)

Communications can be seen as a strategic choice of the elements of the marketing mix which effectively and economically influence the transaction between an organization and its customers, clients and potential customers.

2.2 This concept delivers communications in an utterly consistent manner.

3. Key Issues

3.1 Although this concept has a number of benefits, we need to look at the key issues of applying it in overseas markets as far as your bottled fruit drink is concerned.

3.2 First of all we look at the advertising strategy we can use. Are we going to use standardization globally? That is, are we going to use the same message in all the countries we have targeted? If so, we can do this by using only music and pictures and excluding language, since different languages are spoken worldwide.

3.3 Culture

Another issue of great concern is culture. There are cultural differences in every country and a marketer deciding to market internationally must take this into consideration. Though Integrated Marketing Communications seeks to deliver the same message, the cultural values must also be taken into consideration.

3.4 Economic

Before the concept of Integrated Marketing Communications is adopted in overseas markets, we need to consider the various economic situations in each country. Is the economy booming? What is the employment rate? Will consumers prefer to spend their money on fruit drinks, or buy medicine or vitamins first? Some people believe that the same benefit in fruit drinks can be found in the vitamin itself, so why buy the drink?

3.5 Political and Legal Issues

As far as legal issues are concerned, all advertisements carried out both locally and internationally must be decent, legal, truthful and honest.

3.6 Technology

Recent technological advances have opened ways for consumers to be reached through a number of media such as the Internet and digital TV. We must not lose sight of this, as Integrated Marketing Communications will help us to deliver even our communications in an entirely consistent manner.

3.7 There is a need to adopt this concept because of increased international communications.

4. Benefits of the Concept

4.1 Integrated Marketing Communications give a company the opportunity to link its internal and external communications, thereby understanding the needs of the employees, customers and other important stakeholders.

4.2 There is an opportunity also to link our communications with our distribution partners and provide a co-ordinated and a two-directional flow to our promotional activities.

4.3 This concept will help us to reduce our communications expenditure and yet achieve our aim internationally.

4.4 Integrated Marketing Communications will make it possible to employ one external agency to handle all our above-the-line communication and also bring together other agencies like sales promotion, public relations and direct marketing agencies.

5. Conclusion

To conclude, we at Murdoch & Murdoch would like to suggest that you adopt this concept as it will give you a competitive advantage in marketing your fruit drink internationally.

Senior Examiner's Comments

It is advisable to write a short introduction. However, this student has changed the nature of the question from integrated marketing communication strategy to integrated advertising services.

This is the essence of this question; to standardize or adapt. Can Integrated Marketing Communications be delivered effectively across different nationalities and cultures using an adapted message?

I picked out this answer not because it is particularly good, because it isn't, but simply because it tries to incorporate the IMC concept throughout the answer. Many students attempted this question but the vast majority simply re-iterated their International Marketing notes about PEST factors, media and culture without relating them to IMC.

This is not a trick question; it simply calls for a recognition of how IMC can be delivered internationally and some of the issues that are involved. Namely, to adapt and fail to integrate (or be consistent as this student recognizes) or use a standard message and risk failure due to cultural, media and even local agency inadequacies.

The question calls for IMC but this answer fails to incorporate issues concerning local skills across all the tools of the mix, management issues concerning implementation and control and even issues such as positioning in different markets.

Whilst this question represents more of a challenge than many other questions, students are advised to think carefully about what is required and not just dump standard text book information.

Question 3

You have been invited to visit a local business school to talk to postgraduate students about marketing communications strategies.

Using brands from sectors of your choice and with which you are familiar, prepare notes which explain why such strategies need to change and set out some of the different strategies that might be adopted over the lifetime of a brand.

(20 marks)

Answer - Question 3

Notes for Discussion on Marketing Communication Needs of Brands

1. Introduction

My intention is to provide you with some provoking thoughts and considerations concerning marketing communication strategies, and how they need to be flexible and change over time. This is in the context of brands and the lifetime of a brand and how strategies need to be adapted to the circumstances and customer needs over time.

2. Why Might Strategies Need to Change?

2.1 Maturity and Development of a Brand

A brand goes through a life cycle of development and can be viewed in a product/life cycle context. From here it can be seen that a brand will move along the innovation diffusion of any successful product brand until it reaches decline.

During each stage, marketing communications will be required to do a different job and perform another role.

For example, when Ballantine's Scotch Whisky was first marketed in continental Europe, the job was to develop awareness of the brand and establish its values in the minds of target consumers and potential consumers. Marketing was aimed at selective, prestigious, upmarket image bars and clubs. Personal relationships were key.

After establishment as an image-conscious, high value brand, it was necessary to build brand equity. Lifestyle media campaigns were developed in print, posters, on premise signage, dealer brochures and on television at crucial times of year.

The next stage, taking us into early and late maturity stages, took the brand to a far more extended popular position. It was available through different channels, such as supermarkets and liquor stores. Here mass media was used to underpin the values of the brand.

2.2 Political, Legal and Social Factors

If we examine tobacco brands, such as Marlboro cigarettes, we can see the results of the pressures from political, legal and social groups to influence Marlboro's marketing communications.

Before the advent of the anti-tobacco lobby and educational knowledge of problems associated with smoking, tobacco companies could freely mass advertise.

Marlboro now achieves media coverage through sports sponsorship, attaching its name and image (the cowboy) to clothing. It has had to take a more surreptitious approach.

2.3 Globalization

Globalization and the different consequences and pressures require changing communication strategies to adapt to different cultures and sensitivities. For example in China, Coca-Cola had to change its name to something completely different. Its Chinese name is associated with, or means, 'happy'. Marketing communications had to be adapted to get the message across.

2.4 Technical

This primarily involves the Internet and the Worldwide Web (WWW).

Such innovations cut across boundaries as never before. What you put on your web site can be seen by anyone, anywhere at any time.

If you are a global organization and want to communicate to your audience consistently, what are you going to do?

Siemens decided that it had to adopt English as the language of its company. This allowed consistency of understanding to a wide range of global audiences. Internal marketing communications were brought into play.

3. Conclusion

Mass media advertising with generalized messages is giving way to more customer relationship tailored messages. Brands are just as important as always, but with the advent of databases and technology businesses can get closer to, and form more meaningful relationships with, the customers.

Senior Examiner's Comments

This is clearly an opportunity to use a diagram in order to depict different stages and even label some of the strategies that brands move through. Because this student failed to use a drawing the potency of the answer has been lost.

This answer might have been improved by considering other reasons why brands need to change. For example: wider environmental forces, internal forces, product life cycle impacts through merger and acquisition, brand developments and changes to the core product, competitive actions ranging from heavy SOV to fundamental product enhancements and de-positioning. Above all else, changing customer perception, attitudes and overall needs.

The answer presented here is **not** one that students should model their answers on completely. It does attempt to incorporate many salient points but it lacks depth and breadth.

Question 4

As Marketing Manager in a medium sized company (in a sector and/or country of your choice) prepare a report about how you propose to develop and implement an Integrated Marketing Communications strategy.

(20 marks)

Guideline answer

Introduction

Identification of suitable organization, and reference to current form of communications and associated difficulties.

Define IMC

Explanation of what IMC is and what is to be introduced over which timescale.

Developing Agreement to the Concept

Establish need for internal communication to explain benefits and win approval

Assign CEO/senior director to lead strategic change

Inform and seek support of outsourced providers, in particular marketing communication agencies.

Consult and advise as necessary.

Implementation

Identify resistance to IMC, isolate and persuade

Develop and agree overall plan of implementation (including timescales and costs)

Plan should be stepped as the move to integrated status should be incremental

Agree budgets, set targets, communicate openly.

Agreeing training courses as necessary

Set regular reviews to consider progress.

Evaluation

Appraisal of IMC in terms of the management processes.

Conclusion

General short conclusion making a final few comments.

Answer - Question 4

As marketing manager of the English Plastic Films Extrusion Company Ltd ('EPF'), I am pleased to report on the proposed development and integration of an Integrated Marketing Communications Strategy for the high performance 'barrier' films sector in Northern Europe.

As you know, plastic films have become highly commoditised in the past ten years, with large quantities of simple films now being imported. The effect of these imports is to depress prices in the sophisticated part of the market and to erode our margins there.

With the segmentation and positioning adopted during the recent senior management workshops, we now have established marketing objectives which have been used to develop a set of marketing communications objectives.

The positioning agreed for our 'barrier' films is to be one of consistent high quality combined with superior service.

As you know, the quality aspect means close to zero transmission of gases, vapours and light, combined with strength, in an ultra-thin (and hence low cost) structure. Service means speed of response to new formulation requests, willingness to develop new film 'structures' with food packaging customers, and willingness to produce short production runs.

It is clear that for this strategy to work, full agreement and 'buy-in' is needed from all parts of the company. The enthusiasm and dynamism of the cross-functional teams in the management workshops are an excellent indication that we are on the right track, and something we must build upon.

I recommend that a small team is established, chaired by myself. Since this is a medium sized company with annual turnover circa £25 million, and being typical of the industry, it is assumed that the Marketing Manager reports to the S&M Director, and is the only full-time marketing professional on the staff to develop and implement the Integrated Marketing Communications ('Marcoms') strategy.

The team should comprise members of production, process development, and sales and customer service. It should report to the Sales and Marketing Director. I would anticipate one member from each department, with 'shadows' also nominated in the event of absences.

The team will be briefed with the job of developing the Marcoms strategy in line with the established marketing strategy, and will communicate progress to departmental personnel in face to face meetings on a weekly basis.

The DAGMAR process will be followed (Defining Advertising Goals, Measuring Advertising Results), and will feature the following steps:

- Gain attention.
- Develop awareness.
- Develop comprehension.
- Frame attitudes.
- Create action.

This is particularly necessary since our newer products are little known in the market and few competitive products yet exist. However, where there is awareness already, we will seek to heighten that awareness by emphasizing key brand attributes.

Clearly, the cross-functional nature of the team will encourage company-wide acceptance of the strategy as well as make key contributions, especially regarding technical areas, as well as facilitating integration with other elements of the business mix.

The key stages will be:

- Identification and justification of the marketing message.
- Establishing Marcoms mix (PR, direct marketing, sales promotion, sales force, advertising).
- Establishing budget.
- Selection of media.
- Issue of advertising briefs, where appropriate.
- Identification of target market.

These stages will be processed iteratively, and full integration and use of electronic media within the Marcoms and marketing mix will be ensured.

Measurement in terms of market, money, message and media will be carried out by an outside agency.

Senior Examiner's Comments

Note the absence of an Introduction and how the answer rambles on from one point to another with no clear demarcation.

Many of the points are justified and the scene setting work is very good. Surprisingly, no definition of IMC is offered which would have helped put the answer in context.

The lack of subheadings means that it is difficult to understand the separate points that are being made.

This answer is head and shoulders above most of the responses offered by students. Unfortunately students saw the words IMC and again just reiterated their standard notes. Most of these students wrote about marketing communication plans and would have achieved poor marks.

This student has concentrated on what the question calls for: the **development and implementation** of IMC. Therefore, issues concerning the introduction of new concepts and the management of change are of key importance. Barriers to change and ways of overcoming such barriers using strong senior leadership to the programme direction and credibility were looked for.

There are a number of ways in which this question could be answered. What was important was that students focused on the introduction and implementation issues rather than just what IMC might be.

Question 5

Prepare notes for a presentation to be given to colleagues explaining the nature and role that attitudes play in buyer behaviour. You should explain how marketing communications can be used to influence these attitudes. In particular you should:

Explain the different components of an attitude.

(5 marks)

Describe ways in which marketing communications can be used to shape or change attitudes held by a target market. Use examples.

(10 marks)

Suggest reasons why the development of positive attitudes in the target audience is important for those involved in the management of brands.

(5 marks)

(20 marks in total)

Guideline answer

Understanding Attitudes

3 component structure, attribute orientation, favourable/unfavourable.

Marketing Communications

Minimum of 4 methods, (change attribute, change weighting, introduce new attribute, change beliefs, change importance of attributes, change perception of competitors' attributes, change emotional associations)

Use of examples.

Branding

Might reduce impact of competitors, reduces risk, encourages repeat buying, develops word of mouth communication, enables premium pricing, allows for brand extensions, favourable reception to product development, maintains brand position.

Evaluation

Appraisal of attitude theory or usefulness or practical application or relevance.

Conclusion

General short conclusion making a final few comments.

Answer - Question 5a

To: Marketing Managers

From: Marketing Manager

Date: 5th December, 2000

Re: Nature and Role of Attitudes in Buyer Behaviour

Components of an Attitude

Attitudes are formed over time and are an extension of an opinion. While opinions can be swayed relatively easily through logical argument and case presentation, attitudes are more deeply emotional - based on, and formed from, intangibles.

Attitudes consist of these qualities held by the individual:

- Values and beliefs.
- Experiences.
- Accumulated cues.
- Perception.
- Motivation.

They explain why people act the way they do and why people respond differently to similar situations. They are intrinsic components of a person's personality and difficult to alter. Marketers should encourage a strategy that is relevant to, and fits with, a segment market's attitudes, rather than attempt to change the attitude.

Senior Examiner's Comments

This answer demonstrates where so many students went **wrong.** This explains how attitudes are **formed**, which is very different to the question - which asks what the **components** are.

The correct answer is:

- Cognitive (refers to knowledge, understanding and learning).
- Affective (the degree to which I like or dislike the object).
- Conative (likely actions and behavioural intentions).

These three components underpin the Hierarchy of Effects models that so many students still like.

Answer - Question 5b

Shaping or Changing Attitudes

That said, there will always be a need to shape or change a target segment's attitudes, particularly as a product moves through its life cycle and new markets are being sought to keep the brand alive. Here the focus will be on four ways in which marketing communications can be used to shape/change attitudes held by a target market. All are taken from Kotler and use current examples to explain.

Senior Examiner's Comments

Good attempt here to use 4 methods. This was not asked for in the question but 4 is reasonable in the time period available.

Answer - Question 5c

1. Change or Modify the Product

A product losing market share may need to be altered to change the attitudes of both ex-users and non-users. An example is Persil's new 'colour care' formula which has been **added** to the old Persil product. Persil's advertising message focuses on the improvement and goes so far as to compare the 'new' (or modified) Persil with the 'old' Persil in much the same way as washing powders have traditionally compared their own brand with that of a competitor.

Persil's message appears to be that the product modification has changed Persil so much as to make it a whole new product. The target market is likely to be past users of Persil - who are being persuaded back after switching - and non-users of Persil who are being encouraged to trial the 'new', innovative Persil brand, shifting their attitudes.

2. Change a Product's Benefit

This is an oft-used strategy and can be identified by use of words such as 'fluffier', 'softer', 'stronger than ever'. These words come from Andrex's latest campaign for toilet tissue. The company is advertising exactly the same product using exactly the same campaign style (the cute Andrex puppy) but drawing attention to improved benefits. The campaign is so familiar that Andrex's target market would be for current users thinking of switching brands due to the 'high quality, high price' image of Andrex. To back the improved benefits focus, Andrex included an on-pack 'lower price' promotion to encourage current users to stick with the product due to its quality and (compared with yesterday's price but not that of the competitor) lower price.

3. Draw Attention to a Neglected Attribute

The target market's attitude may be negative due to a focus on a particular attribute that it is not interested in. By switching the focus to another attribute, new interest may be achieved. Volvo, for example, has long focused on the safety attributes of its vehicles - not a feature likely to cause a young male to switch from his current model of zippy runabout. Recently Volvo has moved its strategy focus onto the sleek design of its cars, opening the brand to different segments while maintaining the safety-conscious market.

4. Change Usage Patterns

Breakfast cereals have always, justifiably, been associated with the first meal of the day. Kellogg's has recently positioned cereal as an 'any time' snack and even as an indulgent dessert through its new exotic range. This opens its market to all traditional 'not breakfast so no cereal' eaters and expands its potential markets significantly as even traditional Kellogg's customers are being encouraged to use more of the product.

Positive Attitudes in the Target Audience

The development of positive attitudes in a target market is critical to the success of any brand. Word-of-mouth 'advertising' supplements the brand's campaign in a positive manner. Positive attitudes towards a brand show the market is identifying and relating to the brand, which is critical to its long term success. It shows that people find the brand relevant to their lifestyle, an added-value component to their day - all factors which encourage brand loyalty and long term usage.

Senior Examiner's Comments

The answer to the second part of this question is very good. This student knows about marketing communications and the way they can be used to influence attitudes. All students should be familiar with this level of understanding and be able to give good clear examples. In addition, students could have mentioned:

- Change weighting of an attribute.
- Change beliefs.
- Change the importance of attributes.

- Change perception of competitors' attributes.
- Change emotional associations.

The third part of the answer might have been assisted had there been some focus on what branding represents. The answer is a little too brief and perhaps reference could have been made to competitors, and the forces acting on products and organizations effectively trying to deposition them. Customer tastes and preferences are prone to constant change, therefore by maintaining a positive attitude, not only are current sales more likely to be optimised but should the brand run into problems in the future then the store of positive attitudes and associated brand reputation may well help it through a crisis.

Question 6

Explain the principal means by which marketing communication campaigns for fast moving consumer products, should be evaluated. Consider the effectiveness of three main evaluation techniques.

(20 marks)

Answer - Question 6

To: Mr Kost

From: Mr Pierce

Date: 5th December, 2000

Subject: Marketing Campaign Evaluation

Introduction

It is important that we evaluate the effectiveness of our marketing campaign in order that we can learn from the results as to whether our choice of media is appropriate and also to ensure that the target audience is receiving the message that we want it to receive.

There are various methods of evaluating campaign effectiveness, some of which measure the push, pull and profile strategies. They can also be input into quantitative and qualitative methods. With interactive media there are growing levels of sophistication and accuracy too!

Evaluation Methods

Increased Sales

This is a simple method and does not bear in mind the fact that there are other external factors that affect sales; for example competitor activity. This also assumes that the main objective of Marcoms campaigns is to increase sales, whereas with advertising the aim is to generate awareness. Thus the appropriateness of the measure will also depend on the media being measured. It is also difficult to determine when the effectiveness of a campaign starts and finishes, particularly with purchases that are not regular and require a lot of information gathering before decisions are actually made.

Market Share

Company market share is also a good measure of a campaign; for instance if it increases or decreases. However this may also be caused by external factors - e.g. the issues surrounding Barclays' involvement with South Africa and bad public relations affecting market share.

Measurement against Objectives

This is one of the best ways of not only defining the amount of budget to use for a campaign but also providing the ability to assess it clearly at the end of the campaign. Obviously, for this to be successful the objectives need to be specific, measurable, achievable, realistic and tried. It also helps to determine the media available for use through the amount of budget that can be used.

Changes in Attitude

This is a more qualitative method of measurement, assessing what the target audience's view of the brand values were before and after the campaign. This relates more to a profile of strategy measurement, although it can be used as push and pull.

Audience Reach

This measure determines the effectiveness of the campaign, not just in terms of the whole audience covered, but the specific segment that we were targeting. From this we can determine the effectiveness through the cost of reaching each of the customers, the amount of opportunities to see the campaign that they had and also the wastage. This can determine our effectiveness. Through spreading the campaign and consistent message across various media, we increase the opportunity to see and therefore the likelihood of recall, which is another measure.

Campaign Space

The results of PR are measured in terms of the amount of column inches and the cost that there would have been if the space had been paid for. The results can also be measured in terms of positive and negative PR.

Re-order

Push campaigns may be measured through re-order levels, although these may be skewed as a sales promotional campaign may take product sales from another competitor (with routine buy products that often tend not to have loyalty established) while the price is low. This may mean that both sales and market share drop afterwards as people return to their old brands once the offer is over, or go to another competitor who is running a promotion in retaliation to yours.

This may also not be applicable as people may order large quantities for seasonal fluctuations; such as cranberry sauce at Christmas, or fireworks for 5th November and New Year's Eve.

Loyalty Cards

The advent of loyalty cards means that buyers' purchases can be measured more accurately and these can be related to the promotions on offer. Diageo is installing TV screens in bars to measure the effect of its TV adverts and the purchasing behaviour of the people in the bar.

Telesales

Telesales can record TV adverts, promotions on packs or discounts in papers by having a number to call for information and also a reference to quote, and campaigns can therefore be measured on the calls received. An example of this is the Tango advertisement where a number was given.

Tivo

Tivo is an enhancement of the previous methods in that it can measure what people are interested in and place an advert relating to an individual's interests. It also records whether people fast forward through videos or watch adverts that they like, but obviously this does not take into account the fact that people may not be watching the media as they may be, for example, making a cup of tea.

You can also react with the TV, for example to order a sample product which will immediately be able to feedback the success of the campaign to ensure that responsiveness is measured quickly. If there is a low response, changes can be made quickly.

Conclusion

In conclusion, we can see that the method of evaluation will depend both on the form of media used and also relate to the finances of the consumer and customer attitudes. It is therefore worthwhile to use a variety of methods, but relate them to the objectives that were initially set for the campaign to ensure that success has been achieved.

Senior Examiner's Comments

This answer achieved a good pass mark, if only because of the broad range of techniques offered and basic way it answers the question.

The majority of the techniques offered here are sales oriented and are geared to advertising. The answer could have been improved with a more detailed structure. Perhaps a structure based around each of the individual tools would have enabled a more varied set of evaluation techniques to have been presented. This could then have been followed by a section considering the evaluation issues of IMC which would have enabled the 'campaign objectives' to have been the main concluding point.

Another approach would have been to compare above-and below-the-line methods or qualitative against quantitative approaches. However, a strategic response would have been to consider evaluation in terms of Pull, Push and Profile strategies. Some of these were mentioned in the Introduction; it was a shame they were not developed.

A really good answer would have questioned the validity of the measuring and evaluation techniques. Practical consideration and their associated costs would be of concern to most managers.

Overall, this answer attempts to cover too many techniques and fails to give any real depth of understanding.

Question 7

As an Account Manager at a direct marketing agency, explain why many of your clients have decided to redistribute a greater percentage of their marketing communications budgets away from mass media advertising to other promotional methods. You should also comment on future trends and use examples to illustrate your points.

(20 marks)

Answer - Question 7

To: Marketing Director

From: Account Manager

Date: 5th December, 2000

Re: Adoption of New Marketing Communications Methods by Clients

Introduction

From a review of the nature of business conducted recently both by this agency and by others in the industry, it has been noted that there has been a move away from mass media advertising by a number of our clients. Most are adopting other promotional methods in order to achieve their marketing communications objectives.

I will outline a number of reasons why I believe this change has occurred and suggest some future trends.

Reasons for the Shift

1. Cost and Accountability

In business generally there has been an emerging trend to demand greater effectiveness and accountability for every item of budget spend. This has been stimulated by the larger degree of competition in today's markets.

This has now included the marketing department (partly due to the influence of financial directors who see nothing tangible from marketing).

The ever spiralling cost of mass media advertising coupled with the need for greater effectiveness and demonstrable accountability has lead to qualms over the justification of the mass media advertising spend.

2. Media and Audience Fragmentation

There is an increasing trend in the marketplace to both media and audience fragmentation.

The increasing number of television channels, newspapers and magazines has meant that it has become harder to generate the same reach that used to be achieved with a mass media advertising campaign.

The audience fragmentation, as the audience takes advantage of this extended range of choices, has also made it harder to reach the right people.

As marketers are aware of this they have increasingly turned to these new, non-mass media for their promotions.

For example, painkiller brand Anadin has launched its new Anadin Ultra brand with advertising in niche lifestyle magazines such as FHM and by sponsoring a race team to reach its target male 18-45 bracket, rather than its traditional TV advert approach.

3. Accountability of New Methods

New (or different) promotional methods offer a way for marketing managers to test more efficiently and spend effectively their increasingly monitored budget.

Direct marketing has excellent potential for measuring response, unlike mass media advertising where it is often difficult to relate advertising to sales due to factors such as the Adstock effect.

This is especially important for smaller organizations and charities where it is even more essential to monitor budget effectiveness.

For example, a test promotion by motoring organization the AA ran in 4 formats in different editions of Autotrader. It was then possible to monitor the pound for pound success of each campaign which was not possible with the later TV execution.

4. New Technology

New technological developments such as the Internet have made inroads into the traditional mass media advertising by diverting budgets to create a presence in the new medium.

This technology plus other new technologies, such as improvements in database techniques, have created the opportunity to target and reach the target consumer more effectively, to the detriment of the blanket approach of mass media advertising.

Many financial services providers, such as Alliance & Leicester, have diverted some of their mass media advertising budget to the Internet because the average profile of an Internet user is closely matched to the company's ideal loan buyers; so the Internet is an effective way to focus the advertising at the target segment.

5. Internationalism

The growing number of clients who are working in multiple national markets also influences the decline of mass media advertising, as this form of promotion is often difficult to use internationally due to language and cultural barriers and the high cost of creating the advertising.

Advertising forms with lower creation costs can be more effective, particularly when complemented by better technology such as databases. For example, it is cheaper to develop several executions of direct mail for international use.

Future Trends

Media fragmentation and with it audience fragmentation seem set to continue as new technology facilitates new forms of communication and lowers the barriers to entry of old ones.

Greater measurability of other forms of promotion, such as the work currently being done on developing a system of measuring effectiveness of sponsorship, will tend to encourage the continuation of the move to other forms of media.

As agencies accept the new split between promotion methods, and change their structures to help them cope and survive with this, we will see more clients urged to use other forms of media, either alone or in an integrated campaign.

The increasing awareness of the ability to integrate various forms of marketing communication will also help companies to consider using new promotional methods, knowing they will not have to risk the clarity of their communication to do so.

The current trend of needing increasing budget effectiveness will also continue as globalization of business increases competition.

Increasing globalization of companies' markets will also continue their need to use media suitable for worldwide communication, which currently for most brands is not mass media advertising (only world super brands such as Coca-Cola can currently execute such promotion successfully).

Senior Examiner's Comments

A simple final section that encompasses a number of future issues. The only major omissions concern the nature of competitive markets and the need to find some form of competitive advantage. The drive for IMC demands that brands co-operate with a range of communication suppliers and so it is to be expected that below-the-line techniques will be predominant.

A total of 3 examples (plus a mention of Coca-Cola) is just about OK. When the examples are short and brief, illustrating individual points, then examples of the size mentioned here are satisfactory. Ideally, however, there needs to be more of them.

A mistake that many students made was to describe everything they know about direct marketing rather than take a broad perspective and answer the question about changing marketing communication strategies.

Syllabus

Aims and Objectives

- To develop students understanding of the formulation and implementation of integrated marketing communication plans and associated activities;
- To enable students to appreciate and manage marketing communications within a variety of different contexts;
- To encourage students to recognize, appreciate and contribute to the totality of an organization's system of communications with both internal and external audiences;
- To enable students to be aware of the processes, issues and vocabulary associated with integrated marketing communications in order that they can make an effective contribution within their working environment.

Learning Outcomes

Students will be able to:

- Determine the context in which marketing (and corporate) communications are to be implemented in order to improve effectiveness and efficiency, understand the key strategic communication issues arising from the contextual analysis and prepare (integrated) marketing communications plans.
- Determine promotional objectives, explain positioning and develop perceptual maps, and suggest ways in which offerings can be positioned in different markets.
- Formulate marketing communications strategies with particular regard to consumers, business-to-business markets, members of the marketing channel and wider stakeholder audiences such as employees, financial markets, environmental groups, competitors and local communities.
- Determine specific communication activities based upon knowledge of the key characteristics of the target audience. In particular, they will be able to suggest how knowledge of perception and attitude, levels of perceived risk and involvement can impact upon marketing and corporate communications.
- Select, integrate and justify appropriate promotional mixes to meet the needs of the marketing communication strategies.
- Determine appropriate levels of marketing communications expenditure/appropriation.
- Evaluate a variety of promotional campaigns drawn from different sectors.
- Be aware of the impact and contribution technology makes to marketing communications. Be appreciative of and sensitive to issues associated with cross-border marketing communications.
- Advise on the impact corporate communications can have on both internal and external audiences and their role in the development of integrated marketing communications.

Indicative Content and Weighting

1.1 Strategic Marketing Communications (20%)

1.1.1 A definition and appreciation of the scope and dimensions of marketing and corporate communications.

1.1.2 A contextual analysis understanding and justification for marketing and corporate communication strategies.

1.1.3 The strategic significance and impact of integrated marketing communications.

1.1.4 Identify key (strategic) communication issues that might influence an organisation's marketing communications.

1.1.5 The appreciation and recognition of the importance of ethical and technological influences on promotional activities and to be aware of the social responsibilities organizations have towards the way they communicate with their target audience.

1.2 Developing a Theoretical Understanding of Marketing Communications (20%)

1.2.1 Understanding the key drivers associated with information processing and buyer decision making processes.

1.2.2 Communication issues for internal and external audiences.

1.2.3 The role of personal influences on the communication process

1.3 Managing the Marketing Communications Process (40%)

1.3.1 The determination and appreciation of the prevailing and future contextual conditions as a means of deriving and developing promotional strategies and plans;

1.3.2 The target marketing process as a means of identifying significant promotional opportunities;

1.3.3 Determining promotional objectives and selecting positioning opportunities;

1.3.4 Identify, select and formulate integrated promotional strategies ensuring reference is made to:

1. Push, pull and profile strategies
2. Any existing or proposed branding activities
3. The Internet and e-commerce activities relating to both consumer-to-business and business-to-business markets

1.3.5 Selecting appropriate promotional mixes;

1.3.6 Determining message styles and key media goals;

1.3.7 Deciding upon the level and allocation of the promotional spend;

1.3.8 Managing internal and external resources necessary for successful promotional activities;

1.3.8 Managing internal and external resources necessary for successful promotional activities;

1.3.9 Managing and developing product and corporate brands;

1.3.10 Evaluating the outcomes of promotional activities;

1.4 Evaluation of Different Types of Marketing Communication Campaigns (10%)

1.4.1 Knowledge and understanding of different campaigns from different contexts (incl. FMCG, business to business, services and public sectors, and not for profit organizations).

1.4.2 Consideration of the competitive conditions, available resources, stage in the product life cycle and any political, economic, social or technological factors that might be identified as influencing the development of a campaign.

1.5 Cross-Border Marketing Communications (10%)

1.5.1 Cultural, social and media influences

1.5.2 Organizational type and communication approaches

1.5.3 The Adaption/Standardization debate

1.5.4 Agency structure and support

Note: The words 'promotional' and 'marketing communications' are used interchangeably.

Further study

A wide variety of other texts exist in the specialist subjects of sales promotion, point of purchase, advertising, public relations and direct marketing. These should be used for reference purposes.

Students are also advised to read both the quality press and trade magazines such as Marketing Success, Campaign, Marketing and Marketing Week and to keep abreast of current promotional campaigns.

Reading list

- C Fill; *Marketing Communications: Contexts, Contents and Strategies (2nd Edition)* , Prentice Hall , 2000, Essential Reading
- T Shimp; *Advertising, Promotion & Supplemental Aspects of Integrated Marketing Communications (5th Edition)* , Dryden , 1999, Essential Reading
- T Yeshin; *Integrated Marketing Communications*, CIM/Butterworth-Heinemann , 2000, Coursebook
- *Integrated Marketing Communications*, BPP, 1998, Additional Reading/Resources
- M Solomon; G Barnossy; S Askegaard; *Consumer Behaviour European Perspective*, Prentice Hall , 1999, Additional Reading/Resources
- J Blythe; *The Essence of Consumer Behaviour*, Prentice Hall, 1997, Additional Reading/Resources
- R East; *Consumer Behaviour: Advances & Applications in Marketing* , Prentice Hall , 1997, Additional Reading/Resources
- P Kitchen; *Marketing Communications: Principles & Practice* , Internat'l Thomson: Business Press , 1999, Additional Reading/Resources
- L Butterfield; *Excellence in Advertising (2nd Edition)* , Butterworth-Heinemann , 1999, Additional Reading/Resources
- C Baker; *Advertising Works*, IPA/NTC , 1999, Additional Reading/Resources
- P Kitchen; *Public Relations: Principles & Practice* , Internat'l Thomson Business Press , 1997, Additional Reading/Resources
- L O'Malley; M Patterson; M Evans; *Exploring Direct Marketing*, Internat'l Thomson Learning, 1999, Additional Reading/Resources
- J Jones; *The Advertising Business*, Sage, 1999, Additional Reading/Resources
- D Chaffey; R Mayer; K Johnston; F Ellis-Chadwick; *Internet Marketing*, FT/Prentice Hall , 2000, Additional Reading/Resources
- *Integrated Marketing Communications Practice & Revision* , BPP, 2000, Additional Reading/Resources
- *Learning Cassettes*, BPP, 2000, Additional Reading/Resources

Guideline answer for Question 5.1

Introduction

Role, nature and main characteristics of objectives from a general management perspective.

Promotional objectives

Identification of three types of promotional goals (corporate, sales and communication), their purpose, how determined and range of characteristics.

Role within the planning process

Guide for strategy formulation, determination of the promotional mix, message content, media planning, resource allocation, scheduling, evaluation and feedback.

Evaluation

Appraisal of the usefulness of objectives in IMC.

Conclusion

General short conclusion making a final few comments.

Guideline answer for Question 6.1

Introduction

Definition of marketing channels and outline structure of answer.

Channel members

Types of channel members nature of their relationship with each other (e.g. interdependence and independence).

Need for communication

Explanation of the role and purpose of communication in the channels (e.g. the glue), reduces conflict, improves understanding, focuses attention, increases efficiency, builds trust/commitment, enables the achievement of goals, defines roles, etc.

Key influences on design

Channel structure/design, member attitudes and quality of their relationships, use of technology, climate, competitor communications.

Key Influences on implementation

Balance of power, the actual task, quality of relationships, communication methods used and proposed, resources available, competitor communication strategies etc.

Evaluation

Appraisal of channel communications

Conclusion

General short conclusion making a final few comments.

Guideline answer for Question 9.1

Introduction

Set out structure and form of the answer/report.

The purpose of budgets

Control, appraisal, return, measurement, efficiency and effectiveness.

Process

Internal procedures, co-ordination, timescales, contribution, sharing and brand appropriation, internal political issues and turf wars.

Methods

Percentage of sales, arbitrary, unit, competitive parity, share of voice, objective and task.

The future

Need to adjust amounts to changes in distribution, balance of brand portfolio, competitors, demands of supermarkets for promotional support. Need for processes and procedures to support the brands appropriately and in advance of market and organizational changes.

Evaluation

Short appraisal and prioritization of the various methods and isolation of those issues that are key to us in the haircare market.

Conclusion

General short conclusion about the need for a strategic perspective regarding budgeting.

Index

levels, 59
Lifestyle, 45
Limited problem solving, 42
Logos, 17
Loyalty cards, 5
Loyalty programmes, 5
Lucozade, 46
Market segmentation, 21, 46
Marketing
    elements, 16
  global, 104
  global organizations, 104
  globalization of markets, 104
  international marketing, 104
  mass media, 104
  mix, 4, 16
  multinational, 104
  multinational company, 104
  objectives, 24
  Plan, 13
Marketing communications
  defining, 1
  definition, 6
  objectives, 57
  planning framework, 20
  strategic role, 14
  strategy, 24
  tools of, 2
Marriage
  norm, 34
MCPF, 20
Media, 83
Message
  awareness, 34
  decoding, 8
  decoding a, 34
  impact, 84
  reception, 8
Monitoring, 59
Moral concerns, 48
New products
  bugets, 122
Newspapers, 4
Noise, 7, 8
Objectives, 57
  corporate objectives, 59
  determination of, 59
Oil co
  British Airways, 99
  corporate identities, 99
  corporate image, 99
  Proctor & Gamble, 99
  Shell, 99
Opinion formers, 9

Opinion leaders, 10
Organizational culture, 51
Organizational identity, 50
Own brands, 6, 17
  advertising, 76, 93
  brand name, 93
  corporate identity, 93
  corporate image, 93
  generic branding, 93
  Kellogg, 93
  mergers and acquisitions, 93
  premium pricing, 93
  remind/reassurance strategies, 76
  Sainsbury's, 93
  strong theory, 76
  Tesco, 93
  Virgin Airlines, 93
  weak theory, 76
Pack designs, 17
Parenthood, 33
Pepsi, 16
Perception, 16, 34, 37
Perceptual mapping, 68
Performance requirement
  stakeholders, 61
Personal selling, 2, 131
Planning, 19, 27
  marketing communications planning
    framework (MCPF), 58
  marketing plan, 58
Population, 34
Positioning, 24, 65
Positioning guidelines, 67
Positioning strategies, 69
  cultural symbols, 69
  price/quality, 69
  product class dissociation, 69
  product feature, 69
  product use, 69
  target user, 69
Post-parenthood stage, 33
Post-purchase evaluation, 41
Prestige image, 18
Problem recognition, 39
Problem solving, 41, 42
Product, 16
  innovation, 5
  labelling, 48
Product gross margin
  anticipated turnover, 119
  competitive expenditure, 119
  DAGMAR, 119
  media inflation, 119
  objective-and-task method, 119